Travels With My Daughter

Niema Ash

Published by TravellersEye Ltd

Travels With My Daughter

1st Edition

Published by TravellersEye Ltd 2001

Head Office:

Colemore Farm

Colemore Green

Bridgnorth

Shropshire

WV16 4ST

United Kingdom

tel: (0044) 1746 766447   fax: (0044) 1746 766665

email: books@travellerseye.com   website: www.travellerseye.com

Set in Times

ISBN: 190307004X

Copyright 2001 Niema Ash

Printed and bound in Great Britain by Creative Print & Design

With special thanks to my dear friends:
The Laytons, Cedric Smith and Rosy & Andrew Gibb for being part
of my life and my story.

About The Author

Niema Ash has been described by a perceptive critic as "the ideal author of a travel book: passionate, curious, self-critical and with a rare ability to describe not just the outward appearances of a foreign land but to penetrate, and evoke in splendidly vivid prose, its very essence."

In her first book, *Touching Tibet*, to which the Dalai Lama wrote the foreword, Niema takes us into the spiritual heart of this unique and threatened culture.

"Excellent – Niema Ash really understands the situation facing Tibet and conveys it with remarkable perception."

(Tenzin Choegyal – brother of the Dalai Lama)

"Mesmerising"

(The Sunday Times)

"Thought-provoking and enjoyable…it will evoke a deep desire to go to Tibet"

(Geographical Magazine)

Touching Tibet
Foreword by His HolinessThe Dalai Lama
Published by TravellersEye Ltd, Oct 1999
ISBN: 0953057550

Contents

For my daughter Ronit and mother Rose

In tribute to Victoria Bates

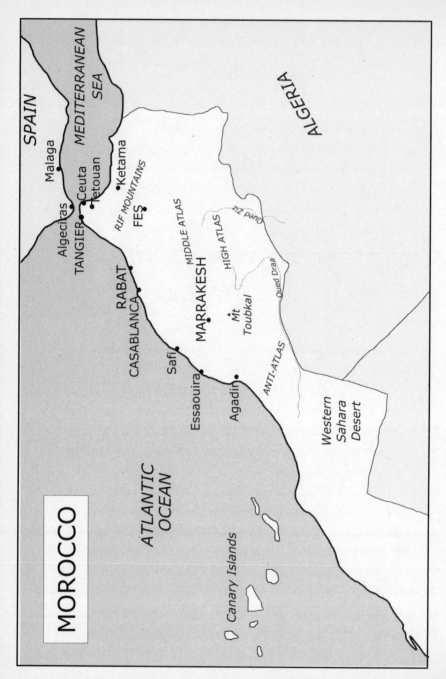

8

Introduction

Travel was always my driving passion. The initiation ceremony marking my coming of age was a journey into the world. Most of the major events of my life happened on the road. I was married on the road, conceived my daughter on the road, turned from girl to woman on the road. I acted, interacted, taught and learned on the road. I was introduced to Buddhism in Tibet, to Islam in Morocco, to Hinduism in India, to apartheid in South Africa. The road was my university, my church, my true love.

How alarming then, while travelling in Africa, to discover I was pregnant. I panicked. Now I would have to choose between travel and motherhood. But I soon discovered that in the heart of Africa I didn't have that choice. I would have to stay pregnant. In desperation I vowed to myself that motherhood would not limit my love of exploration, of experience with people and places, would not curb the adventure. Somehow I would find a way. And so it was.

This book is the story of how I found that way, how my love of travel and adventure was shared with my daughter, Ronit. How she participated in my journey, how that journey became her journey; how we grew to better know and understand each other, how Ronit became my best travel companion.

The adventures described here take place mainly in Morocco, when three women, a fifteen year old girl and an eleven year old boy, travel in a beat-up Volkswagen into the wilds of Morocco. But the book also describes how, as soon as was possible, Ronit was exposed not only to fascinating adventures with countries but, due to lucky circumstances, to adventures with some of the most fascinating and talented poets and musicians of our time, including Bob Dylan, Leonard Cohen, Seamus Heaney and Irving Layton; adventures which shaped both our lives. This book is the story not only of extraordinary travel adventures but also of extraordinary people adventures.

Some readers may be dismayed or even shocked by my unorthodox approach to motherhood, shocked by the risks, the dangers, the daring that Ronit was exposed to, especially in Morocco. But others may be inspired by knowing that motherhood need not be the end to travel and adventure, may find the adventures and experiences described here a way of opening the gates to their own promises of adventure. If it's true that appetite comes with eating, perhaps the tastes experienced here will develop into a wondrous appetite.

Travelling today, in many ways, is easier than when I did it. The possibility is greater now than it has ever been. As Hilary, the renowned mountain climber said, "the greatest loss is not taking the adventure." I hope this book inspires you to take it, or at the very least to participate in the journey of someone who did.

1. Travels In The Womb

"I'm taking Ronit to Morocco for a year," I announced with measured composure, and then held my breath, fingers strangling the telephone receiver, grateful that I was in London and my former husband, Shimon, in Montreal.

"You're doing what?" Shimon hurled at me, his voice hurtling across the Atlantic and exploding with disbelief and outrage.

As my eyes squeezed shut against the sting of his disapproval, and my ear numbed as though struck, I was suddenly reminded of another voice on the telephone, fifteen years before, using those exact words, 'You're doing what?' in that exact tone. I was very young then and in the last stages of pregnancy with Ronit. The doctor had instructed me to phone him as soon as the contractions began, day or night. But I kept delaying the call. I was feeling dislocated, fearful, having returned home to Montreal only weeks earlier after a long, wonderful absence travelling the world, because I needed somewhere to have a baby. The problem was I didn't want to have a baby and dreaded going to the hospital, knowing that once there, I would have no choice. Finally, just after midnight, I phoned the doctor, compounding my fear of the hospital with that of waking him.

"My contractions have begun," I announced brightly, belying my multiple anxieties. I could hear his yawn.

"How long apart are they?" He sighed sleepily, and I could tell he was pondering the perversity of yet another female who insisted on giving birth in the middle of the night.

"They're coming every few minutes." Suddenly he was wide awake.

"What are you doing?" His voice was shrill and I detected an edge of alarm.

"I'm going to have a shower and go to bed."

"You're doing what?" he rasped, spitting that same disbelief and outrage in those same words. I repeated my agenda with dwindling confidence. "You're getting into a taxi and going to the hospital, pronto, right away. I'll meet you there." He hung up.

Shimon and I couldn't afford a taxi, so with heavy heart I woke my father and he drove us to the hospital. An hour later Ronit was born.

Now, fifteen years later, Shimon's voice had that same resolute quality the doctor's had all those years ago, and I shuddered at the recollection, my resolve threatened.

"You're not taking Ronit to Morocco."

"Why not?"

"Why not? I can't believe you're asking that. It's suicidal, that's why not."

He proceeded to recite a litany of disasters involving people we knew; friends robbed of everything, money, clothes, tickets, passports, everything; a close friend imprisoned for months in a filthy cell; female friends, especially vulnerable, harassed and pursued to the point of despair; police extracting bribes; and drugs, drugs and more drugs; the list was endless and accurate.

"And you ask why not? If you want to get yourself killed, that's your business, but what do you have against Ronit? You're supposed to be her mother... And what about school?"

"School's no problem," I said quickly, grateful to circumvent the heavier issues. "She's a year ahead anyway. I'll just take her out for a year. They're used to that in London," I improvised. "It's no problem."

"It's no problem? It's nothing but problems." I could feel his frustration, his exasperation at having no control over my decisions and his daughter's life.

"How about if I take her to Morocco for six months and you take her to Canada for six months," I offered.

"I don't even want to discuss it. If you take her to Morocco, I'm

12

cutting off my support cheques." With that he hung up.

But stopping Ronit's meagre support cheques was hardly a deterrent. It would just mean adding waitress work to my supply teaching to earn extra money, and hitchhiking instead of taking buses and trains to conserve it. It would make things a lot more difficult for us - not really what Shimon wanted, but he had to do something to express his opposition.

I understood his worry. Shimon had never been to Morocco. The sinister stories he heard had fermented in his imagination until Morocco became one gigantic tale of horror, peopled by dark lean men with alligator jaws who snapped up foolish ladies like me for breakfast, saving the succulent ones, like Ronit, for dessert. It loomed like some faceless monster with a terrible heart, unpredictable, unknowable. It was different for me. I had been to Morocco. It was not a life-threatening experience. But I knew it would be impossible to convince Shimon of that. I remembered the terrible fear my parents suffered when I was in Northern Ireland and the Canadian press reported incident after incident of shootings and bombings. They begged me to return, fearing for my life. It was impossible to convince them that I was in no danger; that despite the bombings and shootings, life was entirely ordinary; that imagining the horrors in Northern Ireland was far worse than being there; that life endured with stubborn normality behind the headlines and horror stories. But that was no consolation for Shimon. For him only the dangers were real, and I was being an irresponsible mother by exposing Ronit to them.

I did not accept the charge of irresponsible mother, although I knew a good case could be made to support it. As a matter of fact it would be possible to argue that my being a mother was one long series of irresponsible behaviour, and that this Moroccan trip was only one more irresponsibility in a long list which began with Ronit's conception.

Ronit was conceived while Shimon and I were hitch-hiking from East Africa to South Africa. Shimon was South African. We had met in

Israel and married so that he could obtain leave from the army, which had exhausted him. With borrowed money we flew from Tel Aviv to Nairobi to visit Shimon's sister and then hitchhiked the vast distance to Johannesburg to visit the rest of his family. At that time hitchhiking was the only means of travelling by land. There was no public transportation. Actually there were no roads, only dirt tracks riddled with ridges and potholes. The journey was difficult, bumping through areas where the tsetse fly had wiped out human life with sleeping sickness and the only visible homo sapiens were fierce-looking nomads, seven feet tall, draped in blankets and beads, wandering with spears and cows. For days on end there was nowhere to buy food or find a bed. Not surprisingly, when we reached the civilisation of Dadoma, Tanganyika, (now Tanzania), we splurged on the luxuries of Hotel Dadoma. These included a bedroom with a four-poster bed, silk sheets and a mosquito net.

The contrast with nights spent cramped in vehicles or on the floors of wooden shacks was so intoxicating that I became pregnant. However, this fact did not reveal itself to me until we reached Johannesburg, two and a half months later. Meanwhile, secretly, tenaciously, the child in my womb clung to life. Ronit's survival was nothing short of a miracle.

Outside Dadoma travelling became treacherous. The jungle paths disappeared into rocks, stumps and gullies. I was so severely shaken by the jolting and thudding that I hung on to my limbs and breasts to prevent them detaching. I held my body together piece by piece. Each time we lurched into a crevice or bounced off a stump, the jolt was so fierce that I found myself clutching my guts to stop them hitting the floor. The poor newly-made Ronit was in there somewhere, hanging on. But at least, unaware of Ronit's presence, I could not be held responsible for those early months in my acrobatic womb. It was different later on.

In Johannesburg I discovered I was pregnant. The news was devastating. For me, having a baby was an alien concept, going to Mars was more of a consideration. I wanted only to travel. As a child I was more fascinated by Aladdin and Sinbad than by the Bobbsy Twins and

14

Bessie Bunter. As an adolescent my pin-ups were not movie stars, but maps. Travel was my great passion, my first love, and I wanted nothing to come between it and me.

Africa was only the beginning, the plan was to travel through Europe to Russia and then onwards from there. But I was forced to stay pregnant, abortion was impossible, only witch doctors performed them. Having no alternative, I decided to ignore the whole thing in the hope that it would go away. In my three months working in Johannesburg, and in the following months hitchhiking through South Africa, Spain and France, I never consulted a doctor. When I confessed this to the Montreal obstetrician, in my final month of pregnancy, he drew his eyebrows tight, sucked in his lips, and stared at me in silence. I like to think it was more in wonder than in censure. After an exhausting examination, he mumbled, "well both you and the baby seem to be healthy," and shrugged his shoulders, in a gesture indicating there was no accounting for providence, so if he thought I had acted irresponsibly, he never let on.

I did make one concession to pregnancy: I bought a book on natural childbirth by Dick-Read, a South African doctor. The main fact I gleaned from Dr. Dick-Read was that having a baby didn't hurt. Secure in that knowledge, and with implicit trust, I put the entire matter out of my head and carried on with my vitaminless, doctorless itinerary. Months later, in hospital, torn apart by the cruellest pain I had ever known, sweating and panting and gasping in the agony of childbirth, I felt outraged by the deception. The only time I cried out was in protest to Shimon. "Damn that Doctor Read," I wailed, in indignation. "He betrayed us."

As if the trauma of those first desperate months clinging to life in the hostile jungles of East Africa wasn't enough for the poor, unborn foetus Ronit, she had to undergo a further battle for survival in the aggressive waters of the Atlantic. In my sixth month of pregnancy we sailed from Cape Town to Malaga on a Cunard liner. My plan to ignore the pregnancy was working to perfection. No one suspected my condition. The modest swell of belly was easily concealed under loose clothing, and I had virtually forgotten all about it. I participated in the ship's activities, attending the dances, which I loved, and joining in the games and competitions. When the kicks came, I pressed my hands over the offending area, rubbing it gently, soothing it as though it was a muscle twitch, and waited until it was better.

Our first stop was the Canary Islands, and eager to see volcanoes and hear Flamenco music, I convinced a reluctant Shimon to leave the ship, having been told it would be easy to get another one. For two weeks we tried unsuccessfully to book a passage to Malaga and finally settled for third class passage on a small elderly ship we had been warned against. Third class consisted of two dorms in the hold, women and children in one, men in the other. The dorm was narrow and windowless with two tiers of bunk beds so close together we had to shuffle sideways between them. The mattresses were lumpy and crawling with bed bugs. There was no deck and no food. The other passengers came equipped with baskets filled with sausages and bread. The smell of garlic, combined with the smell of diesel fumes, was nauseating. To make matters even worse, we ran into a storm the first night at sea. Everyone was sick, babies crying and spurting vomit, splattering the floor and walls with undigested garlic sausage. Suddenly I knew I was pregnant.

Although terminally nauseous and unable to eat, I couldn't stop throwing up, my distended belly clenched in spasms of pain from the violent retching. Everything hurt. My aching teeth projected thin needles of pain into my eye sockets and my cheekbones were like rods burning holes into my brain. Shimon searched for a doctor or nurse, fearing the worst. He couldn't even find a first aid kit, or anyone who spoke English. In desperation he carried me onto the tiny, forbidden, first class deck where at least I could breathe fresh air instead of the stench below. For almost five days I lay on that deck writhing in pain, my stomach contracted in a tight fist punching me from within, battering my womb, as the ship pitched and heaved. I thought I was dying and didn't much care. But through it all, Ronit held on, determined to be born.

In a strategically placed mirror, hanging somewhere above the operating table I was lying on, legs forced wide apart by metal stirrups, I watched her being born. Shimon wasn't allowed in the delivery room and I felt abandoned and alone. Ironically, although I was the centre of attention, I was virtually ignored by the efficient medical staff brusque with preparations and crisp utterances like 'dilation', 'uterus', 'diaphragm', 'placenta', as though none of these related to me. It was disorientating having to look up toward the mirror to see something happening down inside myself while glaring lights distorted my vision and brutal, spasmodic thrusts contorted my womb. Engrossed in mastering a body in chaos and satisfying the demands of a doctor I couldn't even see, I was suddenly aware of a gentle cajoling voice nuzzling my ear and a hand soothing my forehead. I looked up into the pained eyes of a young intern bending over me, coaxing me into taking whiffs of gas to ease the pain. I pressed my hand into his with the intensity of a new lover, but refused the gas - losing consciousness was even more frightening than giving birth. Heaving and panting I strained to eject the foreign presence trapped in my womb, while the doctor's voice urged me to keep pushing and the intern's fingers gripped mine, offering the only comfort.

"Can you see the head?" the doctor asked while encouraging me to push.

"No." My voice scratched through an arid mouth.

"It's right here." A finger flashed into view and disappeared.

"I can't see it," I moaned, my muddled brain straining to comprehend the remote fragmented images in the mirror, through the haze of pain and excitement.

"What do you mean you can't see it, the head is out...can't you see the hair?"

But in my confusion I had mistaken the dark patch of hair for my own pubic hair, forgetting I had been shaved.

"Keep pushing," he insisted, "it won't be long."

"I see it now," I said with relief, as a small, dark, fuzzy orb appeared in the mirror, balancing in space.

"Push hard. It's almost over."

Then suddenly through the searing pain, a large fleshy lump, raw and bloody, slid into view.

Minutes later when the doctor lay the lump on my stomach, umbilical cord still uncut, it was shining and beautifully formed, like a rubber doll I had as a child with succulently curved arms and legs, except instead of pink, it was entirely purple. For a moment I felt like the leading lady in a gala performance who had just been handed a bouquet of flowers after the final curtain call.

"It's a girl," the doctor announced with satisfaction. I hadn't thought to ask. "Congratulations!"

"But you told me I was going to have a boy," I protested.

"Never believe what I say," he shrugged, and I closed my eyes against the confusion and dire exhaustion.

I was astonished to see how lovely Ronit was when the nurse brought her for her first feed. Through some magical metamorphosis, the shapeless slimy lump in the mirror had changed into a beautiful baby. She had a full head of black hair, creamy white skin and large dark eyes. I gazed at her with the same wonder I had once watched a nasty-looking egg, splattered with muck, turn into a fluffy yellow chick.

Next day the young nurse on duty tied Ronit's hair with a red ribbon and asked if she could show the baby to her boyfriend. "Just to prod him a little," she explained. She planned on enticing him with a state of the art product. Each time Ronit was brought for her feeding, the nurse pulled the curtain around my bed so as not to offend the three other mothers in the room, none of whom were breast feeding - "the sight might be somewhat repulsive," she explained.

"Mind you, I think it's a good thing," she added. "Cow's milk is for calves, mother's milk is for babies, but then they don't see it like that." At least my mothering met with some initial approval.

18

2. Early Days

As if in revenge for her enforced silence during those desperate days in the womb, the state of the art baby didn't stop crying for three months. Because we were penniless, Shimon and I were living with my family in my parents' two-bedroomed flat. My brother had one bedroom, we had the other and my parents slept in the living room. My brother and father had to get up early for work and Shimon was suffering from a recurrence of the hepatitis he had contracted in the Israeli army. (The night I was giving birth, the doctor had been more concerned about him than about me, he looked so ill.) Rest was crucial to his recovery. I was under constant pressure to keep Ronit from crying and disturbing everyone's sleep. All through the night I rocked her in her crib or in my arms, pacing back and forth in the narrow space between the bed and wall. Worried she would cry, I fed her every time she opened her mouth. It was difficult to sit because of my burning stitches (cutting and stitching were standard medical procedures at the time), and nursing was painful.

The nights were a never-ending agony. During the day, when my mother, brother or father took over the pacing, I tended Shimon who was bedridden and very ill, boiled piles of nappies, sheets, blankets, baby clothes and maternity bras, because my mother said that boiling prevented skin rash.

Ronit didn't need sleep. Her days in the womb had trained her to do without it, but I, without her advantages, craved it, falling asleep in the bath, on the loo, once with my head pressed in the rungs of her crib.

Aside from sleep deprivation, I was deprived of fresh air and social contact. I was unable to leave the house, not being permitted to take an infant outdoors. She was born at the end of November, winter in Montreal. It was considered dangerous to expose babies to the severe cold before they were six weeks old.

After three weeks the situation was unbearable. My eyes were puffy from lack of sleep; my stitches ached and itched at the same time; Ronit wailed incessantly no matter what I did; I was unable to visit friends because she couldn't be left with anyone, not even my mother, as she seemed constantly hungry and in need of feeding. I felt the walls pressing against me and the ceiling descending to flatten me, squeezing the juices from my soul. Motherhood was a desperate affair. I did not go gently into maternity, I was dragged into it kicking and screaming.

One day when Shimon was at the doctor's, and my mother was out shopping, I indulged in a deluge of tears, crying with frustration, with rage, with bewilderment, railing against my fate. I was trapped in a nightmare from which there was no possibility of waking. Ronit was in the living room finally asleep in a rickety old pram, loaned to us by a friend. All at once I heard that piercing relentless wail I had come to dread. It filled my head, pounding in my blood, each mindless 'wha...' stoking a volcano waiting inside me. Suddenly I exploded. I knew only one thing. I had to stop that sound. I ran from the bedroom, rushed into the living room and flung the source of the howling into space. The pram impacted against the wall, teetered and fell over. Ronit rolled on to the floor. I turned my back, stalked into the bedroom and locked the door.

My first reaction was a burst of exquisite joy, a wonderful sense of being young and free, and alive, a relief so overwhelming it was as though I had survived some terrible death and found myself with another chance at life. Then, just as suddenly, I was drained of life, emotionally dumb, feeling nothing, knowing nothing, hearing and seeing nothing. Limp and wilted, bereft of will or desire, I collapsed on to the bed, shattered like a windscreen after a head-on collision.

About an hour later I woke abruptly with a sense of panic and rushed into the living room. Ronit was on the floor, still crying.

Carefully I picked her up, like a broken doll. Her face was crimson with howling and her small fists clenched blue, but she seemed unhurt. I gave her my breast and cradling her in my arms, sang her a song Shimon often sang to her, *Hush Little Baby Don't You Cry*. My mother found us both asleep on the sofa.

Despite a severe case of colic, Ronit thrived, but I was withering. At her one-month check up, the doctor prescribed sleeping medicine. When I balked at giving such a small baby sleeping medicine, he said, "it's not for her, it's for you. She'll be fine, I'm not worried about her, it's you I'm worried about... you need sleep and you need to get out of the house, you look like a ghost." I knew he was right.

When Ronit was less than six weeks old, Shimon and I were invited to a new year's party, at a musician friend's house. Life was trickling back into my veins, Shimon was on the mend, and with the doctor's orders fresh in mind, I decided we would take Ronit and go. My mother protested wildly, raising the objections of cold, of noise, of smoke, of drink, of the late hour, of the inappropriateness of the occasion, "you don't take an infant to a party with crazy musicians. The music alone will make her deaf." As a last resort she tried, "but you don't have a carrier cot... you have nothing to take the baby in and nothing to put her in when you get there." Undeterred, I wrapped Ronit in blankets, placed her in a cardboard carton with holes in the lid for air, and Shimon carried the carton to the party. My mother was in a state of shock.

Once there I put the carton in the corner of an unused room, out of harm's way. But soon afterwards when I went to check on Ronit, I couldn't find the carton. I searched the other rooms frantically, but it was nowhere to be seen. Petrified, I rushed to tell Shimon. Strangely, the thing I feared most was my mother's reproach, she would be terrible.

Not suspecting the contents, someone had removed the carton to the cloakroom. Shimon found it under a pile of coats. Terrified that Ronit had suffocated under the heavy garments, I panicked. Unable to breathe in symbiotic empathy, I leapt at the carton and pulled Ronit out gasping to fill my lungs, fighting a thick barrier like a plastic wedge jammed into my mouth, preventing air reaching my lungs. Ronit was fast asleep and breathing quietly. Rocking her in my arms and slowly regaining my breath and composure, I made a silent vow to be a more careful mother in future. After all, if I hadn't asked for her to be born, neither had she. But being born gave her rights and I had to respect those rights. Only Shimon ever knew of the near calamity. He shared the blame and spared me the full guilt. But, in defending the charge of irresponsible mother, I can't help remembering the cardboard carton.

In retrospect, it seems to me incomprehensible that motherhood requires no special qualification or training - no course, no degree, no certificate, no screening, no short list, not even a form to fill in, or a whisper of advice. Anyone can do it, no questions asked, no skill necessary. Parenthood must be the only job in this category. Even the most menial occupation requires some interview to determine potential and suitability. Yet parenthood is the only job one can't quit. It's a permanent occupation. I soon discovered that motherhood would never go away. Ronit was there forever. I found this relentless permanence especially hard to accept. At times I longed to say, 'well that was nice, I did it, I had this child, but now it's time the job was finished, it's time for her to go.' But she never went, the job was never finished, there was never an end in sight, not even a break.

Motherhood was not only a full-time job, it was a lifetime commitment. No one had ever mentioned this to me before. It came as an unwelcome revelation, and learning to cope with it was a long and lonely process. I had no peer group to help or console me. My closest friends were involved with love, romance, careers and university; babies were an irrelevance, even a bore. The few new mothers I met basked in motherhood. It was an eternal sun bestowing life upon them. At every opportunity they would dwell upon its joys. No detail was too small to fascinate, to savour - disposable nappies, formulas, burping, teething - the involvement was total, connecting them with grand purposes, cosmic designs. They were part of the universal, timeless unfolding. My pathetic attempts to confide my conflict and distress were seen as injections of discord into the harmony of creation. My unhappy confessions were greeted with shock and aversion. No decent mother entertained ideas of wanting out, of wanting to be rid of her offspring, or at least never admitted to them. No decent mother felt shackled by motherhood; it was unnatural, perverse. I could feel the turning away as from a shameful contagion. And so I was forced to work things out on my own, find my own solutions. Perhaps I lacked the gene of motherhood other females were born with and would therefore have to work harder at being a mother. My only assistance came from the printed word. I turned to the bookshelves for understanding and advice.

When she was three months old, Ronit's crying ceased as dramatically as it began. The doctor explained that her digestive system had matured and she would no longer suffer gastric disturbances. Whatever the reason, she became pleasant and compliant. Without the constant background of wailing, I stopped thinking of giving her away. Gradually pleasant sensations crept back into my life. I smelled the beginning of Spring, I tasted my mother's Friday night dinners, I saw colours and felt textures. On occasion I even laughed. It was like banging one's head against the wall - it felt so good to stop.

I even began to enjoy Ronit. She was alert and responsive and the constant changes in her were exciting. The first time I found her sitting up, her eyes meeting mine head-on instead of from a supine posture, I was thrilled by the wonder of it all and even called my mother to report. The books I was reading informed me that Ronit was consistently advanced for her age. Besides, she was pretty, and complete strangers would stop to admire her. Still, new acquaintances, and even many people I had known for a long time, never knew I had a child. I didn't easily admit to motherhood, although I was forced to resign myself to it. With great regret my travel plans were put on hold, although I never ceased to

23

contemplate them.

Shimon and I found our own small flat. We slept in the living-room, Ronit in the bedroom. This arrangement made it possible for us to close the bedroom door and put Ronit out of our lives. Shimon would play the guitar and sing in his rich, plaintive voice, and I would dream about travelling. I made endless lists - lists of the countries I would visit, lists of travel agencies specialising in those countries, lists of travel and guide books, even lists of what I would take. I made and revised my lists, consulting maps, charts and books, while he sang about freight trains and lonesome highways. Shimon much preferred singing about 'that long ribbon of highway' to travelling it. The road for him was a precarious place requiring constant vigilance, fraught with unreliability. He had suffered my passion for travel as something which had to be endured, my wild seed which had to be sown before we could settle. But with as much enthusiasm as I anticipated the next adventure, he anticipated the end of adventure, the beginning of stability. And now he had it.

Shimon was wonderful with Ronit. He could do everything I could and more. Whereas I was happy to dress Ronit in a tee shirt and nappy, he liked to see her in the frilly panties South Africans call 'brookies' and a short dress from which the brookies protruded daintily. Not fully recovered from hepatitis, he often looked after her while I earned money teaching dancing. I had studied dance since childhood and taught it before I took to the road; it was easy getting back into it. When he did recover he worked as a sign writer and practised guitar and I took university courses and continued teaching dance, eventually forming my own performance group. Life, if not as I wanted to live it, was at least becoming liveable and, with compromises and concessions, I was coming to terms with motherhood, although these terms were often incomprehensible to others.

One of the things I resented most about being a mother was having to rise at the crack of dawn. I hated getting up early in the cold grey days of winter, uninspired by the score of routine duties awaiting me. So, as

24

soon as Ronit was able to eat solids, I would leave a selection of food in her cot at night - crackers, celery and carrot sticks, bits of apple, slivers of cheese - so that she would find them in the morning and not disturb me. I also left toys so she could entertain herself.

The system worked beautifully. She would wake up, talk to herself, eat the food she found and play with her toys, while I slept. By the time I got to her she was wet but otherwise content. Everyone was happy with the arrangement until one day when I seriously overslept and my mother paid an unexpected visit. She entered Ronit's room to find her soaking wet, her cot strewn with limp carrots, slimy cheese and soggy crackers, and her arms and legs sticky, anointed with apple juice leaked from her bottle.

"You leave food overnight in the baby's bed?" she accused in killer tones.

"I don't want her to wake me up early in the morning," I confessed, bowing my head to the knife.

"You don't want her to wake you up early in the morning?" she mocked, scornfully.

"What kind of a mother are you?... I'll tell you what kind of mother you are. You're lazy and selfish... That's the kind of mother you are. People will think you're an animal. Only an animal takes better care of its children." Her voice was thick with derision.

I was crushed. Hunched against the pitiless onslaught, I made feeble attempts to gather the bits of food and tidy the cot, while my mother changed Ronit with thrust after thrust of guilt.

"Some mother you have. She doesn't deserve you. Thank goodness you have a grandmother." She was merciless.

I didn't blame my mother, she loved Ronit as only a grandmother could. My behaviour was inconceivable to her. For her the baby's needs always came first. And feeding was the paramount need. I still remember her cackling like a chicken to tempt me into consuming one more mouthful. Grossly irresponsible, I was failing on all counts of motherhood.

Although devastated, I wasn't convinced. Was I selfish and lazy? Was I unnatural? Was I a terrible mother because I wanted to sleep late? By now I had discovered my guru, Dr. Spock, the compassionate baby doctor of the sixties, and clung to his reassurances. He believed in a mother following her instincts. I was following mine, considering my needs as important to fulfil as Ronit's, just so long as I loved her and didn't cause her unnecessary suffering. I was opposed to sacrifices, especially unneeded ones, and I refused to be swallowed up by motherhood. I too had rights and, dispelling doubts and accusations, I became even more determined to preserve them. I would have to find my own way. Meanwhile, I continued leaving food in Ronit's cot. Only I made sure to secure the lid on the juice bottle, and I never opened the door before noon.

3. The Finjan and Bob Dylan : Travel Substitutes

When Ronit was four years old her life changed dramatically. Invaded by an unorthodox segment of society, her nuclear family was suddenly extended, requiring radical adjustments. Shimon opened a folk music club called The Finjan, the word for an Arabic coffee pot, around which people traditionally gathered to sing, tell stories and drink coffee. Each week a different performer was hired as the main act, while Shimon, the house musician, was the warm-up act. It was an immediate success.

In the early sixties performers like Bob Dylan, Leonard Cohen, Joni Mitchell, and Kris Kristofferson, not yet popular, were eager to gain experience and exposure by performing in small clubs. Even seasoned performers like the Blues musicians Sonny Terry and Brownie McGhee and the Black Blues guitarist, John Lee Hooker, were readily available. Shimon and I, both devoted to Folk Music and Blues, found it thrilling to have musicians we had listened to on record, right there in the flesh. It was especially thrilling for Shimon who had never seen live performers in isolated South Africa, and who was, by now, a competent musician himself.

One of his idols was Josh White, the great Blues musician. Even in South Africa, Shimon had every one of his recordings. He could hardly believe his good fortune when one day Josh White came to our house.

Shimon had recently been learning to play some of Josh White's chords and blues sequences. There was one elusive chord he had found impossible to duplicate, the stretch was too great, and he was sure some ruse must be employed to play it. Knowing this might be his only chance, he took the plunge. With the humility of an initiate cross-examining the master, he asked Josh White if he would demonstrate the chord. Josh White drew his guitar to him like a lover and, spreading the fingers of his large black hand over its body, struck the impossible chord. The sound swelled, filling the room like the sound of the great amen. Shimon looked as though he had just seen God.

The Finjan was located in a part of Montreal where hotels were expensive. Since we couldn't afford hotel costs, the financial arrangement included rent-free accommodation with us. We put an extra bed in Ronit's room. She slept in one bed and every week a different performer slept in the other. Her room was small and sharing it necessitated removing her toy chest. Together we selected her favourite toys and squeezed them on to her bookshelf, banishing the rest to the locker. We also emptied one of her drawers and made space in her closet. Although she was not enthusiastic about the new arrangements, she adapted to them without protest.

At first she reacted to the succession of musicians sharing her room, passing through her life, with indifference. Somewhat shy of strangers, she kept a cautious distance, yet made allowances for their presence in small ways like tip-toeing in her bedroom - they had probably gone to sleep not much before she awoke. Essentially she carried on with her life out of their way, while at the same time quietly observing theirs. She was good at entertaining herself. Not especially fond of dolls, she busied herself with painting, drawing, looking at books, or playing with her building toys.

Later, after they had returned several times, she became friendly with some of the performers, even developing an affection for a rare few. She accepted the fact that there was always someone living with us, that a constant stream of people came and went. She learned to live her life around that fact, gradually incorporating it into her existence, just as she learned to live with the constant strumming of guitars, and the acceptance of people she found strange, sometimes frightening.

Ronit was three before she saw a black person - there were hardly any in our neighbourhood, few in Montreal. She was astounded. "Mummy why does that lady have a rubber face?" she asked, bewildered. When black musicians started appearing in her room she reacted with suspicion, convinced they hadn't washed, asking why the palms of their hands were clean and the rest of them dirty. But by the time Sonny Terry and Brownie McGhee performed at the club she had grown accustomed to black skin.

Because Sonny was blind and Brownie lame, and because they were well-known performers, no longer young, who deserved extra consideration, we had arranged rooms for them in a hotel. However, they liked spending time in our flat. I cooked special dinners for them - Sonny's favourite was baked ham and pineapple pie - and on their nights off musician friends would come by for wonderful jamming sessions.

From the very beginning Ronit was more friendly with Sonny and Brownie than with the other performers. They were accustomed to relating to children. Brownie had several of his own including a daughter Ronit's age, his youngest. Identifying Ronit with his daughter, he always referred to her as 'the baby'. Even years later when she was a teenager, he would ask, "how's the baby?" Sonny treated Ronit to special harmonica effects, making his harmonica talk for her. Her favourite utterance was 'I want my mamma'. She would sit on the floor, looking up at him, small and white, her eyes wide, her legs tucked under, waiting for 'I want my mama' with the avid expectation she'd wait for sleeping beauty to spring to life. And he, large and black, his big boot thumping beside her, his gold rings flashing, his eyes smiling down on her, coaxed whoops and hoots and howls from his harmonica until it finally wailed, 'I want my mamma.' Each time he played it, her face lit up in wonder and he laughed his great belly laugh, slapping his thighs in delight. Although she could hardly understand his thick Southern accent, I could sense a connection between them, the unlikely connection of polarities, they communicated through 'I want my mama'.

Whereas Ronit accepted the new life style with detachment and neutrality, warming to it only gradually, I embraced it. I worked at The Finjan right from the beginning, leaving Ronit at home with a baby-sitter on week nights and with my parents, who lavished affection upon her, at weekends, accepting their indulgences for the sake of my freedom.

I loved everything about The Finjan; the atmosphere of the room, intimate with fishnets, brass lanterns and candlelit tables; the late nights; the all-night restaurants; the music; and especially the musicians. Every night was a Saturday night. I never knew the mornings.

By now Ronit was able to get her own breakfast and dress herself for school. She woke me only to braid her long plait and to hear me say, "have a good day at school, and don't forget your lunch". Then she waited for my father to take her to school and I slept until noon.

Plaiting her hair was the one thing I didn't resent being woken up for. I did it lovingly. Ronit's hair was my indulged darling, the fulfilment of my childhood fantasy. No sacrifice was too great for it. It fell like a cascade streaming over her bum, thick and rippling and long, long, long. I would never let it be cut. When I was a child I yearned for long hair. But my mother viewed long hair as an enemy against which she waged a relentless battle. Then one summer at my aunt's farm, when my mother was preoccupied, it slipped by her watchful eye and grew to my shoulders. For one sweet summer I felt like Rapunzel. Then suddenly, alarmed by her terrible lapse, she summoned a hair cutter. I remember screeching in agony as the scissors descended. The poor woman thought she had pierced my skull. My first act of independence was growing my hair long. I never cut it again. Ronit's first act of independence was cutting hers short. It was many years before she allowed it to pass her ears.

For me, meeting a new performer every week was, in a way, like travelling, each musician an adventure, a landscape to explore, a magic encounter. I didn't have to court the exceptional as every real traveller does, the exceptional courted me. I learned to tread softly as though entering a new land, feeling my way into the experience. I had a special affinity with those who not only sang traditional ballads, work songs and blues, but who wrote their own songs. Long after Shimon had gone to sleep, I would spend what remained of the night, ensconced in my wonderful kitchen, listening to their music, participating in their visions, immersed in their poetry. They were like the images in their songs, like

30

the sound of their music, tender, powerful, haunting, original. They were like outlaws with anti-establishment lyrics as their weapons, they embodied romance, mystery, excitement, rebellion. I looked into their eyes, breathed their atmosphere and longed for the unknown yet to be experienced. With the first signs of light I'd slip away, not allowing the shapes of morning to dispel the poetry of the night. In what remained of the day, I would cook for them, ascend Mount Royal in the heart of the city to dream under the weeping willows by the lake, attend to the flat and to Ronit, prepare for my university courses, and wait for the night.

Most of the performers were male. Women found the bitter solitude of anonymous cities strung together by vast stretches of highway, with only a guitar for comfort, too hard for consistent endurance and rarely returned. They fascinated me, these determined, devoted males, these gypsy bards. I was fascinated not only by their talent, by their need to make music, but also by the way they lived, on the edge, exposed and vulnerable, singing protest and love, their lives part of their songs.

Performing at The Finjan was a difficult, lonely experience. Bereft of electronic assistance, of extravagant lighting, of a distanced stage, the performer was alone, impaled by a red-amber spotlight, caged by expectant faces, with just his guitar and his voice. Yet he created sounds and images that went directly to the centre of feeling, enhanced by the intense sensuality he projected. He held up his soul like a mirror and I saw myself in it. He sat on a tall stool, the guitar cradled in his thigh, the fingers of one hand stroking the slender neck, while the other beat a driving rhythm, and I could feel him lower his head into its curves in perfect oneness. When he threw back his head, drawing the guitar to his breast, clenching his eyes shut in some wild ecstasy of music and man, I'd shiver with the embrace. Sometimes I knew I could love him because of his song, such was my empathy, my yearning, my desire to nourish, to hold. I related to the wanderer in him, the seeker, the rebel, and because I was temporarily anchored, I was able to provide an anchor, a small haven, a brief respite. Because the musicians were always on the road, not in one place long enough to make friends, they responded to my extension of care with enthusiasm and affection. In one way they had the effect on me children were supposed to have, they inspired mothering, but unlike children they never overstayed their welcome, their last song left me wanting more. And they inspired much else. They dared to point to a new horizon over which the changing times were taking shape, and I, along with my generation, tuned into their vision, sharing their sense of triumph in breaking new ground. Armed with flowers in our hands and in our hair, 'coils of beads around our necks', and lines from their songs, we embraced the changing times. I became very close to many of them. Some eventually became lovers, some remained my closest friends, and some went on to become famous.

Bob Dylan epitomised many of the characteristics which drew me to the musicians. I first heard him play in New York at Gerde's Folk City, a Greenwich Village club popular with folk singers. Every Monday Gerde's had a hootenanny night where musicians came to perform and meet each other. The standard was high, many now well-known musicians used Gerde's as a showcase, a venue to perfect their performance skills and to be discovered. I don't know if Bob Dylan was scheduled to play that night, because when the M.C., Brother John Sellers, called him, he looked uncomfortable and dragged himself on to the stage, whereas the other performers leapt on to it. The audience didn't know him, he had recently come to New York, and they seemed unwilling to make the effort to listen. After a few songs there were shouts for him to get off the stage. He continued singing through the shouts, looking so thin, I thought I could see his shoulder blades cutting his flesh, his pale aquiline face topped by a jaunty cap making him look thinner and paler. Before his allotted songs were up, he slunk off the stool, and looking like he'd been fatally wounded, slouched off the stage. I was among the few people who clapped, not only because of empathy, but because I thought he was excellent. His voice took some getting used to. At that time it had a rent, rasping quality as though it had been caught on barb wire which tore

32

deeper as he struggled to free it, but it was ideally suited to both his lyrics and his appearance on stage, which were troubled, anguished, conveying a searing beauty. It went straight to my heart. He was deeply moving, unforgettable.

When he came to Montreal, less than a year later, I went to meet him at a down town bar to take him to The Finjan. By now his fortunes had improved. He had a small but devoted following, mainly musicians themselves, who thought he was brilliant. He seemed more assured, that perpetual orphaned look, helpless and bereft, was almost gone. As soon as he saw me he launched into one of those sad funny monologues I was to become so fond of, explaining why he was late. He told me that upon arriving at the Montreal airport the customs officials put him through some intensive questioning - probably because he looked dishevelled and spoke with a rambling cowboy drawl. This came as a shock. "Hey man", he responded to one question, "that ain't none of your business." His behaviour must have seemed so erratic, so surly, so resentful of authority, that the officials decided to search him thoroughly. "Can you believe those mother fuckers, they started poking into my things... my personal things."

He was outraged by the intrusion into his privacy. When the officer had the audacity to open his bag he pulled it away, "hey man you can't do that, them's my personal belongings". He looked at me, took a long pull on his cigarette, and said, "I hate that kind of stuff." Apparently he didn't know they could do exactly that and they did it. He became increasingly incensed as they not only probed his belongings but searched his person. He was at the mercy of authority and he detested it. Through sheer perversity he smiled sardonically and said, "hey man, if it's the dope you want, I got it hid right here...in my harmonica." He couldn't believe what happened next.

"D'ye know what those mother fuckers did... they unscrewed every screw in every one of my harmonicas looking for dope. Those dumb-assed coppers thought I was going to tell them where I stash the dope, those creeps couldn't even speak English." By the time the search was over he'd missed his bus and had to wait over an hour for another one.

"When I got to town I went into a bar for a drink, y'know, just to cool my head, it needed cooling real bad. I ordered a drink and handed the barman a $10 bill. That dood took my good U.S. money and gave me monopoly money for change, y'know that phoney coloured money, he even gave me a $2 bill." I remembered that American money has no $2 bills, and was all one colour, whereas Canadian money has a different colour for each denomination.

"Hey man, what do you take me for, I ain't no fool, I ain't taking none of your funny money. You some kind of a crook, or what? He started hollerin' and screamin' and I started hollerin' and screamin' louder, and he said he was callin' the po-lice. That dood was sure fuckin' with my head. And all those streets were headin' down the hill into the river and I just knew if I didn't sit tight I'd roll right down into that river and drown." He turned to me with a look of total incomprehension, "what kind of a place is this anyway? I sure could use some salvation."

As he puffed relentlessly on his cigarette I wondered if it was possible that he knew nothing about border crossings, customs, countries with different languages, different currencies, if this was his first time out of the U.S.A. I never knew if that traumatic entry into Canada was entirely real or partly imagined or a bit of both, but I loved the story and its dead-pan delivery.

Later, when I got to know him better, I understood that the impression of baffled innocence and inability to fathom the ways of the world, of being a primitive anti-intellectual, as though he'd never read a book, was cultivated as part of his persona. In fact he was astute, knowledgeable, even disciplined. It was his way of keeping people off-balance, of controlling the situation by not letting on if what he was saying was fact or fantasy. I came to accept this and to enjoy which ever it was.

That attitude of incredible naivety when dealing with the

practicalities of life, like he had just stepped into the twentieth century was much in evidence during the subsequent times I saw him in New York. Once I introduced him to Rivka, an Israeli friend of mine. They hit it off immediately. He said he'd never eaten Israeli food and she invited him to dinner. He was delighted by the invitation and was in the process of noting her address. "Eighty-eighth street," she told him. He stopped writing, returned the pencil and paper to his pocket and looked at her with a sad apologetic smile.

"I can't come."

"Why?" she asked confused, things had been going so well.

"I don't go above forty-second street." He paused, then as if in explanation added, "there's some real weird people up there. Forty-second street, that's as far as I go." And that was final.

Another time, inspired by my passion for travel, he said, "Yeah, I'd like to travel...I'd like to see Israel... what d'ye have to do to get there?"

"Well first you have to get a passport."

"How d'ye do that?"

I couldn't tell if he really didn't know, but went along for the ride.

"You go to the passport office, fill out a form, take some photos, pay some money and apply for a passport."

He looked disheartened. "Y'got to do all that?"

"It's not that much."

"I ain't going nowhere if I gotta do all that."

Israel was dropped.

Bob Dylan played at The Finjan and shared Ronit's room. He was the only performer we ever had who people walked out on. (Later, young musicians like Toronto's Murray McLaughlan, who was to became famous himself, vied to sleep in the bed he had slept in.) His rough, gravelly voice with its nasal twang didn't appeal to Finjan audiences and, not knowing what to make of him, they walked out. One night, discouraged by the lack of appreciation, he said to Shimon, "this is the last time I play clubs, from now on I only do concerts. I'm going to play Carnegie Hall. I'm going to make it big." Shimon laughed at the absurdity of the idea.

"Yeah, you and who else?" he teased. Shimon wasn't particularly impressed by Bob Dylan's non-melodic songs, and by his tuneless, often off-key voice. But I was mesmerised by his songs, by his performance style, by the combination of his dishevelled appearance and the careless informality of his music, juxtaposed with the precision of his poetry, the startling bite of his layered imagery, by his raw vital energy. For me the growling monotone voice people objected to was a third instrument interwoven with his guitar and harmonica, producing a tortured sound, counterpointing, complementing, adding a new dimension to his powerful lyrics. I thought he was unique, great. I loved his imagination, his original way of seeing things, his off-beat humour, and I loved what he was singing about, his challenge to authority, to 'the masters of war', his celebration of the young, the powerless, the outcasts.

After one discouraging Finjan performance, when he was hurt by the audience's insensitive behaviour and, pretending it didn't matter, he confessed to me that he was feeling down, achy, depleted. "I'm all twisted up" he said, "I need to untwist real bad." I offered him a massage. He abandoned himself to that massage with the intensity he devoted to his song writing. As my thumbs circled and coaxed the small knots and ridges imbedded in his flesh and my palms pressed and kneaded his pale buttery skin, my fingers reaching into his pain, I could feel his body sigh as it surrendered to my hands. He wouldn't allow the massage to stop; he needed it, he said, to level his head. He kept me at it all night long. When I protested and wanted to stop, he sang me snatches of songs he kept in his head, and told me sad, funny, mad stories. Soon the bed became a tiny island adrift in a surreal stream of consciousness, brilliant flashes suddenly illuminating the dark.

I was enthralled by his stunning connections, the electric leaps from sense to nonsense, the unpredictable twists and spirals of his imagination, as he related the unrelatable. His mind became a collage of images overlapping into new meanings as he laid down layer upon layer of madness and sanity which entwined and interlaced, forming some kind of subliminal sense, moving in and out of my comprehension. It was astonishing - strange, wonderful, exceptional. Soon he didn't have to urge me to continue massaging, because just as he couldn't stop talking it was more than just talking - ideas seemed to be pouring out of him - I couldn't stop massaging - it was more than just massaging, energy seemed to be flowing from my hands, shaping, creating, releasing the wild images trapped inside him. I had the sense that if he didn't expel those images battling in his head they would explode into madness and that my hands were somehow maintaining sanity. I was compelled to continue. It was an extraordinary duet. I massaged him until morning came and he was asleep.

That massage cemented our friendship. (Later he confided that if he ever got rich the first thing he would get was a full-time massage person. I should have applied for the job.) I saw him whenever I went to New York and our times together were a treat. He had an unexpected side to him, which I adored. He liked being the jester, leaping into impromptu capsules of off-beat acting out, tiny improvised performances where he plunged in and out of other realities. He often shared these morsels of fantasy theatre with Rambling Jack Elliott, a musician friend who greatly influenced his music, his style and his behaviour. They were very funny together, breaking into incongruous scenarios of whatever took their fancy.

One summer night when I was in New York, the three of us were tripping through the streets feeling great. Bob and Jack looked like a pair of adopted cowboys, in cowboy hats, boots, worn jeans, guitars and dark glasses. (It was unseemly for cowboys to wear glasses but dark glasses, 'shades' were acceptable.) I was the invisible cowgirl. They were at their playful, fun-loving best, laughing, joking, bouncing off each other. Suddenly we came to a wide square with an illuminated fountain in its centre rising and falling in bursts of colour. The setting was irresistible. They climbed the fountain wall, pulling me after them.

We sat on the wall, our legs dangling over the side, the fountain at our backs, looking down on the passers-by, like kings of the castle. Bob raised his guitar to toast the occasion and began strumming and picking, Country style. Jack joined him. A crowd gathered beneath us. Bob looked down into the raised faces and burst into Shakespeare. "I'm Ham-let," he drawled, cowboy style, with more twangs and licks, "and this here's Or-feel-ye-ah". He pointed his guitar toward Jack who nodded and tipped his hat to accompanying strums and riffs. "Far out," someone yelled. And they launched into a personalised rendition of Hamlet, narrated by two laid-back cowboys sitting around a camp fire and accompanied by Country and Western guitar picking. It was hilarious. A gem. We found the wall strewn with coins.

I was with Bob Dylan, walking down a Greenwich Village street, the first time he was followed by two teeny-boppers. He couldn't be convinced they were following him and kept stopping abruptly to see if they too would stop. When they did, shyly and at a safe distance, he was ecstatic. "I'm being followed", he whooped with joy, "can you believe it, I'm being followed!"

The incident inspired a confession. "I once followed Woody Guthrie... right here in the Village," I said, aware I was unleashing a boomerang.

"Y'mean you followed Woody Guthrie?" He was as stunned as if I had just revealed that I was the Virgin Mary. He idolised Woody Guthrie. Woody Guthrie was his hero, his guru, the formative influence in his life. He modelled himself on Woody Guthrie, he talked like him, sang like him, wrote talking blues like him and his main reason for coming to New York was in the hope of meeting Woody Guthrie, and with luck, to sing him one of his first songs, *A Song To Woody*. He wanted to hear every detail.

I was then fifteen years old. It was one of my first times in New York, and I was smitten by its unlimited possibilities. I had come with my friend, Rhoda Pomp, and while we were exploring the Village, feeling like characters in an adventure story, we came across a poster saying that Woody Guthrie was giving a Benefit performance that night. I was thrilled. Woody Guthrie was one of my favourite singers, a folk hero. I had read his autobiography *Bound For Glory* and his hard travelling was my inspiration. I had to hear him. But alas, when we got to the hall we discovered we didn't have enough money for tickets; we hadn't even noticed the price. As I retreated down the street, bitterly disappointed, I couldn't believe my eyes. There was Woody Guthrie himself walking toward us. I recognised him from the poster. On an impulse we turned and followed him. He went up a staircase at the back of the hall and disappeared behind the stage door. I stood there dissolved in bliss, intoxicated by a rush of excitement, by the magic of New York. I couldn't bring myself to leave that door. Rhoda Pomp and I sat on the metal steps, hoping for a miracle. About half an hour later Woody came out onto the landing to smoke a cigarette. We held our breaths. Suddenly he saw us.

"What you girls doing down there; come on up here and say hello." Feeling like we were climbing the stairway to paradise, we clattered up the steps. I explained that we didn't have enough money for tickets. "I'll fix that," he said, "you just come with me." He led us through the door and to our surprise, right onto the stage. Putting an arm around each of us he introduced us as 'Woody Guthrie and his Bobby Sox Brigade.' I don't know how we survived the joy. He got us chairs and we sat in a corner of the stage feeling blessed. Later he took us for 'eats', "Gotta keep my Brigade in eats," he said. The story was a winner.

The last time I saw Bob Dylan in New York was at Gerde's Folk City, where I had first seen him. Shimon and I were there to check out performers for The Finjan. The word quickly got around that someone was booking for a club. Bob Dylan was talking to us when several musicians approached Shimon, eager to have a word with him. "Your husband sure is famous," he said, impressed.

If for me The Finjan was a substitute for travel; for Ronit it was fertile soil for her responses to life to take root. If for me the musicians had a special magic, for her they were just people who slept in the bed opposite her bed and sat beside her at the kitchen table. When they began to appear on mega stages celebrated by mega audiences she deduced that everything was accessible. Having observed them so closely took the mystique out of their success. She had watched them picking up their guitars like this, playing them like that, it was all in the realm of possibility. No one fazed her, no achievement intimidated her. Soon she was singing on stage with Shimon. She had a pretty voice and could sing in harmony. Then she was asking for her own guitar. But here she ran into difficulty. Neither Shimon nor I were eager to teach her skills. Shimon believed that if she wanted to learn anything badly enough she would do it on her own, just as he had. I didn't adhere to his philosophy but was simply otherwise engaged. She developed a quiet resolve, an extension of the determination she had first exhibited as a foetus, surviving the jungles of Africa and the storms of the Atlantic. Life outside the womb was comparatively easy.

During the first year of The Finjan she asked me to teach her to read. I refused, telling her that if she learned to read at four, she'd be bored when she had to learn at six. She devised her own plan. She asked my friend Dorothy, who was a primary school teacher, to lend her some first grade reading books. Dorothy was happy to oblige. Dorothy visited often and Ronit would wait patiently for the opportunity to ask her what different words meant. Soon she was asking anyone who showed an interest. Defeated by her determination, I relented and helped her.

It was the same some years later when she made the sudden decision to learn pottery. I littered her path with obstacles, telling her I knew no one who did ceramics, had no idea where she could be taught and doubted if such a place existed. Undaunted, she consulted the telephone book. Under 'Ceramics' she found several pages of listings, probably factories and shops making and selling dishes. "Do you teach nine year old girls ceramics?" she asked each one in turn. Most of them had no idea

40

what she wanted, many were French and didn't understand English, but she persisted. Finally at the end of the list she found 'Victoria Ceramics'. Yes, they taught nine year old girls ceramics but she would have to come early Saturday mornings to the other end of town. I hated the idea of getting up early, especially on Saturdays, but I had to acknowledge such perseverance. Each Saturday morning I struggled out of bed, took Ronit to her ceramics class, waited for her, and brought her home. My sacrifices were rewarded years later, in London, when Ronit made almost all our dishes, including jugs, ash trays, even casseroles.

Shimon eventually bought her a guitar but, in accordance with his principles, resisted teaching her how to play it. Although I didn't think so at the time, perhaps he was right because through her own resolution she learned to play the guitar, the recorder and the flute and to read and write music. She discovered that if you want to do something all you have to do is do it. The Finjan years were at the heart of that discovery.

4. The Healing Of Leonard Cohen

When Ronit was eleven, I scraped together enough money to spend several weeks in Ireland. By then I had completed a Masters thesis on the well-known Irish poet and dramatist, W.B. Yeats, and had begun a doctorate. I decided to attend the Yeats Summer School in Sligo and travel in Ireland with research as my excuse. I had been growing increasingly restless. The Finjan was no longer, and I was straining at the bit, yearning for travel. Whereas Shimon thrived on predictability, I withered. He needed home. I needed the road. Without rancour or bitterness we had been steadily growing in different directions.

The trip to Ireland heightened my longing for the road. I returned to Montreal even more restless, unprepared for what awaited me there. Without warning Shimon had left me and was living with someone else. Although I understood his motivations, I was devastated. Trapped, bereft, penniless, I spent the next six months chained to circumstances I was powerless to alter, my travel dreams shattered by unrelenting reality. Then suddenly everything changed. I received a three year Canada Council award, plus travel grant, to complete my doctorate at the university of my choice. My ticket to ride was magically reissued. I packed one bag for myself, one for Ronit and, leaving Shimon with whatever worldly possessions I had, Ronit and I took off for England.

The only material thing I regretted leaving behind was my kitchen with its 'wall of fame'. When Ronit was two we had moved into a larger flat where she and I remained until leaving for England. The flat had a remarkable kitchen. It had a special energy, a special ambience, a well-being where things flowed, things happened. It was spacious, yet snug, with a wall of windows overlooking a wild field, a tract of unspoiled land prohibited to builders, a rare event in the bosom of a city. In summer the field was filled with flowers, birds and sunshine, making one feel expansive, extending the kitchen into a macrocosm of possibilities. In winter it was blanketed with snow, long shadows and cold stars, the kitchen withdrawing into an interior landscape, a secret refuge, cosy, warm, intimate. The skies were never still, moving from serene to angry, blue or grey or pink in the day, black with soft moons or streaks of Northern Lights at night. It was a vista conducive to discoveries, revelations, creations. The kitchen table was its heart, generating life, providing a continuous feast. It was around the kitchen table, folded into black velvet skies, drawn by a circle of candle light into compelling universes, that I fell in love with music, with musicians, with poetry, with friends; it was here that I dreamed my dreams of travel; that I prepared long loving dinners; that I did my work, planning choreography, reading and revising for university exams, toiling into the night on overdue term papers. I remember Ronit waking late one night to find me at the kitchen table immersed in books, notes and typewriter, my eyes strained with the effort of completing a paper due next day. "Papers, papers, papers," she wailed, "I'm never going to university!" But the kitchen gave me energy, stamina, strength to persevere. It was my perfect place.

Late one morning, during The Finjan days, I woke to find a legend boldly inscribed across the kitchen wall. 'This is the one and only kitchen in the whole wide world' it proclaimed, signed 'Ron Eliran', the Israeli singer then performing at The Finjan. I was so taken aback I hardly registered the sentiment, so perfectly in tune with mine. How dare he deface my kitchen wall. Immediately I tried to scrub it clean. But scrawled with an indelible marker, it refused to be eradicated. When I confronted Ron, he was unrepentant. "Why did you do that?" I moaned, "I can't wash it off."

"I did it because it had to be done...It must never be washed off. Everyone who stays here should write something for the wall. It will be a wall of fame, a thank you to this wonderful kitchen."

Shimon agreed and the wall of fame was born. For me it became a celebration of my kitchen, of The Finjan, of the musicians, of my substitute for travel, of all of us together. After I left Montreal I never saw it again, but wherever I went I took that kitchen and its wall of fame with me.

Although the wall provided happy recollections, it evoked one disturbing memory which continued to haunt me. When the now-famous blues musician, John Lee Hooker, performed at The Finjan, spending wonderful hours in our kitchen, I asked him, as a matter of course, to sign the wall. I was taken aback by his adamant refusal. "Everyone writes something on the wall," I protested. But he was unyielding. "Please John," I urged, unable to fathom this stubborn refusal in someone so amenable, "I really want you to sign the wall...I want to remember you being here." But, uncharacteristically, he continued to refuse, and, characteristically, I continued to twist his arm. "Why John? Why won't you sign the wall?" I pleaded.

Finally he offered a lame, "I don't know what to write."

"That's no problem," I said with a sense of deliverance. At that time he had a hit song in circulation called *Boom Boom*. "Just write 'Boom Boom'...nothing else...just 'Boom Boom'...that'll be great." Eroded by my insistence, he acquiesced. "Good man," I said, handing him the felt pen. He clutched it like a child grasping a too-fat crayon, and in slow awkward letters painfully scratched an M...an O...another O and a misshapen N facing backwards. Suddenly it hit me. He was illiterate. He couldn't write. And I had forced humiliation upon him. Mortified, I watched him press another tortured M...O...O and a wounded N into the wall.

"Boom! Boom!" he smiled broadly, his ordeal over.

"Thanks John, I really appreciate that," I said, severely chastened. "Now I'll always think of you when I look at the wall." And I always did, but with a stinging shame.

At first I intended finishing my university degree in Ireland since I was working on an Irish writer. But after attending the Yeats Summer School and spending some time in Dublin, I realised this was not a good idea. It would be too difficult for a woman on her own with a child to live in Ireland. In a country where divorce was not permitted, where men lived with their mothers until they married in their late thirties or even mid forties, and where sexual repression was rampant, I would be too high profile, up for grabs. Even being in Ireland without Ronit gave rise to a plague of curiosity, making me feel as though my bones were being picked. Although I loved Ireland and the Irish, the poetry, the talk, the music, the hilarity, the madness, I knew I couldn't live there. It was too introverted, too incestuous, to give me the anonymity I desired.

I had already suffered unwanted attention in Montreal where the English-speaking community was relatively small and where Shimon was relatively well known because of The Finjan years and his subsequent success as a performer. Everyone knew we had parted, that he was living with someone else. Strangers would express sorrow at our separation. The looks of sympathy and commiseration had been difficult to bear, they were like eulogies at my funeral. I decided on London where no one was interested in me, except for Ruth, my only friend there, and Rosy, whom I had met at the Yeats Summer School and recognised as a soul mate.

I had written my Masters thesis on W.B. Yeats' *Plays For Dancers,* excited by the discovery that Yeats, like myself, was impelled by dance, that it was central to his concept of drama. His fascination with dance and the plays themselves so impressed me that, determined to disprove the critics' claim that Yeats was the greatest twentieth century poet but a failed dramatist, I had convinced The Centaur Theatre, the principal English-speaking theatre in Montreal, to stage two of his dance plays with myself as choreographer and assistant director. That's how I came to meet Brian Stavetchney. He was the main actor-dancer in the plays and quickly became devoted to Yeats and to me. The more we worked together the more I realised how perfectly suited he was to creating the elusive qualities Yeats was after, like evoking those emotions which 'haunt the edge of trance', those perceptions outside the scope of reason, the 'intimacies, ecstasies and anguish of soul life', the 'images that remind us of vast passions'. Yeats wanted his theatre to call up the world of imagination and spirit, to be magical.

Brian had a magic about him. He was spectacular to look at with a shock of frizzy sunflower hair that framed his head like a halo. His long oval face, high cheekbones and startling blue eyes were so striking that even in repose he appeared to be on stage. His face was always alive as though sensing nuances the rest of us were unable to perceive, vibrations we couldn't feel, like a finely attuned animal, alert, responsive, tuned into another dimension. His body was beautiful, long and lean and golden. It was eloquent, able to communicate when he was silent, and he moved it like a dancer even when he was still. He didn't speak much but when he did speak his voice was soft and resonant, rich and melodic on stage. I came to see him as some aspect of Yeats, some incarnation Yeats would have desired. Much later, in the months he was in London, it was Brian who insisted on us forming the Yeats Theatre Company and performing several of the dance plays, the first professional production in London since Yeats' death, and attended by T.S. Eliot's wife, Valerie, and Ninette de Valois, founder of The Royal Ballet Company, among others. I was merely impelled by his energy. Not long after Shimon and I separated Brian and I became lovers, and when I left Montreal with Ronit, he came with us.

My plan was for the three of us to spend the first part of the summer in Greece on the island of Lesbos with my closest friend Aviva, and then for Brian and I to go on to Ireland to attend the Yeats Summer School, for him an exciting bonus. Aviva, Irving and their son David were spending the summer on Lesbos. Irving, considered Canada's leading poet, had been my teacher at university, the inspiration behind my pursuit of Yeats. Leonard Cohen, David's godfather, was also expected. Irving was his mentor and contact with Irving gave him sustenance. Brian, who admired both men and who was a devout reader of their poetry, was

46

thrilled by the possibility of meeting them.

Ronit looked forward to Lesbos. She would be seeing David whom she sorely missed since Aviva and Irving had moved to Toronto the previous year. Although several years older than David they were very close, each like the brother or sister the other never had. I sorely missed Aviva. Since childhood I always had a best friend, friends being the most valued thing in my life. But Aviva was more than a best friend, more than a sister, there was an empathy between us, a twinned connection, that even strangers recognised. Although we looked nothing like each other, she was fair and I dark, although we spoke English with different accents, people confused us, calling her Niema and me Aviva, forgetting which of us they had talked to, which of us had said what, which child belonged to whom.

We never exhausted our times together, always had more to reveal. We shared our most intimate moments, stood by each other through every crisis, were each other's main source of comfort. When Aviva was devastated by the sudden death of a good friend, Irving sent me to be with her. When Shimon decided he wanted to live with someone else, he first told Aviva asking her how best to tell me. I was with Aviva when she gave birth to David, when she fed him his first spoon of solid food, when he locked himself in a car for which there was no key.

It was never an imposition, a burden, to listen to the repetitive agonised sagas of her life with Irving - the much older man she had pursued and was living with - it was a privilege. I loved her 'quick-silver intelligence' (Irving's phrase), her acid wit, her humour, her vitality, her appetite for experience, her generosity with her friendship. If times were bad for me, her presence improved them, and if times were good, her presence made them even better. We gave each other permission to take pleasure from life, a precept adhered to by my parents but vigorously denied by hers. We could be open, exposed, vulnerable, with complete trust. And when we were 'on' we could take on the world, and did. A German poet or was it philosopher once said, *Love is greater than genius*

47

itself and friendship is greater than love. He could have been referring to our friendship. Unlike love, it brought no hurt, no violent mood swings, no desperation. Most importantly it was not an addiction, it was more like a sustaining habit, like a book at bedtime, a great healer. It was its very 'greatness' that made it difficult for others to contend with. Although Irving and I had been friends before I met Aviva, he sometimes couldn't help resenting our special attachment. 'Your wife called,' he would report sardonically. 'You spend so much time with Aviva, why don't you move in,' my mother would complain. But lately we had been living in different cities, and now we would be living in different countries. Our time together in Lesbos was especially precious.

I also looked forward to seeing Leonard Cohen. I had met him many years before at Irving and Aviva's. From the first meeting, Leonard fascinated me with his bitter-sweet attitudes to life, his penetrating humour often entrenched in pain and directed against himself, his beautiful melancholy, his dark mesmerising good looks and his promise of anguish and ecstasy. Perhaps it was because of this promise, made in poems and songs tortured with tender love, yet savagely accurate, delivered in his smoky opium voice resonant with incantation that spanned Rabbinical intoning to Buddhist chanting, that both men and women were to phone him saying they wanted to hear the sound of his voice before taking their lives. He was a magnet for the tortured.

Although he was very young at the time he seemed to peel and discard layer after layer of living, as though he had been on earth an eternity. Yet he could be newborn, child-like, unfallen. Like Bob Dylan his imagination had a life of its own, an original way of seeing things, of yoking ideas, but his was a darker vision, intense, haunted, as though he had visits with doom. Predictably enough he was intrigued by Bob Dylan, by his songs, by his startling imagination, by his rise to fame. He was just beginning to write songs himself and was overwhelmed that I knew Bob Dylan. He wanted to hear every detail about him, especially what it was like to be famous, even to know someone famous. Ironically, he was to find out all too soon. And, to compound the irony, in 1975 Dylan was to dedicate his album *Desire* to Leonard Cohen.

When Ronit graduated from elementary school, Irving gave her a copy of Leonard Cohen's poems with the inscription, 'Now that you have graduated, let Leonard Cohen do the rest!' He asked Leonard to autograph the book and Leonard added, 'Yeah, let me do the rest!' He was drawn to Ronit's undefiled girlhood and made me promise to keep her in white until she was old enough to marry him. But a photograph I have of them at this time looks like they were already married. Such was the oneness between them, the similarity of expression, of unseen internal forces shaping the external image. Caught by the camera in a moment of intense connection, they were two aspects of one reality. Ronit looking outwards in innocent wonder, entering life, Leonard with his arm around her shoulder, protecting her from what he had already lived.

For me the most striking thing about Leonard was a compelling kind of madness, and a genius for infecting others with it. Both Aviva and I were especially susceptible to this seductive charisma and an experience we had with it was so intense, so bizarre, so magical, that it remains one of the extraordinary happenings in my life. It was made possible not only because of Leonard's unique power, but because Aviva and I were together, experiencing it with him.

One of Irving's qualities I found most attractive was his interest in younger writers. No matter how busy he was he found time to offer encouragement and advice, even financial assistance to the promising young poets who regularly sought him out. Leonard Cohen was such a young poet. His zaniness, 'the joker high and wild', the gypsy-boy, complemented Irving's essential sobriety; his pale aristocratic inheritance, Irving's robust peasant roots. They were drawn together like the joining of night with day. Leonard had a profound regard for Irving's talent as a poet and a deep love for him as a man. Irving considered Leonard to have 'the purest lyrical gift in the country', and cherished him as a friend. Leonard fascinated Irving; his tortured sensibility, his mystical yearnings, his affinity with pain, his Christ-like suffering, were diametrically opposed to Irving's pragmatic vigorous solidity, his refusal to turn the other cheek. Leonard brought Irving in touch with an ethos Irving could not otherwise reach. And, in turn, Leonard drew strength from Irving's vast resources of stability and health. Leonard's first book of poetry was dedicated to Irving.

Later, Leonard expanded his literary activities to include novels and then turned to writing songs and eventually to performing them. Although from the beginning he achieved popularity in the States, especially as a song-writer and performer, he wasn't successful in Canada except among a small group of admirers. Canada refused to recognise his talents. Every grant, every award, he applied for was denied and everything he published, every performance he gave, received a negative review. Discouraged by repeated rejection he left Montreal and went to live in New York. Years later, when, as a successful super star with several gold albums, he returned to Montreal to give his first big concert, he was still steeling himself against the anticipated negative response. Aviva and I found him in the dressing room composing a terse reply to the inevitable bad review he knew would appear in the 'Montreal Star'.

"Why do you bother?" Aviva asked. "The London Times says you're great, the New York Times says you're fantastic, you get international rave reviews, why do you care what the pathetic little Montreal Star writes?"

"Because", he answered sadly, "my mother reads the Montreal Star. She's convinced I'm a failure."

I came to know Leonard through my friendship with Irving and Aviva. I met him often at their home before he became famous, and then at least for Christmas once he was famous. He believed in maintaining traditions, said they were his anchor in the chaos of existence. Even if it meant flying from one side of the world to the other, he never failed to share the Christmas spirit with his dear friend Irving, and with Aviva and David. Ronit and I would come as well, and the six of us would usher in the Yuletide with blessings for peace and love. After dinner Leonard would lead us in various ceremonies and rituals, depending on what esoteric philosophy he was involved with at the time. One year we incanted the mantra *Om Mani Padme Hum* by the light of a single candle, entranced by the sound of the Tibetan words: *God in unmanifest form is like a jewel in the centre of a lotus, manifest in my heart.* We chanted invocations for peace and love until, in a semi-hypnotic state, we could feel our energies merging with the cosmic energies in an overwhelming energy of universal love. Even Irving was captivated.

It was Leonard who first introduced me to Tibet, an introduction that was to become an obsession. Leonard emanated a contagious magic. He was a master at evoking mystical atmospheres, creating strange moods where all things were possible. Like a magician he wove a spell impelling sceptic and believer alike to surrender to it. His writing and his music had this same compelling power. Like Aviva, I was especially receptive to these charged atmospheres. He once told me that I was a 'familiar', that force which is conducive to the creation of magic, like the black cat whose presence assists the clairvoyant - the catalyst that makes the magic happen. I had never considered that possibility but I was pleased he had. Leonard moved in and out of my life at intervals which became further apart the more famous he became.

The event I referred to earlier occurred one cold Montreal night. My friend Tom phoned telling me he had managed to procure some magic mushrooms. Leonard had introduced both Irving and Aviva to magic mushrooms, the love drug, and they reported huge ecstasies, delights of phenomenal proportions. I was a coward when it came to drugs. I even avoided aspirin. I didn't smoke tobacco and rarely drank alcohol. Even when Shimon and I were travelling in Spain and a free bottle of wine came with every meal, we left it untouched. But the mushrooms intrigued me. They grew in Mexico where the Indians used them for religious, spiritual and magical rites. Friends I knew had swung in hammocks for months on end waiting for the magic mushroom to mature. I took the plunge.

Before leaving for Tom's I phoned Aviva to convey my anxieties.

"You're going to have a super time", she assured me, "one of the most fabulous times of your life. Lucky thing. Phone me and tell me how it's going. Better still, come over. Leonard is in town. I'm sure he'd love to see you."

"I'll phone and let you know", I said, reassured. I crossed the threshold of Tom's living room as though stepping on stage for my big performance. Tom, detecting my stage nerves, said he wouldn't take any mushrooms so that I could rely on his sobriety. Tom radiated a Rock of Gibraltar dependability. He was raised on a farm in Saskatchewan drinking milk straight from the cows. I swallowed the mushrooms with total confidence.

By the time I phoned Aviva I was deep into the delights she had promised. Tom's spartan living room was alive with paintings composed of tiny points of light, with music becoming dancing sound, with colours singing in a rainbow arc. I was the heart of a magic lantern.

"Aviva, everything is beaming diamond light."

"Beaming diamond light," Aviva repeated.

"Tell her to bring it here." It was Leonard's voice.

Tom and I arrived in a cocoon of silver snow flakes while I was at the peak of my trip and sat by the log fire splashing warmth in colours of gold. The room, usually lovely, was exquisite with its Indian table composed of tiny pieces of mother-of-pearl, radiating light, like a chest of jewels. Irving and Leonard sat on the pale gold sofa and I knelt beside them gazing into their faces, exhilarated by my crystal vision. "What do you see?" Leonard asked.

"I see a dance of words ... solos ... duets ... trios ... spiraling from your lips, spinning to the table ... winding among the jewels ... filling with light ... then sparkling up to Irvings lips ... letters embracing, entwining ... leaping, pirouetting as they danced back to your lips, arching higher and higher ... growing more luminous as they passed from lips to lips. " I spoke slowly, my words shinning, images shimmering with revalation.

Aviva, Irving and Leonard took turns asking, "Now what do you see?" and then began adding their visions to mine, in a shimmering cascade of words until the words began to rotate in a kaleidoscope of images, brilliant upon brilliant, our laughter whirling in the air like sparklers spinning, spiralling up and up, riding my contact high. Tom remained apart, blinded, unable to enter the magic circle as it sped faster and faster.

Suddenly Leonard raised his hand. The kaleidoscope stilled. His voice echoed from a solemn cavern deep within him. "Friends," he said gravely, "I must reveal to you a problem I have, which I was unable to share until tonight."

"The problems of Leonard Cohen, a legend in his own time, do not exist", Aviva chanted. "A man who can have everything he wants, success, money, fame, women, is no longer entitled to have problems."

"Can you have all the women you want?" Irving asked, his mouth pursing with admiration.

"Yes. It's like magic. I enter a crowded elevator and point. When I reach my floor the woman I pointed at follows me."

"And that's a problem?" Irving intoned. "I should have such problems. It sounds more like a paradise."

"Yes, that's a problem. Because now that I can have any woman I lay my finger on, I can't make love to any of them. I haven't been able to have an erection for almost a year."

"You," Aviva gasped, "guru of love, every woman's rising star, the man with the golden organ. You haven't been able to have an erection?"

"Yes," Leonard said, his eyes dark with shame. "I'm a fraud."

Suddenly I felt a wild exhilaration. "On this night we have the power to magic your erection back."

Leonard had laid his finger on me. His response was immediate. As though pronouncing a prophecy, he said: "Tonight shall be remembered as the night the erection of Leonard Cohen returned to earth". His voice

53

resounded with the power of miracle. "Henceforth virgins dressed in white will light candles to commemorate the miracle, proclaiming, 'Leonard Cohen's erection is alive. Magic is afoot.'"

Leonard, the orgy master, cracked his whip and the sparks burst into flame.

"We shall have an erection competition." He was inspired, intoxicating. "The men will stand side by side, penises exposed. The ladies will dance naked before them."

He spoke like a medium manifesting a vision. And we all submitted like novices to an all-enveloping spiritual mystery. "I have never won anything in my life. But tonight I shall be the winner, my competitors will bless me with success."

He proceeded to conjure up the dance.

"First you will move sensuously, encouraging, coaxing erection. Woman as seducer. Then your dance will become a ritual of growth, of procreation. The goddess dancing a fertility rite to encourage a fruitful yield. The men will partake in a ceremony of manhood, a contest of virility. The first man to achieve erection is the victor." He wore the robes of prophet.

Leonard put a record on and lit several candles. The music glittered in its own elaborate choreography through the firelight and candlelight. Aviva peeled off her clothes, eager to partake in the ritual. She adored Leonard and loved yielding to the power of his baroque imagination. Besides, refusing him would be like the tides refusing the moon. She became a beautiful sprite, surrounded by an aura of light. I removed my blouse, my breasts powerful in my hands, but retained my skirt, swishing silk against my thighs, my purple stockings and my Chinese slippers winking sequins. Leonard graciously permitted the transgressions. Three limp penises lined up against the wall. Tom's eyes were downcast, like a Samson, his hair newly shorn, or a cowboy, fresh from the prairies, suddenly naked in Sodom or Gemorah, not daring to behold the twin wickedness, yet fatally drawn to the decadence, an Adam doomed to partake in sin. Leonard's white skin stretched porcelain thin over a slender frame, helpless on the cross of his body. Irving was an immovable mountain, his limbs thick tree roots, planted firmly in its base, his legs astride, a Colossus ready for battle.

Leonard raised his arm signalling Aviva and me to dance. We moved first like belly dancers in a harem, navels flashing, bodies rubbed in perfumed oils. Then we became Everywoman, the temptress, the enchantress, dancing a timeless seduction. I see Aviva become Eve, then Helen of Troy, then Lolita; I am Cleopatra, Mata Hari, Jezebel. Breasts, belly, thighs, rocking, swaying, tempting invisible maleness. Hips pulsating deep into the journey of seduction, searching for the golden stud, Adam, Caesar, Christ. Then slowly into rituals of fertility, kneeling, blessing the earth, arms lifting in spirals from earth through rain and sun. Palms reaching to the sky in an invocation of growth.

Leonard watched like a caged bird, its beak open in a silent mating song. Irving watched, steeped in poetry, and Tom like a displaced cock unable to crow. Aviva and I danced together, a ballet celebrating the female, withdrawing from the male, the mesmerised trinity deaf to our rhythms, their penises cobras who had forgotten how to be charmed.

Then slowly, very slowly, I danced to the sofa and folded into the gold, beckoning Leonard and Irving to either side of me. Tom sat facing us bathed in redemption as Aviva sensing his discomfort climbed into his lap and perched on his knee, smiling like a child in the Garden of Eden. I felt newly born, my body fresh like morning sunshine, but blessed with an ancient miracle, the power of healer. Beside me Leonard's penis lay like a broken bird. Carefully I took it in my hand. As it nested in my fingers, I saw its mouth open and begin to sing. I listened to the notes of a birdsong.

"The bird is singing." I smiled up at Leonard. Then I heard another call, faint, distant. I covered Irving's penis with my other hand. Yes. A mating call. "Two love birds, two song birds," I crooned.

"And you are creating the music," Leonard said. I sat between them cradling their music in my palms, feeling them fuse into a single instrument and I its maestro. I, who could hardly bang out chopsticks, began playing like a virtuoso, fingering the pipes, simultaneously, alternately, my hands embracing, strumming, stroking, plucking flecks of golden light, my fingertips seething with tattoos of sound as music shuttled through my fingers. I could sense the hushed audience enthralled as I tossed my head and played for the universe, feeling the music in my nostrils, hearing it on my tongue, tasting it through my eyes. I was an inspired musician playing a divine organ.

Irving and Leonard closed their eyes, released into perfect attunement. Aviva's smile, Tom's blessings, swelled the notes, as we created magical harmonies, mysterious chords, fierce rhythms.

"It's the sacred music of the spheres," I said with wonder. Wild sounds tamed by my hands into cradlesongs and beating wild again. And I, pulled by the pipes into pools of music flowing between us, knowing every thought they knew, feeling every thought they felt. One hand on the crucifix, one hand on the song. Touching where they could not. Feeling for them, through them, into them, composing, orchestrating, their music exploding in my hands. Union. Communion. The older poet giving to the younger his strength, his potency. And the younger poet giving to the older, his youth, his love. And I the altar, the temple, the wishing well of their love. They create through me. Madonna. Tara. Sheba. The birth of the Young King. And Leonard is born in my hand, and grows through me, through Aviva, through Irving, through Tom. Erect.

"Standing ovation!" Leonard shouted, rising. We applaud, celebrating Leonard's erection, as candles ignite all about us in thanksgiving and commemoration.

5. The Man Who Wouldn't Talk

Ronit took the idea of a new life in a new country in her stride. She didn't complain about leaving Montreal except for the separation from her father and grandmother (her grandfather was no longer alive). However, she was easily reassured when I promised both her and Shimon that if she was unhappy I would return her to Montreal and that, in any case, she would visit often. The idea of living in England appealed to her. By now horses were her passionate interest. For several summers she had gone to a horse-riding farm owned by a friend and had learned to ride and to care for the horses. She had won ribbons for showjumping and she longed to be with horses. We both had the mistaken notion that England would provide that opportunity. As it turned out we were always so short of money that she went riding only a few times in the years she was there.

We all looked forward to the trip. Brian had never crossed the Atlantic, neither had Ronit and I was happy to be travelling again even if it wasn't the kind of travel I had in mind. Our ticket to Greece had a London stop-over. We stayed with Ruth, persuading her to join us in Athens. I had met Ruth through Aviva. They had been childhood friends. Aviva would be delighted to see her. In Athens we decided to rent a car and drive through the Peloponnese so we could see something of the mainland before going on to Lesbos. Brian was especially anxious to see Olympia and declaim in the ancient amphitheatre. None of us spoke any Greek and once leaving Athens and driving in the untouristy villages of the Peloponnese, we found few people who spoke any English. It became increasingly difficult to communicate even on the basic level of finding food and a place to sleep, until Brian conceived the brilliant idea of miming and dancing our needs.

His performances worked wonders. The Greeks adored him. They were so responsive that he went from the expression of simple needs to conducting entire conversations, able to convey complex ideas non-verbally.

Once we met Costa and Yani, two young Greeks, both deaf mutes. Brian was in his element. They invited us to an old-fashioned dance hall where people still danced only in couples. There were few females present making Ruth, Ronit and me very popular. Costa kept asking Ronit to dance and although he didn't especially appeal to her, she complied. After one very slow, very close, dance she said, "I don't want to dance with him any more. He keeps touching me in a creepy way."

But when he asked her again, I convinced her to oblige on the grounds of compassion. "He has enough problems being deaf and dumb, don't give him any more. It's only a dance. You'll never see him again. Bring him a little joy."

But I was wrong and she was right. He put his hand into her tee shirt and down her jeans, holding her so tight she was unable to free herself. She was in tears. Brian took Costa aside. He pointed to Ronit and formed his arms like a cradle, swaying them from side to side, rocking the cradle, indicating that Ronit was young, still a baby. Then, pointing to me, he rocked the cradle again miming that I was big, the mother and Ronit was small, the child. He reinforced the message improvising additional mother and child mime. Costa nodded in understanding, indicating surprise that I was Ronit's mother and that Ronit was still a child - at thirteen she was taller than me. The realisation put a new complexion on things. The boys became models of decorum. Costa apologised first to Ronit, than to me, falling on his knees and begging forgiveness. He continued to dance only with Ruth, politely, respectfully.

Brian's mime had triumphed.

He was eloquent and inventive with a remarkable talent for externalising subtle perceptions through movement. Our Peloponnese trip was wonderfully enhanced by his ability to make contact with people and to elicit warm response. He got so good at his mime-dance creations, polishing them into mini entertainments, mini silent movies and was so inspired by the response they evoked that by the time we returned to Athens to board the ship for Lesbos, he had made a massive decision. He decided to give up talking. In one of his last verbal communications he explained that he wanted the discipline of expressing himself only in movement, the experience of internal meditation, of 'noble silence'. He had a captive audience on the ship and communicated and entertained around the clock, developing his silence into a fine art. During the two day voyage all the passengers grew to love him. He was deluged with wine, cheese, sausage and inviting looks, accepted by the Greeks like a family member. Considering this was his first time with foreigners, he was spectacular.

Everyone grew to love him, that is everyone but me. Ronit enjoyed him, Ruth was amused and impressed, but I grew increasingly disenchanted and needy. At first I sympathised with his experiment, but when I realised he wasn't going to talk even to me, I began to resent it.

He was high on a solo flight from which I was excluded. When he wasn't performing, he was silent, absorbed in thoughts I couldn't share, enjoying his internal meditation. Rather than appreciating his noble silence, I became increasingly jealous of it. It was like a devotion to a new love. I wanted him back. Ronit, on the other hand, went along with him, relishing his complicated communications, patiently interpreting his desires. "Brian says he's not having lunch with us, he's eating with that Greek family, you know the one with the little girl who wears that big bow in her hair. He says we should bring our wine and join them after we've eaten. The father is teaching him to play the bazouki."

Besides, I became weary of the sympathetic looks and sad smiles which said to me 'you have such a fine young man, what a pity he's a mute.' When the boat docked I didn't mind having to make all the travel arrangements, a taxi into town, bus tickets from town, food, schedules, while he entertained, but I did mind his total preoccupation with his new love.

By the time we got to Molivos, the small fishing village on Lesbos, I felt totally alienated by Brian's refusal to talk, and hoped that meeting Irving, Aviva and Leonard, would induce him to give up his vow of silence. But it didn't. He remained silent, preferring his art, foregoing the contact he had so looked forward to, for its sake. There were several Westerners in Molivos. Up until now he had performed almost exclusively for Greeks. Trying to communicate with Westerners through movement was a new challenge, stretching his capacities, making him even more remote from me. We stopped making love. I felt hurt and rejected as his silence consumed him, leaving little for me. I needed his attention feeling vulnerable after my separation from Shimon. There were longer and longer periods of silence as I stopped trying to decipher what he was thinking and stopped bothering to tell him what I was feeling. I spent more and more time with Aviva.

When Lloyd, a New Yorker, began to pay me attention, I found it a relief to detach myself from Brian. I began to disappear with Lloyd and brought him, instead of Brian, on our outings to secluded beaches and remote villages. It was a joy to have verbal contact. Brian seemed unconcerned. There were many people intrigued by him, Westerners who appreciated his experiment with silence and Greeks who, thinking he was mute, paid him special attention - they could never comprehend that his silence was deliberate. I spent more and more time with Lloyd encouraged by Aviva who resented Brian's treatment of me.

Then suddenly a note appeared from Ronit. It read: 'First daddy, then Brian, now Lloyd. What do you think I am?' I sprang to attention, shocked. I had been so entrenched in my involvement with Brian and Lloyd that I hadn't bothered to see how it was affecting Ronit. I was forced into some serious considerations. I had to reassess my motherhood. After all I had a daughter to consider, a daughter whose feelings I had been blissfully oblivious to, concentrating on my problems, first with a husband, then with lovers. How ironic. I was always teaching Ronit to be aware of the needs of others. Thank goodness she was able to articulate her anxieties. She refused to be invisible. I made my own vow, vowing to devote myself to her needs. I was reminded of the cardboard carton incident many years before when I had vowed to be a more careful mother. That vow was in dire need of renewal. I had taken Ronit from the father she loved, from the love of her grandmother, from her friends, from everything familiar, and was bringing her to a strange land with people she didn't know because it suited me. I suddenly appreciated the trauma I was subjecting her to. I decided to stop seeing Lloyd immediately and that once my relationship with Brian was ended, there would be no men in my life until Ronit was secure in hers. Affairs of the heart would be on hold. She would be my focus. That was her right. From the cardboard carton days I always tried respecting her rights just as I wanted her to learn to respect mine. I felt much better after sorting out my priorities.

That evening, fortified by the zeal of a new resolution, I announced to Brian that I didn't want him to come to the Yeats Summer School with me. He said nothing, but slowly, very slowly, his eyes widened, the blue turning to black, and his mouth opened forming a great "Oh", in the terrible sadness of a bewildered Pierrot. He rose to his feet and began to dance, slowly, intensely, his body vivid with regret. Then he took my hand and looked at me, his face a knife-edge of pain. And I realised I had no right to keep him from the thing he so much wanted, to spoil his dream. I was, in a way, using the Summer School as one parent, in the throes of rejection, uses a child, as a weapon against the other. Finally I struck a bargain. We would go to Ireland together but once he was ensconced in the Summer School, we would go our separate ways, have our own rooms, own schedules. His eyes filled with tenderness and he embraced me so completely my resolve was almost done in.

When it was time for Brian and me to leave Lesbos for London and Dublin, I made final arrangements for Ronit. She would remain with Aviva and David for most of August, then a friend would take her to the port, making sure she was safely aboard the ship to Athens. In Athens, Tamila, another friend would meet her, and take her to the airport. She already had a ticket to London. Ruth would meet her in London and I would be at Ruth's several days later. The arrangements did not intimidate her.

She looked forward to travelling on her own. (Was it in the genes?) But I had some bouts with my conscience, defending the long-standing charge of irresponsible mother. I knew that neither Shimon nor my mother would approve. She was only thirteen. But I won the battle. She was armed with travellers' cheques, hidden cash, telephone numbers and an incredible resourcefulness, besides she had learned enough Greek to make herself understood. The Greeks were honest, gentle and incredibly helpful. She would be fine. It was her psyche that needed protection and care at this time of her life. If she exhibited emotional dependency, fragility; physically, she was robust, independent, confident. Or was I breaking my vow already, putting my needs before hers? I walked a thin line. It was hard balancing, getting it right. She kissed Brian and me goodbye with a happy smile.

When we got to London I insisted that Brian organise our tickets for Dublin. If he didn't want to talk that was his decision, I wasn't going to serve it. He was no longer being indulged by a soporific Lesbos. This was the real world. I was determined to make him accountable. The fiasco at Heathrow strengthened that resolution. Although I had warned against it, he boarded the plane in Athens wearing almost see-through macramed shorts, made for him by a Greek admirer, a thin cotton shirt with an embroidered edge open at the chest and held together by a sash, and a pair of leather thongs - a great outfit for Greece but hardly appropriate for Heathrow. As he danced his way into the customs hall, I made sure to enter a different queue. When the customs officer questioned him he would make no verbal response but could produce no identification indicating he was mute. When the officer asked if he could talk, he nodded his head indicating that he could. Baffled and annoyed, the officer took him away. After a difficult search I discovered he was being held in the detention centre. When I was finally admitted, I found him looking bright and cheerful despite a body search and brusque officials. I explained that he had taken a vow of silence. 'It's part of his religion' I improvised. They had no idea what to do with this information, but since he had enough money for his stay in England, and a return ticket to Canada, and not wanting to be accused of religious discrimination, they released him. The officer in charge gave his attire a last scathing glance, but being English, said nothing.

I had booked our tickets to Dublin by phone but insisted that Brian collect them and pay for them. It was important that he did this right because if he didn't we would miss our connections and the opening of the Summer School. It was his first time in the West End of London, the main downtown area, so I was understandably apprehensive. Before he left I made him promise to phone me. I devised an ingenious plan.

"I know you won't talk," I said, "but I'll ask you questions and you click your tongue once if the answer is yes, and twice if it's no. That way I'll know if everything went alright, if you got the tickets and if there's anything I have to do." By this time I wished I had gone for the tickets myself, the principal didn't seem worth defending. I could see that Brian wasn't convinced by the plan, would it be violating his silence? But for the sake of peace, he relented.

On edge I waited for his call. One hour. Two hours. Three hours. Four hours. But no call from Brian. Surely he would have called had he got the tickets. Something must have gone wrong. By now the ticket office was closed. We were supposed to leave early next morning. What was I to do? Why hadn't I left him in Lesbos dancing for the Greeks?

Suddenly the phone rang. "Did you get the tickets?" I shouted into the silence. One despondent click, "yes". What a relief. But why had it taken him so long to call? "Are you alright?" Two clicks, "no". No?

"Are you hurt?" One click. Oh my god, he's hurt. "Where are you?" He couldn't answer that. Quick, rephrase the question. "Are you in the hospital?" One click. My god, he's in the hospital. Suddenly a woman's voice.

"I'm nurse Murphy. A very kind couple found your husband unconscious in Regent Street. They called an ambulance and brought him to hospital. He injured his head and required several stitches. He's fine now and we're arranging for a taxi to take him home. He'll be right as rain after a good night's sleep. But do have a doctor check the stitches in a week or so. Nothing to worry about."

I was so overwhelmed I couldn't think what to ask. I thanked her and she hung up. Within an hour Brian was home, looking pale and subdued but proudly producing the tickets.

When I finally unravelled the story, told to me in mime and dance punctuated by guilty clicks, I learned that all went well until Brian collected the tickets and was on his way home. On Regent Street he was suddenly inspired. He would treat the English to some street entertainment as he had so often treated the Greeks. Only London was not Athens. The English were not only indifferent, but disapproving, even hostile. They hurried past him, their eyes averted, as though by looking at him they would be condoning some obscene activity. No laughter, no cheers, nothing. Brian grew more and more determined to make them respond, to bring them joy. Finally, executing a mad desperate twirl, he went smashing into a lamp post and fell unconscious beneath it. Then the English responded. They were good at tragedy, not so good at comedy. My poor Brian, he was learning the hard way. I put him to bed with kisses.

The Yeats Summer School in Sligo was a very verbal affair with lectures, seminars, discussions, analysis and readings. Brian's non-verbal stance didn't go down well. It was a thorn, an irritant to the professors, the literary critics, the Yeats experts. But there were also the poets. Some of Ireland's finest poets were present. For them Brian was a wonderful enigma. Some, like Seamus Heaney, Brendan Kennelly, and Jimmy

Simmons, considered joining him and forming a non-verbal contingent. Two camps developed, a pro-Brian camp and an anti-Brian camp. The professors were impatient, they had no time for him; the poets admired him, wanted to imitate him, invented their own soundless scenarios, discussed the advantages, the possibilities inherent in silence, the space between the words. I watched from a distance, enjoying the fray but unable to be objective, not knowing which side I was on.

The natives of Sligo responded much as the Greeks had, with delight. Once walking down the main street of Sligo I noticed a crowd and approached to investigate. In the middle of the crowd Brian was mine-dancing. I watched him for a while impressed. He was miming the pathos of two lovers separated by some overwhelming force, his own version of Romeo and Juliet. The crowd was enthralled. As he built up to the climax, I wondered how he would end the performance, there were no curtains, no lights and the drama was so intense it required a grand finale. Suddenly there was the shrill scream of a siren. A police van sped up to the crowd and screeched to a halt. Two policemen burst from the van descending on Brian, pulling him into it. Brian was unrattled. The police became part of the performance. With raised arms, like a helpless Christ, he submitted to his executioners. Then from the back of the van he saluted his cheering audience as he was driven off. It was the perfect ending. His offence turned out to be obstructing traffic. He was released with a warning and a smile.

For the entire two weeks of the Summer School Brian remained silent, but his presence was increasingly felt. The police encounter transformed him into a minor folk hero - the Irish being prone to the creation of folk heroes. His salute from the police van became a badge, a password, a salute to him. People saluted him on the streets. In the school he was asked to give illustrations of mime, dance, performances of Yeats.

Seamus Heaney, later to become the dominant poet of our time, a noble laureate, suggested that he present a dance from one of Yeats' plays - a surprise performance for the closing ceremony of the school. Brian was delighted.

He decided on the climatic dance from *At The Hawk's Well*, one of Yeats' dance plays based on Irish mythology. He would dance the young hero, the warrior Cuchulain, seeking the well of eternal life. 'He who drinks, they say, that miraculous water, lives forever.' I would dance The Hawk Woman, the Guardian of the well, who lures Cuchulain from the well just as the mysterious waters bubble up and begin to flow. 'She is always flitting upon this mountain side, to allure or to destroy.' Cuchulain resists the Hawk Woman but finally, hypnotised by her dance, follows her, forsaking his chance for immortality. We practised all afternoon, improvising costumes and music, mainly drum beats and strange discordant sounds. The well, true to Yeats' directions, was represented by a square of blue cloth. We painted our faces white to suggest the masks Yeats wanted for the plays.

That night Brian danced Cuchulain, strong, magnificent, his shins laced with leather thongs, his hand clutching a spear. I danced the Hawk Woman, an embodiment of the bird of prey's cruelty coupled with a woman's beauty, dressed in grey/black with a shawl whose dark fringe unfurled to suggest malevolent wings. 'It flew as though it would have torn me with its beak, or blinded me, smiting with that great wing.' My cry of 'Taka!' intermingled with the drum beats, the wild sounds. A bitter yet heroic duet, making tangible the 'imagery of emotion', ritualising a universal quest with mythological significance 'beyond the scope of reason'.

The most powerful moment came when Cuchulain stood, his back to the well, hearing its water bubbling up, but unable to turn from the Hawk Woman, her power compelling him to abandon the well. In a last heroic effort to free himself from her, recollecting his past conquests as a Warrior King, he slowly raised his wrist and warned:

"Run where you will,
Grey bird,

You shall be perched upon my wrist.

Some were called queens and yet have been perched there."

Brian's voice shattered the silence, rich, intense, passionate, defiant, agonised. The audience held its breath. Brian had spoken.

The magical power of the play exploded with the miracle of his voice. The play, the dance, Yeats, the poetry, Brian, me, the poets, the school, we were all miracles together. And Brian's silence was over.

6. Victoria

It was at the Yeats Summer School, the first year I attended, the year before the Brian event, that I met Victoria. I had quickly become friendly with some of the Summer School leading lights, mainly the Irish poets and writers like Seamus Heaney, Brendan Kennelly, John Kelly, and especially friendly with the poet, Jimmy Simmons. This was primarily due to the fact that the Summer School literary elite were based at the Imperial Hotel in Sligo, a grand Victorian building by the river, with splashes of faded elegance. I had been corresponding with Brendan Kennelly, who was then director of the school, and he had convinced me that this was the place to stay.

He was right. Staying at the Imperial Hotel afforded me special privileges, like easy access to the Irish poets to whom I was immediately drawn. I adored their fun-loving generous spirit, their informality, their refusal to take anyone, including themselves, seriously, (even the great bard, the paymaster, was hardly spared), their inherent modesty, even shyness, and their sense of melancholy laced with humour. They were wonderful. In many ways they were like my musicians. They had that same ability to flood the soul, to excite the senses, to arouse with delicacy, with nuance, with startling images; they exuded that same quality of precarious balance, of living life on the edge, high and wild. They personified a line from a song written by my friend, Jesse Winchester, '*if you're treading on thin ice you might as well dance.*'

They were themselves a kind of poetry, as though the poetry of the written word had somehow shaped itself to their own beings. However, the Irish poets were more articulate, taking a wild pleasure in words, their conversations often shot through with poetry - words leaping out of sentences, evocative, musical, delighting my ear accustomed to Canadian flatness - and they were more gregarious, more lusty, relishing the contact

68

of a good scrum.

The hotel had a comfortable lounge, with a fireplace, which was host to nightly adventures of unlimited potential. After the official activities were over, usually close to midnight, the poets, critics, the literary giants of the Yeats universe would gather here to sweep aside the world of letters, of footnotes and references, and indulge in social riot. And I gathered with them. "This room is the only reason I come to the Summer School," Jimmy once confided. The drinking was phenomenal and inspired a fierce hilarity spiked by monologue, dialogue, anecdote, and raucous choruses, sung and spoken, reeking with nostalgia and rocking with laughter until tears rolled and collapse was imminent - in an unbridled desire to break the good times barrier. After hours the Yeats Summer School was one grand Celtic celebration, and I suspected that this was its main attraction for many of its devotees.

As for me, it was hard enough to get used to the fact that prominent Yeats scholars, critics whose books I had studied and quoted, and before whom I trembled, like Richard Ellman, Frank Kermode, John Unterecter, Norman Jeffares, were actually there, lecturing in the flesh, but to see eminent American and English authorities pissed and unpredictable, incited by their irrepressible Irish counterparts, inhibitions soaked up by Guinness, liberated from academia in an extravagant blast of spontaneity, was a jolt to my notion of the order of things. At the same time I realised I was being allowed a coveted behind-the-scenes glimpse. Had I witnessed Yeats himself dancing a Guinness-sodden jig, or belting out *Danny Boy*, I wouldn't have felt more privileged. I was party to a marvellous confession and I savoured every minute of it. I rarely got to bed before the sun came up, lest I miss a single witticism, a single stagger, a single belch. I marvelled continuously at the punctuality of the lecturers during the early morning sessions, and their lack of tell tale morning-after signs. They were true professionals.

Early in the first week, during a break between lectures, I was standing in the crowded corridor, talking to a group of fellow students, when Jimmy Simmons, who had a connoisseur's eye for the ladies, led me away with unexpected urgency. "Come with me for a minute. I want to show you someone." He pointed out a girl standing in a small alcove, half-hidden by a plant. "I've been watching her from the first day," he confided. "She's painfully beautiful, so beautiful she makes my heart ache."

He looked intense, struggling with some concept, as though finding the words for a poem, "I can feel her fragility, her tremble. It's as though her body doesn't conceal her soul." I understood what he meant. She had a haunting solitary beauty, her face mobile, vulnerable, her eyes surprised, slightly frightened, her mouth controlling a quiver, barely perceptible, her body alert, slender, waif-like. She gave the impression of a doe poised to flee.

"She certainly is beautiful," I confirmed. As though aware of some threat, she inched further into the plant.

"I'd love to know her, to see what sort of creature she is, what land she comes from. But I'm too timid. I'm afraid if I talk to her she'll vanish."

"So you want me to do it for you?"

He looked at me shyly and nodded. "You won't startle her, she'll be easy with you."

"I'll be glad to talk to her."

"You don't mind?"

"Not at all," I said with an Irish accent - it was the only Irish phrase I could say.

"She looks like someone I'd want to know." I started toward her.

"Not now," Jimmy stopped me. "Wait until I'm gone."

I watched for her after the lecture and made my approach as she was leaving the building.

"Hi. My name is Niema," I said in my brightest Canadian manner. "Did you enjoy the lecture?" She looked at me with the hint of a smile, her lower lip trembling slightly.

70

"Yes, very much, did you? But it would be far better if the lectures were held outdoors. Don't you think?"

Although I shivered inwardly at the thought of sitting in the Irish damp, I agreed. I walked along with her. She didn't seem to mind. She told me her name was Victoria and that she knew very little about Yeats.

"What brings you to the Yeats Summer School?" I asked.

"I wanted to get away from London... somewhere in the country... and this seemed like an interesting thing to do...learning about Yeats...I admire his poetry...for some reason I've been reading a great deal of Yeats lately. When I heard about the Summer School in Ireland, it seemed the perfect thing to do." She spoke in hesitant short phrases, unsure of where they were leading, as though voicing ideas for the first time.

"Where are you staying?" I asked, anxious to move away from Yeats and on to easier territory.

"In a little bed and breakfast."

"Do you like it?"

"Not really, the room is fine...but the landlady is a bit of a snoop ... she comes into my room without knocking...I think she wants to catch me out...she probably thinks I'm hiding someone." A small nervous smile hovered as she spoke.

"That's terrible," I said. "You don't want to be hassled by a snoopy landlady. Besides you're away from all the fun and the poetry." Then impulsively, "why don't you move to the Imperial Hotel? That's where all the action is, parties, sing-songs, poetry readings....all the Irish poets stay there and they're great."

"Is that where you stay?"

"Yes. It's wonderful."

"I didn't know about it."

"It's not too late," I said with such eagerness I surprised myself.

"I suppose there's nothing to stop me from moving," she said, picking up on my enthusiasm. "It would be a good idea to leave that landlady, don't you think?"

"Definitely. How long will it take you to pack?" I said, springing into action.

"Not long, half an hour."

Her ability to take the plunge, sight unseen, impressed me. "I'll pick you up in an hour. How do I get to the house?"

She was really pleased now, smiling and almost at ease. "Thank you very much."

I liked her a lot.

I helped carry her few belongings to the hotel, sat her in the lobby and went directly to the desk to check her in. Then something happened I hadn't counted on. "Sorry the hotel is full. Booked solid. There's nothing available," the receptionist said apologetically. My heart plunged like a stone. How awful. Victoria had left her room at my insistence, she had trusted me, I was leading her on to bigger and better things, like some self-proclaimed pied piper, and now there was nowhere for her to stay. I was humiliated.

"We may have a room in a few days," the receptionist said, attempting to sooth my visible disappointment.

A few days. What good was that? I felt ill. Then suddenly I had an idea. Why not invite Victoria to stay with me until a room became available? I had a double room. "Can she share my room until then?" I asked, hopefully.

"I can't see why not," the receptionist answered, pleased that a solution was at hand. "I'll book her into your room and when something becomes free we'll move her."

Then I remembered. My room had only one bed - a fairly large bed but still only one. I disliked sleeping with anyone except lovers, not even with friends or family, and Victoria was virtually a stranger. But never mind about me, I deserved to suffer, I was responsible for this mess, what about the innocent Victoria? What if she hated the idea of sharing my room, my bed. We hardly knew each other. I shrivelled with embarrassment.

I was nervous about telling her, placing her into this impossible situation. Why hadn't I checked first? It was acutely painful. But my fears proved groundless. Victoria was delighted, bubbly and excited like a schoolgirl. She loved the idea of sharing my room and my bed, so much so that when a room eventually became available, she asked me, very tentatively, if she could continue to stay with me; she said she found it comforting. I was touched. She had an incredible sweetness about her, child-like, affectionate. How could I refuse? Besides I didn't want to refuse. Her bright intelligence coupled with an original perception about the lectures, the seminars, the people, fascinated me. She added a new dimension to the Summer School. I loved her wistful observations, her daring - she would ask the most provocative questions at question time - her sense of adventure, her unpredictability, her strange blend of shy and strident, the mischievous glint in her eye when she knew she was being impossible. She was an enigmatic being. We became inseparable. Friendships at the Summer School were quick and intense, like those made travelling.

She took to Jimmy immediately. She liked listening to his Irish lilt, the way he put words and ideas together. He made her laugh and she made his heart ache. They bounced off each other. They both adored the outdoors and, growing restless during lectures, would often slip away for a walk. They liked walking and would go on long walks at every opportunity, returning deep in conversation. Sometimes I would go with them, mostly I didn't. But I took pleasure in their being together.

Although Victoria and I spent much time in each other's company, I knew very little about her. She seemed reluctant to talk about her life in London and I didn't press her. Then one day a postcard was delivered to my room. I read it before realising it was for her. One line was bewildering. 'I've been asked to lunch with Noel Coward and Zaza Gabor - she's passing through London.' It was signed, 'Alan'.

"Someone is putting you on Victoria," I said handing her the card.

She read it. "No. It's genuine," she said quietly.

73

"Genuine? How genuine can having lunch with Noel Coward and Zaza Gabor be?"

She looked embarrassed, as thought caught in a guilty secret. "I'm married to Alan Bates," she said lowering her head. "He's an actor...he knows these people."

"You mean Zorba The Greek, Alan Bates?"

"Yes." I could see she was becoming uncomfortable, agitated. "I'd rather you didn't tell anyone...I'd rather people knew me as myself and not as Alan Bates' wife."

I was stunned. Had she told me she was married to the Duke of York, I couldn't be more surprised. She didn't fit my idea of a film star's wife - not that I had ever met one - she seemed so unpretentious, so modest, at times even awkward, so careless of her dress, her appearance in general, there wasn't a smidgen of glamour adorning her person, and she seemed so interested in things untrendy, difficult ideas, unpopular philosophies, things without shine and glitter.

"How come you're married to Alan Bates?" I asked, incredulously.

"Pure chance," she replied.

"It's better than winning at roulette," I quipped in an attempt to dispel the disquiet I could feel gripping her, mouth twitching, body tightening.

But, then, gradually, the story unfolded. She had been born into a poor East End London family but, determined to escape the poverty, she had taught herself skills, took courses and read profusely. She loved plays and poetry. She learned secretarial skills in order to earn money and got a job in a West End London office with connections in New York. Going to New York was her great dream and she eventually saved enough money for an extended visit. In New York she stayed with a girlfriend who lived in a shared flat in Manhattan. One day her friend decided to have a party and, since she too was new to New York and didn't know many men, she decided that each of her flat-mates, Victoria included, would have to invite three men. "I didn't know three men,"

Victoria admitted, "but that afternoon I had seen a play with Alan Bates and I was very much taken by him."

"You and every other woman who saw the play," I commented.

"But I decided to do something daring. I decided to phone the theatre and invite him to the party. It was strange really, had it been any other night he couldn't have come. But that was his one night off and he came - I guess he was curious."

"And you ended up getting married?"

"I didn't want to get married. I never intended getting married. I'm very jealous of my freedom and my privacy. Besides we come from very different worlds. I didn't like his world...especially the acting world... didn't fit into it...didn't want to."

She paused remembering something. "When Alan brought me home to meet his parents...his family lives in Derbyshire, D.H. Lawrence country...very beautiful...his mother was sitting on the patio...most elegant...sipping a glass of sherry...when he told her we were getting married she dropped the glass...it shattered into a hundred pieces....I guess I wasn't what she had in mind."

Later she told me that she and Alan had twin sons under a year old. "How did you manage to get away from London with two babies?" I asked, remembering the bind of motherhood.

"Alan is taking care of them," she said casually. "He has some time off. I don't think being an actor gives one special privileges...do you?...he has to get up nights to change nappies just like I do...I'm an artist too in my own way, everyone is...we share the responsibility of the twins. Alan agrees. He's very helpful."

When I moved to London I saw Victoria often and met Alan and the twins - Ronit was often their baby-sitter. Alan was one of the finest, most gentle, most generous people I had ever met, and I often marvelled at the patient way he dealt with Victoria's unbridled unconventionality, her wild riding roughshod manner, her distrust of his fellow actors, her disdain for what she considered their indulged, ego-inflated lives, her

75

exasperating principles, her loathing of what she considered middle-class pampering. For example, she wouldn't have any help in the house, although she barely did the housework or cooking, disliking both. Chairs were piled high with a confusion of clothing, papers and books, the bathroom walls were streaked with a blend of talcum powder, face cream and red paint - the latest of the twins' artistic endeavours – but she refused to allow money to make domestic life easier. I remember her going to the doctor's surgery to get booster shots for the twins, standing with one baby under each arm, waiting her turn in the queue, exhausted.

"Why don't you get a private doctor to come to the house? It would be so much easier on you," I suggested.

"I don't believe in it," she said, her tone precluding further discussion.

Victoria had a gentle influence on my life and her 'Neem...please...' could easily bend my resolve. 'Neem' was her pet name for me. Spoken like an affectionate embrace it filled me with a happy warmth, silencing any objections.

"Neem, please take one of Tinker Bell's kittens, she's so pretty, her name is Tiger Lily, Ronit will adore her."

"No Victoria. Ronit will adore her, but I'll end up cleaning the litter. And what about when I'm travelling?"

"I'll look after her. Oh please Neem, do it."

I did it.

Or, "Neem, you must go to the tricologist," when I complained of dry hair. "He'll get you sorted, treat your hair, give you yeast to make it healthy. Neem, please, you must go."

I went although I had never heard of a tricologist. Apparently neither had most people I knew.

"I telephoned to you this afternoon but you were not there," my Hungarian friend, Piri, said.

"I was at the tricologist's."

"I didn't know you went to one of those," she said, with what I

76

considered exaggerated concern, then she added sympathetically. "You have big problems? I didn't know that. What is wrong?"

"Not big problems...it's just that my hair has been really dry this past while. He gave me a special treatment."

"Dry hair? And for that you have to get special treatment?" I was beginning to feel ridiculous.

"Well, dry hair can be a serious problem." I defended my visit to the tricologist's.

There was an awkward pause.

"I didn't know people go to a psychologist because they have dry hair."

Aside from going to the tricologist and getting a kitten, Victoria permanently altered an important aspect of my life. She got me to change my hair style. No easy matter. My hair was my one large vanity. All my life I had longed for it to be straight and bemoaned its crumpled curliness. Then I discovered I could straighten it. While wet I would roll it onto oversized rollers and blow it dry, or if in a hurry, I'd iron it straight (little wonder it needed a tricologist.)

One evening Victoria and I arranged to meet Alan at a Greek restaurant for dinner. She loved Greek food. Both she and Alan were vegetarians, although she would always pluck bits of meat from my plate, and Greek cuisine had a good choice of vegetarian dishes. I had washed my hair for the occasion, combed it out, and was preparing for the roller ritual when the phone rang. It was a long distance family call from Canada. I lost track of time. When it was over I calculated that I had just enough time to wet my hair and iron it straight, rollers were out of the question. Suddenly the doorbell rang. It was Victoria.

"Sorry I'm early," she said. Victoria was usually early or late, rarely on time. "Just give me ten minutes to iron my hair, it's dried while I was on the phone and gone all miserable and curly."

She turned to look at me and her face flooded with joy, as though beholding a vision.

"Neem, your hair is beautiful...please Neem, you musn't straighten it." She paused dramatically. "You look like an Egyptian princess." Had anyone else said this I would have rushed for the iron, Egyptian Princess indeed. But coming from Victoria I dared to be flattered. Surely Victoria would know. She not only had access to the most glamorous women in the world but contact with royalty. I looked in the mirror. My hair had divided into a multitude of strands, each strand sprung into a coil. My face was stranded amidst the coils. I shrugged. Still, if anyone could recognise an Egyptian princess it was Victoria. I never straightened my hair again.

Victoria always intrigued me. Instinctively I loved her but I never understood the fierce ambiguities of her nature, although I learned to accept them, even to cherish them. She was an enigma with her insatiable appetite for experience, for ideas, for art, for literature, for stimulating discussion, and her lack of interest in the routines that bind existence, her inability to organise the daily rituals of living, her inability to direct, to focus or even to acknowledge her own unusual talents, although she was quick to encourage and support those of her friends.

Abstract concepts were her passionate preoccupation. They were more important to her than daily realities. One moment she was consumed by Gurdjieff, the next devoted to iridology. The preparation of meals could wait, the laundry could be ignored, but the reading of John Donne or W.B. Yeats could not be neglected. Her spirit thrived on ideas, they were the fundamentals of her life and her engagement with them was total.

One of her most fascinating characteristics was an exciting inconsistency. It was impossible to anticipate her. Just when I'd be convinced she was fiercely independent, she'd become awkwardly self-conscious, so unsure of herself that she seemed to dissolve in a puddle of dependency. At times she was like a musical instrument, so tightly strung, so finely tuned, that the merest whisper could provoke a dissonant twang.

Once when we were in Paris together she seemed lost and awkward.

We had gone to visit the Louvre and I could tell she was feeling crushed by the paintings, they had evoked some terrible insecurity. I could hear that twang encroaching upon the silence, see it in tiny darts around her mouth. She had that pained, trembling look and I was about to suggest we leave, when I noticed a lovely young man looking at her with that special brand of French appreciation. "He fancies you," I pointed out, hoping my saying this would not make her even more self-conscious, more awkward.

"I fancy him too," she said unexpectedly, and with a marvellous directness went up to him, smiled that small winsome smile of hers and said, "I would like to invite you for coffee."

Victoria wasn't like other friends who grew vague and undefined if we were separated for long periods of time. The thread connecting us was never broken. Time did not create distance. She had stamped herself upon my being. She was always there, close, integral, and when we'd meet again there was no hint of strangeness, no need to restate, to renew - the intimacy had never faded, it was fresh, vital.

If the Yeats Summer School failed to bring me new literary awareness, new intellectual discoveries, it succeeded in something more profound - it brought me new friends. One of the dearest was Victoria.

7. Aviva

Aviva's phone call came the night before Ronit and I were leaving for Morocco. I was deep in sleep, exhausted by the massive task of clearing the flat for friends to move in to. Aviva's voice exploded into my torpor in short thrusts, tight with panic.

"I must see you...I've got to get out of here... Can David and I come...I'm feeling desperate."

I sat up in the dark trying to determine where I was. Sobs burst into my ear and I was suddenly awake, in London. Aviva was in Toronto where it was evening, unaware she had woken me. I read this as an indication of acute distress.

"I'm leaving Irving." Tears dulled her words. "I know you've heard that before, but this time I'm doing it." Her voice, forced through a knotted throat, shrank with pain.

"Aviva, slow down. First of all stop crying, for one thing it's costing you two dollars a sob."

The attempted laugh slid into another sob and I could hear her taking deep breaths to steady herself.

"I'm trying not to cry, it's too indulgent crying long distance." She spoke between spasms of gulped breath, like a child who has been crying too long and can't stop. "But I'm so miserable and so frantic. Is it alright if we come to London?" Her voice usually full of sparkle was flat and lifeless.

"I'd love you to come," I said through her stifled sobs, "but Ronit and I are leaving for Morocco tomorrow morning. We're driving down with Annilee in her car, mostly pleasure, a little business... I wrote you." I could feel her disappointment, heavy and silent, like I was delivering news of a death. I had a sudden flash.

"Come with us! You and David can fly to Spain and meet us in

80

Malaga. We're taking a week to drive down so you'll have lots of time to get yourself organised. There's enough room in the car. It's perfect. You have the summer off. We'll spend some time on the coast of Spain and then cross over to Morocco." By now I was buzzing with excitement, delighted by the possibility. "Please come. I really want you to."

Aviva was one of those special people with whom it was a joy to travel, bringing a freshness of vision, an enthusiastic energy and a sense of wonder and adventure to every experience. We had great times travelling together.

"Morocco is the last place I want to go to," she said despondently.

"Why?" I asked surprised, knowing she was partial to the exotic, especially if re-enforced by sunshine.

"Arabs are not my favourite people. Remember Rus was picked up in Morocco and kept in a hole of a prison until Cedric raised money for bribes." At least she had stopped crying. "It's dangerous travelling there, especially with David." She sounded terminally weary.

"I've been to Morocco many times," I said, "and I'm not only intact but singing its praises. And David isn't exactly a babe in arms. Besides I'm taking Ronit and she's not that much older. Aviva, it's exactly what you need to get out of yourself, a totally new experience, to say nothing of sunshine and sea. I promise you, you'll love it, and it would be great for Ronit and David to see each other. We'll have such fun together. Come on, do it."

"I'm desperate to get out of here and I'm desperate to see you, but I can't cope with Morocco. Not now. It frightens me. Everyone says it's a nightmare place, and at this moment my own nightmare is enough to contend with... I'm feeling so rotten." Her voice dissolved into a sigh and then into tears. I knew that the conversation was an effort for her but by now she was an essential part of my journey and I persisted.

"Aviva, I've been there and I'm going back. It's a fabulous place, it's not frightening, it's fascinating. I know Morocco and I know you, you'll love it."

One week later an emotionally fragile Aviva, pale and exhausted, arrived in Malaga with an irritable David and, in an uncharacteristic state of passivity, was allowing herself to be taken to Morocco. Just before embarking on our drive down the Spanish coast and eventually to Algeciras where we would get the Ferry to Morocco, she and I went to a café to talk. Normally effervescent and enthusiastic, responsive to her surroundings, she was subdued, indifferent, immersed in pain, her blond hair limp, her blue eyes ringed with black.

"It seems that I always involve you in this never ending saga between Irving and myself. But you're the one person who knows what I'm talking about, and knowing that you love Irving makes it easier for me to talk about him." She sipped her coffee for strength.

"I'll begin at the beginning." She took a deep breath and began twisting what was supposed to be her wedding ring. "You know how every summer Irving goes through this song and dance routine about how what he wants most is to travel by himself, with a small knapsack on his back, sitting on a shore in Italy, or climbing a hill in Greece; how he's not free to do this with David and me around; how he can't make impulsive decisions, explore whatever excites him at the moment because of us; how he has to get away from the house in the suburbs, the whole family scene I've created and be by himself alone with the wind and the sun and the sea and his muses."

"That sounds like Irving," I interrupted. "He wants his 'wifey', his 'maidel' serving him munchies cosy by the television, and he wants to be the unencumbered bard, wandering ancient burial grounds, composing verse under a gnarled Hawthorn tree, untamed, romantic, free. I'm not putting him down. I'm sure it's a dilemma for him, needing the energy he gets from being alone and in contact with nature, experiencing people, especially female people, on his own - the raw material for his poems - but also needing the nourishment and comfort he gets from wifey Aviva. You're the catalyst who provides the conditions for him to transform that raw material into poetry."

"You know how much I respect his poetry," Aviva said.

"Not only respect it, but serve it."

Aviva shrugged her shoulders. "It's true. I've tried to create the perfect environment for him to write in. I cherish his creative spirit, his privacy, protect him from disturbances, even try to give him his freedom, ...within limits," she added.

"What are the limits?" I asked.

"The string of women he dangles before me. You know the syndrome. He'd rub my nose in his mistresses' perfumes until I grew so familiar with their scents I'd wait up late at night to sniff his clothes, like a lovesick dog, to see which one he'd been with. Night after night I'd make myself ill imagining how he was making love to someone else. Then I'd become so desperate to be with him that I'd drive myself to phone the woman I thought he was with, and when she'd answer the phone, I'd say nothing, I'd stand there, not breathing, the phone pressed into my ear, just wanting to be where he was. Next day I'd go to teach my class in sunglasses, looking ridiculous, to hide my red swollen eyes. I'd make some silly excuse about having an eye infection. The number of eye infections I've had would make some optomotrist a wealthy man. I'd become insanely jealous. I despised myself for it but I had no control. Jealousy took over like a demon. I was possessed. You know only too well the sick deranged things I've done." She stared into her coffee.

As the waiter refilled our cups, I remembered a poetry reading Irving had given at McGill University. It was on the occasion of receiving an award for his contribution to Canadian literature. It was a high-powered event, complete with newspaper reporters and television cameras. Before the reading there was a reception arranged by the awards committee. Aviva was radiant that night, greeting friends, writers, officials, sparkling with pride. When we sat listening to the introductory remarks honouring Irving, she looked like a peacock spread grandly in a front row reserved seat. Then suddenly she caught sight of Marta, Irving's long-time mistress, entering the theatre. Aviva's face, serene with happiness, splattered, its tiny muscles contracting spastically, her eyes unfocussed, her mouth darted wildly, like the lines of an electro-encephalogram. She twitched in her seat like a trapped rabbit. Irving stood on the stage, a powerful captivating presence. The third poem he read was from his newly published collection. "My next poem is entitled, 'Marta's Child'". He paused, raised his eyes to the audience and in a voice resonant with emotion said, "I dedicate this poem to my dear friend, Marta." A sob broke from Aviva's throat and, in a chilling rasp like a primeval death rattle, she choked "Bas-tard!", stumbled down the aisle and escaped. It was over in seconds. Irving continued to read, compelling, eloquent. I found Aviva in the ladies' room, weeping like a child whose puppy had just been crushed by a car. She came home with me.

"Aviva, I know only too well the terrible grief Irving's ladies have caused you, but you must know by now that none of them has ever been a threat to you. You're the only woman he wants to live with. He loves you. He'll never leave you for another woman." I said this with the assurance gained from long conversations with Irving.

"It's not a matter of leaving me, it's a matter of living with me, it's a matter of me living with myself. I can't live with the awful humiliations he puts me through," she said miserably, focussing on the ring she was twisting. "Recently, though, he has been making an effort. He insisted he was no longer seeing Marta or anyone else. I believed him. After all he is beginning to get on. There's a limit to his energy. Things were better between us than they've been for a long time. Then last month he began the old refrain about how he has to get away on his own and travel with a knapsack on his back. This time I told him to do it, and there was no laying on of guilts. I really wanted him to go and to go with my blessings, even though we had decided to stay home this summer. We sold our house and had to find somewhere to live then pack and move. His going off meant the burden would fall on me, yet again. I hated the idea. Not my choice of a holiday. But I wanted him to have the experience he'd been longing for. Serving genius, I guess you'd call it."

"Feeding it with a silver spoon," I corrected. It was an old argument between us, Aviva's subservience to Irving's poems.

Her finger had become red and swollen but she went on twisting the ring, grinding it into the puffy flesh as she continued. "The very same day Irving was booked to leave for Italy, I was booked to have a mole removed. Nothing serious. I tried to change the appointment so I could see him off, but I'd have to wait too long for a new one. He left for the airport alone, both of us disappointed that I wasn't going with him. As I was waiting for the taxi to take me to the hospital the phone rang. It was the nurse, relieved to catch me in time.

The doctor had been called out on an emergency and my appointment would have to be postponed. I was delighted. I took the taxi to the airport instead, excited like a kid by the idea of surprising Irving, resenting every red light in case it would make me late. I got to the airport just as he was heading for the plane. Some surprise. He was walking arm in arm with Marta, smiling from ear to ear." Aviva clenched her stomach at the recollection. "My vision blurred and I didn't know what I was seeing. I remained doubled over as though I'd been punched, icy cold. Then suddenly I was boiling hot, my blood pounding with shame, and outrage. I felt I was burning up. Somehow I made it home. When I walked into the house the first thing I saw was Irving's jacket, spread out on the bed, abandoned at the last minute. I went insane. I grabbed a carving knife and plunged it into the soft leather, slash after slash, screaming 'bastard! bastard! bloody fucking bastard!' Then like a madwoman I tore his clothes from the closet. I ripped apart the sweater knitted for him in the Aran Islands, I shredded the silk embroidered shirt I had given him for his birthday, I dismembered his favourite suit, amputating arms and legs, I sliced through the tails he wore to receive the Governor General's award, still wrapped in polythene. I really went mad on his underwear, hacking at the crotches, tearing them out with my nails. For what seemed like hours, I cut and tore, mutilated and stabbed, all the while shrieking 'bastard! bastard! bastard!' I was certifiably insane. Totally deranged. The only way to stop me was to stun me with a mallet. I went on maiming and screaming until my arm couldn't lift the knife, lurching like an epileptic gripped by a seizure, my eyes blind lumps, my throat like sandpaper, raw from screaming. Not even a handkerchief had been spared. I fell on the bed like a scrap of Irving's battered clothing, panting and wailing, 'bastard, bastard,' on and on, like a lament for the dead. I cried myself incoherent, spent to the point of paralysis. But with some miraculously intact fragment of sanity, I knew one thing, knew it with the clarity of a new bell, I had to leave Irving. I had gone to the edge and I was terrified. I couldn't survive another such scene. I had to get away from him. I had to get out of Toronto. When I could make it to my feet, I dragged myself to the telephone and called you."

8. Ketama Where Even The Files Are Stoned

There were five of us crossing by boat from Algeciras in Spain to Ceuta bordering Morocco: Aviva, David, by now eleven, my actress friend Annilee, Ronit who was almost sixteen and myself. I was the only one who had been to Morocco before. The others suffered varying degrees of fear, from Aviva, who didn't want to go at all because, like Shimon, she was terrified by the tales of horror she had heard, and whose terror was absorbed by David, to Annilee, whose fear of Morocco was tempered by a delicious curiosity, to Ronit, who was eager to go, inspired by my stories, but nonetheless apprehensive. Crossing over the narrow channel of water that separates Europe from North Africa, Aviva cast suspicious glances at the boatful of dark brooding Moroccans, many in shabby western clothes, some with flashing gold teeth.

"They look a mean lot, really sinister," she whispered, "like a bunch of cut-throats." She moved closer to me. "Niema, tell me again that it's going to be alright."

"Moroccans look better in Morocco," I assured her. In their long jelabas and kaftans, headdresses and babouches on their feet, they looked exotic, even noble; in baggy pin-striped trousers, soiled white shirts and dusty shoes, with swarthy complexions and short-cropped hair, they did appear 'a mean lot'. Aviva looked miserable, plagued by doubts of herself as a responsible mother. I had persuaded her to come, but my credentials in that capacity were at best questionable. She hardly spoke during the crossing but sat very close to David searching desperately for some way of escaping Morocco. But it was too late. The boat docked in Ceuta and from there we climbed into Vera, Annilee's beat-up Volkswagen Beetle, and drove directly to the Moroccan border, a few miles away.

Ceuta belongs to Spain although it is geographically part of Morocco. Crossing the border into Morocco was a plunge backwards in time. Suddenly we found ourselves immersed in a biblical landscape. Hooded figures in long robes carrying straw baskets on their heads and backs, walked along the road. The women wore yashmaks, veiling their faces so that only their dark eyes could be seen, their heads protected from the sun by long red and white striped shawls. Although it was July and hot, both men and women were entirely covered except for their feet which were bare. When Aviva saw the little grey donkeys, with small boys and bundles bouncing on their backs, a dash of hope sweetened her despair. Perhaps things wouldn't be as bad as she feared. In any case the worst was over. We had arrived, the anguished anticipation was ended.

By the time we stopped in Tetouan for a quick look around and lunch, Aviva had begun to relax. She was beginning to feel safe at least inside the car, and allowed herself the luxury of looking out of the side windows instead of keeping her eyes riveted ahead, as though this would help us get through the enemy territory unharmed.

Our first Moroccan lunch was an unmitigated success. The low benches we sat on were covered with embroidered materials and the walls hung with hand-woven carpets. We lay back among pillows and were served on low round tables. The atmosphere was undeniably exotic, not nouveau exotic; it was the real thing. We were the only tourists, the other diners were Moroccans, and Aviva, always in search of the authentic, was thrilled. Earthenware dishes of beef tagine, a Moroccan stew with prunes and nuts, lemon chicken with olives, and mutton couscous were placed before us. David regarded the strange exhibition with suspicion. "I'll have chips," he announced and refused to eat anything else. We dined in style, lingering over the flavours, wondering at the delicate herbs and spices.

"I must learn to make couscous," Aviva said, watching the grains absorb the spicy sauce, the saffron turning them golden. "It's delicious." Despite herself, her usual responsiveness to the promises of experience was gradually returning.

"Hey mom, look at those guys," David said, too loudly, "they're squeezing their couscous with their hands, it's gross." Mom flinched.

One of the couscous squeezers rose and patiently approached our table.

"May I sit down?" he asked politely. With a sense of history he demonstrated how Moroccans traditionally ate couscous, rolling the grains between the palms of their hands to form little balls, and plunging the balls into their mouths. We all tried, but only Ronit succeeded.

Ronit was the one we turned to for anything requiring practical skill. Perhaps it was because she was studying subjects like auto-mechanics, carpentry and pottery in school, whereas we had studied Latin, drama and sixteenth century English Literature, excluding Shakespeare. Later, leaning into the pillows, sipping tea made with fresh mint and poured ceremoniously from Arabic teapots with long curved spouts, we all relaxed. Aviva was smiling. It was going to be alright after all. The sinister had become delightful. I was temporarily vindicated.

Back in the car we drove toward Ketama. Ketama was an enigma I was interested in exploring. It was a town in the Ketama Valley in Northern Morocco, between Tetouan and Fez. In the valley, which was several miles long, growing marijuana was legal, smoking it was legal, but taking it out of the valley was entirely illegal. Moroccan jails were filled with people of all nationalities who had failed to export hashish, made from the marijuana, out of Ketama. This was the area where all the Moroccan hashish that was smoked throughout the world came from. I had never been to the Ketama valley, but had met people with impressive stories of how they had spent months on farms watching the snow melt on the mountains, being served Moroccan food on silver trays, and smoking as much of the best hashish as they wanted - all for free. I had always wanted to see for myself if this phenomenon really occurred or was some kind of group fantasy. Not that I was all that interested in hashish, but I was intensely curious, intrigued by the bizarre arrangement, and couldn't resist the adventure.

My previous visits to Morocco had taken place during the winter months when the Ketama Valley was cold. Since I had come to Morocco for warmth and sunshine, I had passed on Ketama. This time, however, it was summer and hot and we had a car, so inspite of Aviva's protests and forecasts of doom, reminding me, as though I could forget, that our friend Rus had been arrested in Ketama, I convinced everyone that the opportunity was too good to forego.

The road through the mountains was narrow and winding but good. Driving along smoothly and uneventfully we were surprised to see a new Mercedes. There were two Arab teenagers in it and I idly wondered what they were doing with a Mercedes. We passed small villages lazy in the afternoon heat, with men in jelabas and headdresses sitting in shaded cafes, sipping mint tea and playing cards. It was hot. Ronit kept dropping off to sleep. I felt myself growing drowsy, mesmerised by the heat and the rhythm of driving. Suddenly my reverie was shattered by a loud crash.

"What was that?" Aviva was instant panic. As I was devising an answer, there was a succession of explosions – gunfire! Frantically David rolled the windows shut. Aviva knew immediately she had been right all along. We never should have come. She hugged David protectively. Up ahead was a small village. We could see a roadblock and a crowd of people. We were forced to stop, gunshots ringing about us. Even I, in the role of bringer of calm and interpreter of Arabic good-will, was scared. My God, what had I done? What had I led us into? Our car was surrounded.

"What is it?" I shouted in my best French to a face pressed against the window.

"A wedding. Come see."

I could taste the relief, sweet as honey as I echoed, "a wedding", my head bowed in salvation.

Coming toward us down the road I could see men on horseback riding fast and shooting rifles. Yes, a wedding. I opened the door and stepped out. The others followed cautiously, not entirely convinced.

David remained inside. He couldn't be persuaded that rifle shots had anything to do with weddings and begged us not to go. But we could see men dancing and grew excited. A Rif wedding - what luck! Even Aviva didn't want to miss out.

The Rif people, some of the original inhabitants of Morocco are Berbers, still living in the Rif Mountains and maintaining their own traditions and dress. Crowds of men were gathered along the narrow road. There were no women to be seen. The bridegroom appeared, dressed in white, on a white horse, looking splendid, accompanied by rifle blasts and dancing. Then the music began. Pipes and drums.

Strange wailing music threading through the mountains. The dancers formed into groups and each group in turn danced around the mounted bridegroom, stamping and leaping, their rifles held above their heads. The road leading through the village became the stage on which this ritual was enacted.

We were invited to stay for the wedding festivities which went on for several days. I wanted to stay. Annilee did as well. The others were hesitant, unconvinced. David had the car doors locked. Aviva had that pained inward look which lack of trust inspired. Ronit was not feeling too well: a stomach bug she had picked up in Spain. So when the road was clear, Annilee and I bowed to majority will. We departed amid smiles and handshakes and renewed offers to share the wedding feast. "Perhaps next time," I promised. Waving royal goodbyes we drove off through the village.

Back on the road another Mercedes passed us. There was no other traffic. It was late afternoon and beginning to cool a little when we entered the Ketama Valley. The countryside was dry, burnt out, with nothing growing except colourless weeds. We drove slowly, the paved road turning to dirt road and back again. In one place where road conditions forced us almost to a standstill, young boys startled us by diving at our car, yelling "hashish! hashish!" and waving great brown lumps at us. Again David quickly rolled up the windows. It was as

91

though they were hawking melons or fish, or any of the various things Moroccans sell to passing cars. Only these hashish vendors were disturbingly persistent, pounding on our windows and clinging to Vera. They had to be shaken loose before we could continue, somewhat shaken ourselves.

Another Mercedes. It seemed to be tailing us and we pulled over allowing it to overtake. Instead it moved alongside us. There were three young Moroccan men wearing jelebas inside the car, smiling. One brought his thumb and forefinger together, forming a little circle and waved it toward us. Soon the other two were making the same circles with their fingers. It looked obscene. "Ignore them," I said expertly. "Pay no attention to them and they'll stop." But they didn't stop. They went on waving circle after circle. Finally they passed us, eagerly waving their obscene little circles out the windows. We looked straight ahead, impassive, so as to give no encouragement. They tried desperately to get our attention, blocking the road with their obese Mercedes, driving very slowly, not allowing our chubby little Vera to pass. "Just keep ignoring them," I cautioned, aware of the ineffectiveness of my tactics, but unable to devise a more productive strategy. Rattled by the unsolicited attention but pretending coolness and aloofness, we arrived in Ketama.

I remember once meeting a young Moroccan in a hotel in Marrakesh. He wore magnificent clothes, an exquisite jacket embroidered with silver threads on a black background, a silk batik shirt and hand-stitched trousers which flowed into soft leather boots. He looked superb. Incongruously he carried a black briefcase, such as salesmen sport, spoiling the Prince-of-Arabia image. Outside the hotel his Mercedes Benz shone lavishly. I asked him where he came from. He leaned toward me and whispered, "Ketama". It seemed that if one came from Ketama, one had to whisper the fact. "I'm here on business," he confided. Suddenly I understood what his business was, and why he looked so affluent. I saw him later that day sitting in a cafe with an American couple and their baby, in the new French section of town. He did not greet me. The husband looked like a well-scrubbed astronaut and the wife like the girl next door, in gingham and calico, the baby was straight out of an advert, with blond curls and starched bonnet, gurgling and bouncing on a yellow playhorse. The briefcase had changed hands.

We had arrived in Ketama. The road sign said, 'Ketama Village', but we seemed to be in the middle of nowhere. All we could find was one ornate hotel, with an oversized swimming pool set in a large garden. The hotel was completely out of keeping with the villages we had been passing which were primitive, with no signs of modernity. It belonged in the wealthy westernised suburbs of Casablanca. Aside from the hotel there was a large, modern petrol station, several small shops, and a tiny cafe. Was this Ketama? It was nothing like what I expected. Was it really a town or merely a facade, a front for something more ominous? While we were pondering our disappointment, a policeman came up to us, checked our passports, as though we were entering a foreign country, and kept them, telling us they would be returned when we left Ketama.

As I sat in the car wondering about the passports and what to do next, concerned that the sun was setting and it was beginning to grow dark, and contending with Aviva's 'I-knew-we-shouldn't-have-come' look, the Mercedes which had been hassling us on the road, pulled up. One of the boys approached me. I had the most approachable look. My long dark hair and dark eyes were so common that I could look Italian in Italy, Spanish in Spain, Moroccan in Morocco; with black net stockings and a beret, I could even look French in France.

"Do you speak English?" he asked, in a friendly French-Arabic accent.

"Yes," I replied curtly, not wanting to encourage conversation.

"Why didn't you speak with us? We were telling you that we have zero-zero hashish," he said, making the same obscene gesture. "You know, zero-zero, the best hashish."

93

A sudden flash of comprehension. The boys weren't being obscene, the small circles they were making were little zero-zeros. They were merely imparting information. I began to laugh. They laughed with me. Even Aviva laughed. We all laughed except for David and Ronit. David didn't get the joke and Ronit was feeling ill.

"Would you like to come to see our farm? Me and my brothers we invite you."

"Yes, why not?" I said immediately. This was exactly what I had hoped for, an invitation to stay on a hashish farm, and it was happening only minutes after our arrival. Annilee nodded agreement. Ronit moaned softly. Aviva was unwilling and David had his eyes targeted on the hotel. We managed to convince Aviva, promising to bring her and David back to the hotel if she had any doubts. I felt safe. I knew that Ketama was heavily policed. All the farms were known to the police. Everyone in Ketama was known to the police. Even we were known to the police.

We followed the Mercedes a few miles down the paved road and then turned into a dirt track heading into the hills. The sun was slipping into darkness. A slim crescent of moon was visible in the sky. Soon the last rays of light faded and the evening nuzzled softly against us. The dirt road disappeared and there was no longer any road, only rocks, holes and ledges. We twisted and swerved and bumped dangerously along the rough terrain. It became difficult to drive. Annilee struggled to keep Vera from giving up. Night fell, dark and starless. Where were we? We seemed to be climbing along a mountain gorge and could see the black outline of mountains. Darkness and silence in a hostile landscape. Aviva grew increasingly nervous. My earlier vindication was now on hold.

"I don't trust those Moroccans. We must be mad following them. Please let's go back."

David pleaded to go back. He had visions of opium dens and white slavery. Ronit was hunched over, stoically enduring, wanting to arrive anywhere. Annilee who had been eager about the adventure, was becoming edgy.

"Where are they taking us?" she asked, "I can't keep Vera going. They said it was five kilometres, we've already gone more than ten."

Where were they taking us indeed. I could feel Aviva's tension intensifying in the darkness, and Ronit's stomach-ache growing worse. My confidence began to crumble. Shimon's litany of disasters recited on the telephone leapt at me with a vengeance, girls who disappeared forever, guys cut up and dumped. I was the one responsible for bringing three females and two children into this deserted moonscape. And before us lurched three Arabs, with who-knows-what ideas. Shimon was right, if I wanted to take chances with my life that was my business, but why involve other people in my private risks? The doubts piled. When would I stop jumping off cliffs and yelling it hurts?

"If we don't get there in a few minutes we'll turn back," I said without conviction, acutely aware that we didn't know where back was. The boys, sensing our loss of faith, urged us onward with more zero-zeros. Suddenly, to our great relief, lights spread out before us. A village - thirteen kilometres later.

We pulled up beside a large dilapidated farmhouse and climbed a flight of rickety stairs to a veranda, almost tripping over human bodies strewn on the wooden floor. There was no electricity, only two candle stubs, spiting splinters of light. The bodies stirred and separated into one female and two males - catatonic Italians. The beam of our flashlight picked up odd bits of clothing, papers, tin cans and spilled sardine oil.

Aviva's relief at being rescued from rape and worse quickly converted to distress. Her face looked pale and pinched in the thin light.

"We can't stay here. This is gross. Let's go back," David urged, yearning for clean sheets and locked doors. His face seemed to have grown smaller, and his eyes larger. I gave him a hug.

Ronit, Annilee and I continued following the boys, more in desperation than in hope, while Aviva and David froze, refusing to go a single step further. We turned a corner, a door was opened, and out of the shabby surroundings, as if some genie had rubbed a magic lantern, a large lovely room, furnished in Arabic style, appeared. Thick Moroccan carpets, round brass tables hammered with intricate designs, and low benches covered with embroidered materials and strewn with pillows, transformed the chill of decay outside, into a glowing exotica, inside.

"This is your room now. Make yourself welcome," one of our hosts said with a broad smile.

David and Aviva were coaxed back with the promise of instant departure if they disapproved. David's eyes grew even larger as they surveyed the room, lingering on the Arabic teapot and the silver dish of oranges and nuts.

"You mean we can stay here?"

"Yes, if you want to, we've been invited to stay," I replied, entirely vindicated.

"Sure thing I want to," he said, releasing his mother's hand. Aviva gave her verdict by collapsing into the pillows.

Almost immediately dinner was brought to us by the women of the house, nodding welcome. We hadn't eaten since our Arabic lunch and were famished. Two large ceramic dishes heaped with tagine and couscous were placed in the centre of the table, a stack of round Arabic breads, beside them, and waiting on a Moroccan tray, a bowl of dates, a pot of mint tea, and chunks of hashish. The house boy did the serving.

We ate Arabic style, scooping sauce, vegetables and meat with pieces of bread. Even David dug in, not insisting on his own plate as he had during lunch. It was hard to believe that only hours before he wouldn't touch Arabic food. Aviva's emotional see-saw balanced at the tranquil position, secretly grateful she was spared the difficult journey back.

"This must be good for us, all these whole grains and vegetables," she said exuding relief, and watching with obvious pleasure as David, who was addicted to junk food, dug into the couscous. Ronit was feeling better, a combination of the homeopathic medicine I had given her, and the fact that her guts were not being jolted. Annilee was thankful that by some miracle, Vera was intact. David was simply glad to be alive and

96

eating, and my doubts began a quick vanishing process.

After dinner our three hosts joined us. They had changed from jelabas and headdresses into jeans and white shirts. We could see them properly now. Abdulla was tall and lean, attractive with his dark moustache and flashing eyes. Amal was slightly younger and heavier with scars on his face. The third brother was not much older than David, wiry with a closely cropped head. They were completely at ease with us. They told us they were Berbers, not Arabs. The Berbers had been conquered by the Arabs and forced to convert to Islam. They have the reputation of being honest, honourable, proud people.

"Better?" Abdulla asked. "You didn't believe us. You were afraid," he teased.

"You told us it was only five kilometres," Annilee pointed out.

"You would not have come if I told you it was thirteen." Abdulla spoke the best English and did most of the talking. We talked as tea was poured. We discovered that Abdulla's heros were Yasser Arafat and Bob Dylan. I toyed with the idea of telling him that Ronit and I knew Bob Dylan, but somehow it didn't seem relevant. Instead I asked why they had invited us to stay.

"We like visitors. We practice speaking different languages. We learn. And that is the way we do business. We never ask you to buy anything. But maybe one day you have a friend who wants to do business, then you remember us."

Amal told us that his favourite visitors were British, Canadians and Danes. "In between are the Australians and the Germans, and bad visitors are Americans and French. We never invite them." He picked a good lot in us. Annilee was English, Ronit and I Canadian, living in England, David Canadian, and Aviva Australian, living in Canada. Winners, the lot of us. I asked them how they knew we weren't Americans.

"I see your car licence," Abdulla said, "then I hear you speak and I know."

The youngest brother, Ahamed didn't speak much English but he smiled a lot, especially at David. Aviva asked about the Italians.

"The girl is called Leila, not her true name, it's an Arabic name she likes to have," Abdulla explained.

He said she had been staying with them for a month and was remaining indefinitely. Next day she told us she was a philosophy student in Italy. "I come to Ketama to cool out," she said, " I love the farm. I smoke all the time." She explained that the two Italian boys were her friends, recently arrived, who were "doing a run". We learned more about that later.

After tea the pipe was filled. Slowly the excitement and tension of the day dissolved into sweet sleepiness. Blankets were brought. The low benches became beds with comfortable foam rubber mattresses. The beds were made up silently by two young girls, who were shy and hardly looked at us. Warm water and towels were brought for washing. After making sure that we lacked nothing, the boys wished us a good night. Left to ourselves, we stretched out languidly, deeply content. David was ecstatic with relief. Abdulla and Amal were not abductors, instead they were like older brothers, warm and friendly, paying him special attention. We settled down to sleep and sunny dreams. Our first day in Morocco was over, *Hamdulelah*, thanks be to God.

Next morning we woke early and washed standing on stones in a clear cool stream coming from the mountains. Then, eager to see where we were, we took a short walk and were greeted by an incredible scene. We were in a lush green valley, surrounded by high barren mountains. The sight of green was cool and refreshing. Until now the countryside had been dry, bleached colourless by the hot sun. We soon discovered that the emerald green terraced fields were marijuana fields, growing up the sides of the mountains and in the valley as far as we could see. We returned to the house intrigued.

The houseboy prepared breakfast, first brushing the lumps of hashish left from the previous night on to the floor, then serving us strong sweet coffee with Arabic bread and jam. After breakfast we decided to explore our surroundings. The house was more interesting in daylight. A pungent cooking smell greeted us as we stepped from our Arabian Nights room, which David traced to a small internal courtyard. The courtyard contained sheep and chickens as well as two squatting women cooking on small camping stoves. It also contained a cot on which a mother, a baby, and a small goat were curled up together. Leaving the house, we walked through the village, feeling the heat increase dramatically, as the sun rose in the bright blue sky. Under a tall shady tree a group of boys were gathered and as we passed they invited us to sit with them. Ronit and David shared a rock. The boys appeared to be working, sorting baskets of dried plants and leaves. "You must work too", one of the boys said, showing Ronit how to make kif, smoked by Moroccans. She helped with the kif-making while we watched. I found it somewhat disconcerting that what she was told to throw away was what Westerners smoked as 'grass'. I've always been opposed to waste. Only the tops of the marijuana plant were kept, the rest was discarded. Later the tops were mixed with a special black tobacco and sold as kif in kiosks throughout Morocco. Most Moroccans smoked kif, hashish was for export. The boys passed kif pipes as they worked. They ranged in age from ten to early twenties. "This is my work - smoking," Abdulla had said the night before when David asked him what his job was on the farm, envisioning milking cows or tending sheep.

"Smoke with us," one of the older boys said, offering Annilee the pipe.

"It's too early," she ventured as an excuse.

"Everyone smokes here," he said amiably, "everyone is stoned. The horses and cows eat from the fields, they are stoned too. The chickens eat kif. Even the flies are stoned."

After watching the leisurely kif-making process for a while, we made our way toward the fields. The marijuana plants were taller than we were. Women and girls were working in the fields. They smiled at us and waved. One young girl stopped to touch Ronit's long thick plaited hair, which fell along her breasts to her thighs. "Zwine", she said approvingly, "beautiful". Old women and small girls carried huge bundles of cut marijuana plants on their heads and backs. The women and girls did all the work. "If a man does heavy work, he's called a woman", Abdulla explained later, when we questioned the work arrangements, "the men make the business".

Returning to the village we chatted with clusters of men and boys gathered under trees, smoking in the shade. They told us they never drink alcohol; unlike smoking kif, it's against their religion. Everyone smiled at us and offered kif. We refused, having agreed not to smoke in public places. "We don't smoke tobacco," Annilee offered as an acceptable explanation, not wanting to offend - besides it was true.

The village consisted of about a hundred houses with corrugated tin roofs, one shop which sold Coca Cola, to David's delight, apricot jam and tinned sardines, and a school. We heard chanting coming from the school and approached cautiously, not wishing to disturb. To our surprise we were signalled to enter by the teacher who was wearing a long, rather dirty jelaba and who looked stoned. Seated around the teacher on a dried mud floor were about twenty small boys, eight to ten years old. They too were dressed in jelabas, some torn and ragged others patched and carefully mended. They chanted beautifully from the Koran, reciting from broken little slates held on their knees, their voices pure and melodic like choir boys. They hardly noticed us, engrossed in their chanting, slowly rocking back and forth, deeply stoned. Aviva pulled David closer and, unusual for him, he submitted. I shuddered, somewhat unnerved, but listened with fascination. There was no other sound.

We returned to the house in time to watch our hosts line a suitcase with hashish for the two Italian boys 'doing the run'. "Small business," Abdulla said, with a hint of disdain, "too much hassle, but we do it for Leila's friends." He told us that they know every make of car and how to fit each one with hashish. "We like cars better, that is big business, it's worth to take the trouble." When the suitcase was finished it seemed impossible to tell it from a straight one. The thin sheets of hashish were perfectly moulded to the shape of the case under the re-glued lining. The high quality of the craftsmanship was impressive. Bits of hashish littered the floor. The houseboy swept them away.

Next morning we were taken to the hashish factory, a little white house with two rooms, on the edge of the village. In one of the rooms the hashish was made. There were bags of hashish powder set side by side on shelves and sacks of dried marijuana on the floor. We sat on the sacks and were served tea. Aviva noticed two books among the sacks and picked them up. One was a copy of *Shelley's Selected Poems*, and the other *Teach Yourself Logic*, both from the Hornsey Public Library in London.

Abdulla initiated us into the hashish making ritual. We took the whole dried marijuana plant and with forefingers and thumbs stripped off the top leaves and flowers, allowing the coarser leaves to remain on the stem. We were instructed to do this slowly with one long stroke. After we had collected a sufficient amount of the dried leaves on a plastic sheet, we were shown how to clean them, discarding the ones which were burnt or yellow. We gently crumbled the remaining leaves and flowers and put them on a muslin cloth stretched tightly over a large basin. Next we moved our fingers very gently through the crushed marijuana in order to release the pollen. Only the pollen was collected in the bottom of the basin, a thin layer of brownish-green powder. This was gathered into a small heap and we were shown how to press and knead the pollen with our fingers until it became soft and pliable and was eventually moulded into a dark lump of hashish. This was zero-zero quality, made from only the purest pollen. About half a kilo, one pound of leaves and flowers were required to produce the pollen for a marble-sized piece of hashish. We were told that one man worked five hours to make a kilo of hashish from the time of picking the plants.

The price of zero-zero in London was about fifteen times the going price in Ketama. We left the factory with the sense of having participated in a unique adventure. David didn't quite understand its significance but

101

was caught up in the mystery and awe. Ronit was especially excited, not least by the illicit overtones, and pleased by the new skill she had acquired, but realised it would be difficult to discuss it with her school mates, and impossible to put it to use. Where can one get a job making zero-zero?

We spent the rest of the day lying in the sun, chatting with the boys who spoke English or French. They spoke openly, candidly answering our many questions. The atmosphere was free from any sort of hassle. There was no pressure of any kind brought to bear on us. Abdulla's favourite utterance was, 'as you like'. If he suggested something and we were not agreeable, he nodded his head, raised one hand, lifted his shoulders to his ears and said serenely, "as you like". The choice was ours.

Especially surprising was the fact that there were no sexual innuendoes, although, except for Leila, we were the only visible ladies in town. We wandered about trailing feminine grace, a bouquet of wild flowers unpicked in the fields of grass. Our initial reaction was relief but soon we began to wonder at our lack of appeal. Even Annilee and Aviva, both with blond hair and fair complexions, features usually irresistible to North African men, elicited no special overtures. Where were we going wrong? After all we must be desirable verified by the fact that, except for Ronit who was too young, we've all had husbands.

Aviva still managed to have one, in her fashion. As a matter of fact Annilee rather fancied Abdulla, and was frankly puzzled by his non-preferential radiant smiles and friendly attention to all the ladies as well as to David. With curly yellow hair and violet eyes, she was unaccustomed to male indifference. Abdulla grinned, but revealed nothing. We concluded that they were all too stoned to make any sexual efforts. A profusion of sunshine and kif made for a laid-back existence. We began to lay back.

9. Senor Barba

Ketama gave me time to pause, to gather my energy, to change gears from Europe to North Africa, to reflect. If I had been waiting for a more leisurely occasion to assess various ambiguous experiences, which had occurred en route, Ketama was that occasion and 'Senor Barba' that ambiguous experience.

On our way through Spain we had been camping in the hills, avoiding the coast raped by tourism. However, as we approached Algeciras we took the coast road. Trying to catch a glimpse of sea through high rise apartment blocks and wall-to-wall hotels, I was startled by a sign saying 'Mijas', pointing into the hills. Mijas? One minute. I knew Mijas. As a matter of fact I knew Mijas intimately. Funny, I had not thought about Mijas for years. Now, there it was. We stopped the car while I remembered Mijas.

My connection with Mijas went back a long time, over fifteen years. Ronit was still in the womb having barely survived that battering by the turbulent Atlantic on our journey from the Canaries to Spain. I had disembarked in Algeciras only half alive. But after several days of struggling to maintain my equilibrium on streets which insisted on rocking like the sea, I was suddenly recovered and anxious to explore Southern Spain. However, having survived the sea, a new hazard developed on land. Wherever Shimon and I went, we inspired uproarious hilarity. Children shrieked with laughter when they laid eyes on us; adults choked trying to stifle bursts of laughter, girls giggled uncontrollably into their fingers. There we were, ambassadors of good will, prepared to love everyone and everything, but each time we entered a village or town we became the butt of some cosmic joke. Children followed us in the streets with taunting laughter. Women, leaning out of windows, hastily summoned relatives to enjoy the fun. Laughing faces pressed into the windows of cafés - we didn't dare sit outside - to witness the joke first hand, as word quickly spread. It was unnerving, impossible. True, at that time, Southern Spain was relatively untouched by tourism and the inhabitants of villages and small towns were unaccustomed to encountering people other than themselves. Still we were recognisably human. We were even dark haired and dark eyed like the Spanish. What could be provoking such merriment? We considered various possibilities. Shimon was over six feet tall and I was only five feet. Were we a sort of Mutt and Jeff, a Little and Large joke? Perhaps that could justify the odd snigger but surely not inspire fits of jubilation. Our clothing seemed to be in order, at least nothing was showing which shouldn't be. What was it?

After a few days of painful exposure we made several useful observations. Women and girls did not wear trousers, and jeans were unheard of. Only cowboys wore jeans. That is cowboys and me. Worse, my jeans were designed like men's with a front zipper. That zipper excited howls of laughter. Did it sprout a you-know-what companion? Also men did not wear shorts. Shorts were for little boys. Shimon was wearing shorts. But most significant of all, men did not have beards. Only Jesus Christ had a beard. Shimon's beard triggered turbulent outbursts of laughter. A self-proclaimed, tall, thin Christ with hairy legs, dressed like a child in short pants, and a small cowboy disciple with bosoms and who knows what apparatus concealed behind a zip. We were the funniest thing that had entered Andalusian life since Mickey Mouse. Well, I was able to wear a dress and Shimon to wear long trousers, but what about the beard, the major source of amusement, the punch line to the joke? Shimon was attached to his beard, so was I. We wanted it where it was. Would peasant pressure force him to shave?

One day we went to Gibraltar to escape the torment of Spain. After all Gibraltar was British. We were sitting in a restaurant dejected, because contrary to expectations people were still Spanish and still laughing, when suddenly we saw, sitting at a table at the other end of the restaurant, another misfit sporting a beard. He saw us at the same moment.

Shimon and he rose spontaneously, and with preordained inevitability moved toward each other and embraced. It was love at first sight. The three of us laughed and hugged and pulled beards. It turned out that our fellow transgressor was South African, like Shimon, and lived for part of the year in a little mountain town called Mijas, close by. His name was Jeffrey but he was called 'Signor Barba', Mr. Beard, - what else - by the locals, in recognition of his amazing appendage. He invited us to Mijas. At first I resisted. We were on our way to Granada and I didn't want to delay the Gypsies and the caves and the Alhambra. But he was insistent and finally, starved for sympathetic human contact and persuaded by Shimon, I agreed to go - for one night.

I couldn't believe Mijas. It was exquisite. A small white village with narrow cobblestone streets, high above the sea, a tiny locket set in breasts of hills. From the patio of Jeffrey's small villa we could see the Atlantic, the Mediterranean and the straits of Gibraltar connecting them. Jeffrey's girlfriend, Susan, was a dancer, like myself, and he was a sculptor and an artist. Shimon too was an artist. It was perfect.

Shimon sang and played his guitar on the patio and we listened and watched the oceans move in and out of each other's arms. We didn't leave the next day nor the next, nor the next or the next. When we finally did leave for Granada Jeffrey and Susan came with us.

One day when we were still in Mijas, Jeffrey showed us a farm house and a large tract of land he was intending to buy. Even at that time and with our limited knowledge, the price seemed ridiculously low, something like $700. He told us that for $400 we could have a house built next to his with acres of land. But we had no money. Neither did he. He worked as an architect in London for several months of the year, just long enough to enable him to live in Spain for the rest of the year. He disliked the work but had forced himself to do it in order to buy the farm and hoped to earn enough money from the farmers harvesting the fruit on his land so he would never have to work again. He considered himself a professional dropout, a hippy bum and was making provisions to sustain that life-style. He must have sensed a great affinity with us because he was determined that we become neighbours and made us promise to send the money when we got to Canada. He would arrange everything. Under the influence of Jeffrey - he was good looking and persuasive - and Mijas, and the oceans, we promised. But by the time we got to Canada Ronit was born and Shimon was sick and we were too poor. It was impossible to save $400. Eventually we gave up trying.

We said goodbye to Jeffrey and Susan with genuine sadness, but convinced we would return soon, promising to send the money and vowing never to lose touch. Well, we didn't return, we didn't send the money, and we did lose touch. Eventually Mijas became a place in my memory and even the memory grew increasingly dim. And now, suddenly, fifteen years later, Mijas had somehow materialised, it was real, in the flesh. Little white Mijas with its small cobblestone square where women drew water from the well while donkeys waited patiently, where one woke to the smell of fresh bread, where men climbed the long road from the sea with baskets of fish on their backs, where I had spent lyrical days with Jeffrey and Susan and Shimon, where we had regained our confidence as being certifiably human, even loved. I had returned to Mijas.

The road to Mijas was now paved. There were no peasants with rope-soled shoes and baskets of fish, only long lines of cars. Then came the full shock. Mijas. Souvenir shops, a bloated car park, a museum with 'the smallest things in the world', irritated honking on the narrow streets, the smell of petrol fumes, and tangles of tourists. Mijas, speedy, buzzing, cluttered. The setting was still beautiful, but my Mijas was gone. I wanted to leave immediately in order to preserve a shred of memory intact, but the others persuaded me to ask about Senor Barba first. Ronit was especially insistent, she loved experiencing bits of my past.

She and I searched out the most authentic shop we could find, with the oldest shopkeeper, and with little hope of success I asked if he knew Senor Barba. His eyes lit up. I had spoken the magic words. 'Senor Barba', he sang out, yes, of course he knew Senor Barba, everyone knew him. But Senor Barba was no longer there. He had left some years before.

"*Donde?*" I asked. Where is he? Closing his shop, he signalled us to follow him. Suddenly I found myself in Jeffrey's small villa. It was now surrounded by other grander homes but I could still see the oceans embracing from the patio. I pumped the man's hand with excitement. An old man came out of the house and we were introduced as amigos of Senor Barba. He greeted us with great enthusiasm.

Although my Spanish was pathetic, I understood him. "*Senor Barba*", he said, savouring the words and nodding significantly, "*Senor Barba, mucho dinaro*", much money, "*muchas casas*", many houses. Then he pointed all the way to the sea and made a sweeping circle with his arm, "*todas Senor Barba.*"

All Senor Barba's. "*Todas?*" I asked in disbelief.

He nodded to assure me, "*todas...todas.*" He spoke with pride, without a trace of resentment. Senor Barba, who had come from some foreign land and had lived in his village for many years, was now part owner of Spain. This pleased him. It amazed me. Jeffrey, the hippie bum who preferred dabbling with paint in his mountain village, to real life and career in the big metropolises, was now a millionaire. How did that happen? I asked where Senor Barba lived and was told he had his own 'urbanisation' in Estapona, down the coast toward Algeciras. I was given his address. I left stunned by the encounter.

It was almost ten o'clock, but still light. We decided to find Jeffrey in Estapona. Spaniards go to bed late. On the drive there we wove delicious fantasies. During our trip through Spain, Ronit, Annilee and I had been sleeping in fields and eating mainly bread, olives and cheese, saving our money for Morocco. For the past few nights David and Aviva had joined us camping in fields. David had been protesting wildly, complaining about the primitive conditions, the small menus with smaller choices. What if Jeffrey invited us to stay in his house and we could take hot showers? What if he fed us a meal with shrimp, maybe lobster, even paella, or hamburger and chips, David's private fantasy. The 'what ifs' grew more elaborate as we drew closer to Estapona and increasingly hungry.

When we finally located the urbanisation it was after eleven o'clock and dark. I became hesitant. A new 'what if' reared its head, what if Jeffrey didn't remember me? After all here I was, arriving without warning, late at night, after fifteen years and I was bringing four people with me. It was a bit much.

Even at night the urbanisation looked lovely. It was right on the sea, dotted with swimming pools each shaped differently and filled with flowers and trees. Each house was built differently as well. At least it was done with good taste. We found Jeffrey's house and knocked. A young girl came to the door, his daughter. She informed us that Jeffrey and Susan were out, but when I told her I was an old friend, she invited us in, saying she would get them. We waited in their elegant living room which for me became more like a dentist's waiting room, as I grew increasingly nervous with each passing minute. How would he receive me? Would he recognise me? Would I recognise him? And how would he receive the others? What was he expected to do with us at that time of night? Suddenly he came through the door. He looked at me for a moment and took me in his arms. He held me for a long time and we both laughed.

"I was afraid you wouldn't recognise me," I said, relieved.

"But you haven't changed one iota. It's remarkable."

"You've changed," I said, "you're more handsome."

He was tall, brown, with longish sun streaked hair, bright blue shirt, white immaculate jeans, a touch heavier, but in superb condition, like one of those perfect lifeguards on his night off. He looked radiant, overjoyed at seeing me, and delighted to see Ronit.

"So this is what happened to that lump your mother was hiding. Well, well, well," he said embracing her.

He even kissed Aviva, and Annilee, and shook David's hand warmly. Rather than being put off by our sudden arrival, he seemed to welcome it. Then Susan arrived. Susan was a different story. She looked worn and thin, her face lined and tired. Life hadn't given her what it had given Jeffrey. She looked like the good time was over and she was paying the bill. She too remembered me and said that, strangely enough, they had been talking about Shimon and me a few days earlier. A ripple of guilt skimmed my conscience, Shimon and I had stopped talking about them years ago. She was pleased to see Ronit. Although not full of kisses and sunshine, she received me kindly, Ronit and David as well, but she all but ignored Aviva and Annilee.

As soon as he discovered we hadn't eaten, Jeffrey invited us out to dinner. Susan didn't want to come and he didn't waste time persuading her. We had a midnight, moonlight feast by the sea, in a restaurant owned by Jeffrey. Giant charcoal grilled shrimp, my beloved lobster with butter sauce, octopus, a variety of meats and salads, even David's coveted hamburgers and chips, and of course, paella and champagne. It was splendid. Jeffrey managed to improve on our fantasies. Ronit and David played ping-pong and overdosed on the pinball machines – their mutual addiction - since it was all for free, and we talked and laughed, Jeffrey expansive, exuberant, luxuriating in the company of three attentive females. Aviva became increasingly witty the more champagne she drank. She could be very impressive and Jeffrey was impressed. Annilee grew more entertaining, improvising a South African accent, to Jeffrey's delight, and I, basking in exquisite relief, just grew more adoring. We were good value. Jeffrey was loving it. Did he fancy Aviva, or was it Annilee, by now I couldn't tell. We too were loving it - the food, the sea, the moon, the champagne, the laughter, the vigilant waiters, and Jeffrey. It was a love affair all around.

After dinner we walked through Jeffrey's urbanisation with arms around each other. "It's my sculpture, my work of art," he said, "and you are here to share it, isn't that just wonderful?" We hugged him with sheer joy. He led us to one of the smaller villas apologising for its size; it was the only one he had the key to and he didn't want to wake the manager, but the next night we would have a "special villa". Aviva had already warned David to suppress even a shadow of disappointment no matter what we were offered, if indeed, we were lucky enough to be offered anything, and on no account to criticise or complain. But the villa Jeffrey gave us that night was so grand the precaution was unnecessary. "I didn't expect anything like this," David gasped. It was built on different levels and all the rooms led to the sea. We could step from our bedrooms on to a shore lined with flowers and palm trees. The rooms were spacious with beamed ceilings and large windows, beautifully furnished in Spanish style. There were two bathrooms with hot water. After Jeffrey left we laughed and danced, leaping from shower to bath, splashing in the hot water, too excited to sleep, unable to believe our good fortune. "Imagine what he'll give us tomorrow," David said. We couldn't imagine.

Next morning we waited for Jeffrey to take us for breakfast as he'd arranged. As soon as I saw him I knew something was radically different. It was definitely the morning after. The glow was gone. At breakfast the 'special villa' did not cross his lips. Instead he said, "Susan mentioned something about you catching a boat from Algeciras to Morocco today. What time does it leave?" He didn't even lower his eyes. I could tell David was just about to say, "you said we were staying here tonight," but Aviva silenced him, probably with a kick under the table.

"It leaves at 1:30," I said.

"Then you'll have to hurry to catch it. You'll need time to organise the tickets, there's always confusion at the ports."

"Yes, we'd better get ready," Aviva said.

"I'd like to say goodbye and thank you to Susan," I added. We were all busy pretending it was business as usual.

"Oh... Susan had to leave early. She sent her goodbyes. I'll convey your thanks."

He drove us back to the villa and waited while we packed, helping us arrange the bags in the car, and giving us fruit for the journey.

"Don't wait fifteen years before you visit us again," he said, giving me a big hug.

As we stood by the car saying final goodbyes, pretending all was as it should be, I knew I couldn't leave without at least gleaning one bit of vital information.

"Jeffrey, last time I saw you, you were a hippy bum, now you're a millionaire with a yacht and a plane. What happened in between?"

He smiled. "I'm still a hippy bum in my heart if not in my pocket."

"It's the pocket that intrigues me."

"Remember when I told you to buy that land?" Yes, I remembered. "I couldn't stop what happened. It happened inspite of me. Shortly after I bought the farm I found myself in the middle of a land boom. My land became so valuable that I sold it, then I bought more, sold that, bought, sold, and before I knew what was happening I was rich. And believe me, I didn't have much talent for it. I just happened to be in the right place at the right time." He paused. "Had you sent me that $400 the same thing could have happened to you."

I thought about the $400 as we drove toward Algeciras. Would I have been rich too? Somehow I don't think so. I wasn't meant to have a spare $400. I still don't. Probably never will. And I never did own anything worth owning. Probably never will.

Rushing to catch the Algeciras boat and engulfed in the subsequent Moroccan events, we didn't have much opportunity to reflect on Jeffrey. But now, laying back in the sunshine of Ketama, the Senor Barba affair took on a new clarity, as Aviva and I dissected it. The mystery of our sudden enforced exit cleared. We decided it was Susan who instigated it, probably insisted upon it. We were sure she had seen it all before. Jeffrey entertaining the ladies, feasting upon their attention, while she wilted on the sidelines. She'd probably had enough of that. More than enough. Jeffrey's obvious pleasure in the company of women didn't spring from nowhere, it required practice. Aviva could relate to that. Neither did Susan's lined face, her strained appearance, her permanent sense of grievance, they too were the result of precedent. Aviva could relate to that as well. But if Susan was paying the bill, she had made sure we shared it.

10. Less Than Zero-Zero

It always surprised me how quickly travellers developed small routines wherever they visited, even if they were only staying a few days - morning coffee at a particular cafe, afternoon walk by the sea, or a stroll through the town or village, drinks on a particular terrace watching the sun set. Routines imposed a cosiness, an order, on to the strange, the uncertain. Routines made things safe. After three sheltered days on the farm framed by a gentle routine devoted to morning coffee, afternoon mint tea, evening pipe and stories and in between bathing, sunning and talking - dividing into pairs, Ronit and David, Aviva and I, Annilee and a young Moroccan she fancied - most of the psychic, emotional, even physical knots we had arrived with had dissolved into the familiar. Even Aviva was ready to venture further afield and assail the road into Ketama.

Aviva did, however, have a huge incentive. She wanted to visit English Tom, more specifically English Tom's twelve year old son, Matthew. English Tom and Matthew had been living close to Ketama village for over a year. Mohammed told us about them the night we arrived, thinking that the knowledge of Westerners living nearby would provide us some insurance. When I asked, in a feeble attempt to introduce some humour into our humourless arrival, if English Tom was called English Tom to differentiate him from all the other Toms living in Ketama, Mohammed said, "No other Toms. He is called English Tom because he is English, and we like him to be English, and he likes to be in Ketama." I couldn't fault that.

Although I had no particular desire to meet fellow Westerners, I was curious to know what kept English Tom and Matthew in Ketama for so long. Aviva had more powerful motives. With her perpetual concern for David's well-being, still struggling with the guilt of exposing him to Morocco, she was overjoyed by the possibility of meeting another boy his age from a similar culture. Perhaps the meeting would inject some normality into the madness of Morocco. Perhaps they would discuss baseball or bicycles or comics or even compare England and Canada. Perhaps Matthew would make Morocco easier for David. She couldn't have been more mistaken.

In daylight the drive to the village was not the demon it had been in the night. Reprieved from our blinding anxiety, the rocks and ditches were merely a nuisance instead of messengers of doom. It was hard to imagine that only days before, the landscape had been filled with terror; now it was not only benign but grand, and we smiled and smiled as we gazed gratefully upon it. But as so often happened in Morocco, the benign and the terrible were inextricably woven into a tapestry of surprises and shocks.

English Tom's house consisted of one long room with a broken stone floor. The furniture was less than sparse. It was almost non-existent. Two narrow beds on either side of the room, a small table, a damaged chair, several cardboard boxes - that was it. The streaky white-washed walls were bare except for a shelf containing discoloured plastic dishes, two blackened pots, an onion and a small bruised camping stove. A nail driven into the wall was draped with faded jeans, dishpan grey shirts and a matching towel. There was no evidence of running water. The one window was small and shuttered against the sunlight and heat. In the semi-darkness Matthew lay stretched out on a bed, half naked, his arms by his side, his eyes fixed on the ceiling. He remained motionless as English Tom, hunched over the table, his hair hanging over his eyes, greeted us with, "Oh, you're Mohammed's lot. Mohammed said you'd be coming. Find yourselves a seat." He wiped the hair from his eyes and nodded toward the beds. Matthew said nothing but was aware of our presence because slowly, very slowly, as though he could hardly bear the exertion, he drew up his knees so that Ronit and I could sit down - his concession to the advent of company. I thought he might be ill, he looked so thin and pale and his eyes were ringed with dark patches.

The springs groaned as Aviva, David and Annilee sat on the bed opposite us. English Tom was busy preparing something in a small cracked bowl and doing battle with his fallen hair. "My son Matthew," he said, nodding toward the bed but not interrupting his mashing and grinding. Matthew fluttered his fingers. We perched uncomfortably on the beds, feet straining to reach the floor. Aviva, normally chatty and inquisitive, was silent. I searched for something to say.

"Have you been here long?" I asked awkwardly. It was hardly better than "do you come here often?"

"About a year," English Tom answered.

"In this same house?" I asked trying to sound casual. The place looked like they had moved in that day.

English Tom registered my surprise. "We keep intending to do something about it, fix it up, but we never seem to get that together." He reached for something on the shelf. "I had enough of houses and getting things together in England. Here we're just drop outs. It suits us fine." He spoke slowly, absorbed in his preparations.

I scanned the room searching for some manifestation of Morocco. In every Moroccan home, even the poorest, there was some evidence of colour, some comfort, some warmth - a rug, a wall hanging, an embroidered cushion, decorated pottery. Here there was only the chillum English Tom had taken from under a pot and set on the table – a largish Moroccan pipe bound with a cloth.

The door opened and for a moment sunshine flooded the room. Two young Moroccan men entered and a shaft of sunshine stayed. They greeted us in the traditional Moroccan manner. "Jamal", the first one said, extending his hand, "labess."

"Niema", I replied receiving his hand. After touching my hand he touched his to his heart, bowed his head slightly and smiled. It was a warm intimate gesture and I was pleased. The introductions made things more friendly - English Tom was certainly no master of old world charm. Sensing David's uneasiness, the Moroccans lingered over making his

115

acquaintance - they had a sixth sense with children.

"Labess king David. You speak Morocco?" Jamal asked, smiling fondly.

David shook his head.

"You like couscous?" David nodded. "You like couscous, you speak Morocco." He ruffled David's hair affectionately.

David actually smiled and ventured, "Ronit speaks Morocco."

"Ah Ronit", he said, vibrating the "R" on his tongue, "speak to us some Morocco." Ronit reeled off a little item she had put together from words and phrases Mohammed and Abdulla had taught her, like "I have no money", "I have one really crazy friend," perfectly reproducing the guttural sounds and inflections of Arabic speech and superimposing a touch of dramatic intensity. It meant nothing but sounded great. The boys roared with laughter and slapped their thighs. Nothing could have been funnier. Aviva kicked off her sandals, hugged her knees to her chest and even glanced hopefully at Matthew. I was beginning to experience the first ripples of a diluted well-being.

Ignoring the laughter and general merriment, English Tom rose from the table, tying his hair back with a leather thong. I knew that meant business. He slammed the door shut, banishing the ray of sunshine. "Let's get on with it," he announced, waving the chillum which he'd carefully stuffed with a large quantity of the mixture from the bowl. I admired his long thin fingers. "Great stuff. My own special brew and none of that wicked tobacco" - this for our benefit. "Ladies and gentlemen we are ready to partake," he announced formally. "Places please." It was as though the childish games were declared over and the players ordered to prepare for serious activity. I thought of the biblical reference to becoming a man and putting away childish things. The Moroccans arranged themselves on the floor, propped up against the wall, ready for becoming men.

Unlike the sepsi, which held a small amount of hashish or kif, and which most Moroccans smoked, the chillum was for committed

116

smokers. I had been introduced to the chillum during my first visit to Morocco, and had once smoked from it. The hit had been so powerful I nearly fell over backwards. That was the point of the chillum. The others had never seen a chillum and they eyed it with varying degrees of suspicion and interest - Aviva with hostility, Annilee and Ronit with curiosity, David with anguish - some new instrument of torture. Although he appeared to accept our smoking with bravado, he was secretly terrified we would slip into some other world and leave him helpless in an alien landscape. Ronit had seen a variety of pipes back in Canada when Shimon had carefully supervised her debut into the marijuana smoking world, but the chillum was a new experience.

During The Finjan days Shimon and I had been knee deep in marijuana. Almost all the musicians smoked, it was part of their message, part of the changing times, the protest, the flowing skirts, the long hair, the beads, all of which I loved. However, it did not occur to either of us to smoke. We didn't smoke cigarettes and, happy to be let off the hook, presumed we wouldn't be able to smoke marijuana. I remember one of the musicians saying sardonically, when he discovered we had been to the Middle East and hadn't smoked kif, "then what did you go there for?" Eventually, however, if we weren't to be considered police informers or worse, it became impossible not to try marijuana.

Shimon was initiated by Cedric Smith, one of The Finjan musicians who had become a good friend. Shimon admired Cedric and I adored him, not only because of his tender, compelling voice and the originality of his songs and the concept of his 'Perth County Conspiracy' band-music blended with poetry, dance and mime, spiked by the alternative lifestyle of band members - but because he kept me laughing. He had a quick, zany, off-the-wall wit and augmented it with a profusion of accents which he dipped in and out of at will. When he was on a roll he had me aching with laughter. (Years later, when he turned to acting, people would phone him just to listen to the message on his answering machine.

117

It was an event. He was offered acting roles on the strength of it.) Cedric could convince us of anything and when he waxed lyrical about the wonder of listening to the Beatles with earphones after a few tokes, Shimon found him irresistible.

"Their music is married to marijuana," Cedric explained, "the perfect coupling."

That night Shimon agreed. The following night, however, either Shimon smoked too much, or too enthusiastically, or the grass was too powerful, because he became severely nauseous. Cedric walked him around the block, hoping the fresh air would make him feel better. But Shimon grew worse. Whether due to anxiety, or the seafood spaghetti dinner, or some mysterious physical reaction, he became so ill that, unable to breathe, he asked Cedric to take him to the hospital. Cedric resisted knowing that bringing him to the hospital would mean his arrest. Throughout the sixties hospitals in Montreal were obliged to report anyone smoking marijuana to the police and the police were obliged to arrest the smoker. The punishment was considerable, often prison, and the criminal record permanent. But Shimon, convinced he was dying, preferred risking jail and a criminal record to death.

The hospital was close to where we lived and Cedric persuaded Shimon to walk there, promising that if he still felt as desperate when they arrived, they would see the doctor. But if the walk didn't cure Shimon, the emergency room did. The sight of bloated faces, blood soaked bandages and mangled limbs, made him feel better fast. He returned home fully recovered. However, his taste for marijuana suffered a set-back, and it was a while before he could listen to the Beatles as they were meant to be appreciated.

Some years later, when Ronit reported that kids at school were sneaking marijuana smokes, Shimon, recalling his initial terrifying experience, told her that if she was ever tempted to try marijuana he would smoke with her. The offer was made in strict secrecy. Had the school authorities got wind of it, a terrible scandal would have resulted.

My mother would have been even less forgiving, her recriminations fierce, 'you're turning your own child into a dope fiend'. And how could I blame her? Although I was in agreement with Shimon, in my heart of hearts I didn't like the idea of Ronit smoking grass. Not for any moral reasons, I didn't consider it dangerous or addictive - that was just establishment propaganda - it just didn't sit right - and she was so young. Eventually Ronit was tempted and eventually Shimon did smoke with her. But she didn't find the experience especially sensational, and perhaps because the mystery was tainted by availability, her temptations were infrequent.

But now, in Ketama, smoking was part of the occasion. Hadn't she made her own zero zero? Besides she was older and I trusted her sense of self-preservation. Jamal showed us how to smoke the chillum, covering the bowl with a cupped hand and inhaling deeply. He passed the chillum to each of us in turn. The Moroccan boys were experts, as was English Tom. I choked, exhaling a rush of smoke. Ronit managed a delicate draw, Jamal shaking his head, disapproving of her caution, encouraging her to inhale. Dismissing the chillum with a flick of the wrist, Aviva passed, more for David's sake than her own. Only Annilee came close to satisfying Jamal and he gave her a grudging thumbs up sign. As the pipe made a second round, Matthew suddenly showed signs of life. He rose on one elbow and signalled for the chillum. Inhaling deeply, his poor lungs filled to bursting like an overstretched balloon, his chest becoming so distended the ribs erupted like knife blades. He held the smoke until his eyes bulged, then exhaled in an angry blue cloud, sputtering and gasping for breath. I watched in alarm as he collapsed onto the bed, his eyes withdrawing into their sockets, his cheeks sunken, his face even paler.

David watched with a mixture of fear and envy. Envy because Matthew was accepted as a man in the world of men, while he was still a boy corralled by a circle of females. Aviva's eyes were fixed on Matthew as though witnessing a macabre horror show but unable to look away, then riveted on David in an effort to protect him with her gaze. I glanced sideways at Ronit. She sat, back to Matthew, absorbed in braiding and unbraiding the strands of wool tying her plait. The room was thick with smoke. David sat as motionless as Matthew and almost as pale, his speckled blue eyes dark with misery. He was hating the visit. There was no talk of baseball or bicycles here. As a matter of fact there was no talk at all. The Moroccans were suddenly silent. I couldn't even make eye contact with them. Annilee giggled erratically. Ronit looked up as though seeing her for the first time. Aviva began to twitch. I was entirely sober. It was time to go.

As we left, the Moroccans smiled dreamily, English Tom, his head on the table, his hair over his eyes, raised one hand and waved vaguely. Matthew made no response. He seemed oblivious to everything and everyone, but was apparently aware of our departure because slowly, very slowly, he stretched out one leg, then the other. David cast a last anguished look at Matthew but drew a blank.

11. Irving

We left Ketama heading for Casablanca via Fes. Entering Fes was like putting one's head in the door of a massive oven. The heat blasted at us sudden and parched. But Fes, one of the oldest of the Moroccan Imperial cities was one of my favourites. I knew the others, especially Aviva, would love it, particularly its medina, the old city encircled by walls arched by magnificent gates, enclosing a maze of alleys crammed with bazaars, mosques, fountains, workshops and every possible market. It was Morocco at its best, miraculously unchanged over the centuries. The camp site was on the outskirts of Fes and surprisingly luxurious. We made arrangements to stay. I was right. Everyone loved Fes. Even David, terrified at first by getting lost in the labyrinth of lanes, jostled by stubborn donkeys who refused to give an inch, soon enjoyed being rescued by young boys who led us out of the tangle of twisted alleyways, pulling him by the hand. He even began to relish the thrill of being lost, coming suddenly upon a tannery with men wading in vats of purple and red dye, or a fountain ornamented with mosaics, or a metalworker hammering a silver tray, or an ancient harem window bulging like a false eye, crafted of wood, to conceal the viewer, or a perfumery smelling of rose, sandalwood and jasmine, knowing that the boys would always lead us to safety.

None of us could keep away from the medina, wandering under the shaded bazaars roofed with cane and tree branches, peering through the doors of mosques to catch a glimpse of cloaked figures prostrated in prayer, drinking mint tea in ornate tea rooms, browsing through the souks making and selling every conceivable craft, the air rich with the mingled odour of spices, incense and kif. It was the stuff of travel dreams.

Fes was the essence of old Morocco and it kindled a special light in Aviva's heart which burned a little brighter each day. Despite her bitter expectations, she found herself not only unthreatened but with an intuitive ability to connect with Moroccans. Unlike Annilee, whose behaviour was often out of touch, unsure of her responses, Aviva was perfectly attuned. She had an ease and empathy which the Moroccans related to with warmth and humour, and she quickly developed some endearing techniques. Instead of recoiling when some merchant rushed out of his shop and took her by the arm in an attempt to entice her inside, as Annilee sometimes did, unsure if she was being flattered or aggressed upon, Aviva would put her hand on the man's shoulder, look into his eyes, smile, and say something like, 'today my husband permits only bananas and beer' walking off with the promise 'but perhaps tomorrow'. No one was offended. When a shopkeeper wuold see her inspecting some article, and in an attempt to sell it tug urgently at her sleeve, with the inevitable 'for you student price', she would respond by tugging at his sleeve with a corresponding 'for you student price' and offer up an old comb or a tired sandal. They would both laugh. Her appreciation of the bargaining ethic gave her an additional affinity with the merchants. After four days in Fes she had the syndrome licked and did the closing on all our purchases. She got an olive wood hair clasp Ronit wanted down to a third of the asking price with sandalwood oil thrown in.

However, it was inevitable that at times she would retreat from the colours, smells and tastes of Morocco and return to her preoccupations in Toronto. The light would dim as she was sucked into a vortex of inner darkness, her eyes pale, her features dulled with pain, reliving the well worn deceptions, humiliations and fears, silent and alone. But only once did she allow herself a public indulgence. Driving to Fes, during a particularly hot tiring patch, I caught a glimpse of her staring at David, her eyes filling with tears, her face creased with sorrow. She moved closer to David and drew him to her, gazing at him with raw pathos, probably imagining his fatherless future. She shivered, hugged David hard and began to weep. David responded with confused tenderness. Fighting his own tears, he patted her back, pleading "don't cry mummy, don't cry mummy", again and again, over and over, until he wept helplessly with her.

I said nothing. We had agreed that she was not to torture herself with searching reviews and analysis. She was to stop the merry-go-round of her mind, the circle of questions, accusations and probings, the obsessive re-run of painful scenes, like the compulsion to prod the raw place where a tooth had been, preventing the healing. She was to release herself into experience without intellectual censure, to enjoy with the senses, to allow herself to become strong in the present before encountering the future. But how could I not forgive the occasional lapse?

She did well in Fes; the profusion of activity, flavours, textures, shut out all other input. A day in the medina was satiating; it overwhelmed the senses, insisting on the present, leaving nothing for the past. But on our last night in Fes, Aviva suffered a small relapse. We were sleeping on air mattresses in the open, too hot to crawl under the tent. I was aware of Aviva tossing and turning, unable to sleep. Finally, she rose quietly and wandered off. When she didn't return I went to look for her. She was sitting under a tree gazing up at the moon through twisted branches. I sat beside her. After a while, almost in a whisper, she began to talk about Irving. Although there was little new to reveal, I knew she had to speak it aloud, to test it against the mosaic of Morocco.

She told me how she had first met Irving when she was very young and had just escaped her mother's stranglehold by coming to Canada. Raised by a mother impossible to please, who undermined her with constant disapproval, and a father who was wrapped in books, oblivious to her existence, she found herself attracted to older men. During her first week in Canada someone took her to the 'open house' held every Friday in Irving's living room, to enable poets to read their poetry and exchange ideas. Aviva was an avid reader of poetry and had an on going love affair with words. Words were her passion. Irving was not only an older man, but a master with words. The die was cast. Although married with two children it wasn't long before he was celebrating her feminine attributes in poetry.

"I was his first major infidelity. I guess he became addicted to infidelity," she reflected sadly.

"And you picked up that addiction, you became addicted to his infidelities. Sometimes when no infidelity existed you imagined one," I suggested.

As though the word 'infidelity' itself was enough to unleash a torrent of tightly-reigned grievances, Aviva succumbed to a tortured recounting of Irving's affairs with other women, her eyes clouding with pain. "Aviva, no one knows better than I what you have suffered, but you must admit that sometimes you grossly overreacted. There were times when your jealousy was evoked by your own insecurities and not by anything Irving did, and there were times when you gave him a hard time not for something he was doing, but for something he had done." Although I loved Aviva dearly and sympathised with her terrible torment in her traumatic union with Irving, I wasn't unaware of her part in creating the traumas. I had seen her wretchedness, her desolation, and my heart ached for her. But although Irving never complained to me, I had seen his misery too, understood his grief. And I knew that often Aviva was oblivious to his pain. Sometimes Irving was the innocent victim of her jealousy tantrums, but he patiently endured her frantic behaviour and bitter retributions, accepting her jealousy as an inevitable fact of his life, and accepting his punishment philosophically, as payment for his part in creating it, behaving not only with dignity but with generosity. I reminded her of a time in Ireland several years back.

Aviva, Irving, David, my friend Tom and I had toured Ireland in a hired car, before I was due at my first Yeats Summer School. In Dublin we met the Irish poet Brendan Kenelley, head of the Summer School, and chatted about Yeats and Irish poetry. Brendan apologised for his limited knowledge of Canadian poetry. "There is only one Canadian poet I remember reading," he mused, "I don't know his name, but I remember a poem he wrote - it's about a girl pissing behind a bush."

124

"I'm that poet," Irving boomed with a touch of bravado.

"And I'm that girl," Aviva added with pride, always eager to share his success. The revelations resulted in a round of drinks at the pub.

While discussing our trip through Ireland, Brendan told us about a unique poetry festival held each year in a Galway castle and urged us not to miss it. The castle was originally the home of a Celtic poet king, who once a year invited the poets throughout his kingdoms to a special feast held in their honour. The feast was served by the players and musicians of his court who also entertained the guests with music, poetry, plays and stories. The Galway festival was the recreation of this ancient tradition. Our plans included a trip to Galway where we intended renting a cottage by the sea before taking a boat to the Aran Islands. We decided to head there earlier to attend the festival.

On the threshold of the castle we were welcomed by a guard of honour and ushered into the entrance hall. Mead was served in stoneware mugs by girls in long velvet gowns, their breasts spilling on to lace, while strolling players wearing embroidered tunics and sandals with silver buckles, strummed on lutes and zithers. The entrance hall glowed with the light of torches held in wall brackets and an open log fire. By the time dinner was announced by the page we were in a festive mood, warmed by mead, pleasure and high spirits. As I was climbing the stone stair well to the banqueting hall, I found myself beside the guard of honour. I had a sudden impulse.

"We have Canada's poet laureate here with us tonight," I whispered, as though confiding a choice secret.

"And who might that be?" he asked.

"That man over there," I pointed to Irving, still drinking mead and chatting with one of the serving maids. "His name is Irving Layton, a truly fine poet."

The banqueting hall was magnificent, set with an enormous wooden table, candles in brass holders their light reflected in pewter mugs, silver goblets, flagons of red wine and fresh flowers. A fire blazed in the hearth. We took our seats to the music of dulcimers, lutes and zithers. Wine was poured. Then suddenly a thunderous clap on the drum. We all fell silent. "The King of Connacht!" the page announced.

The king entered wearing a gold crown, his shoulders draped by a purple cloak held at the breast by a Celtic cross, a gold-hilted sword at his side. As he took his place at the head of the table, the page lifted his goblet, "to the King of Connacht." We all raised our goblets. The king rose to salute us, his goblet meeting ours. "Poets of the four provinces of Ireland, I welcome you to my castle." Another page entered bearing a tall thick candle set on a marble slab. The king spoke." Each year I light a candle to honour a poet from one of our kingdoms. Tonight I dedicate this candle to the renowned bard, famous throughout the land, Irving Layton, and ask him to rise." Everyone clapped. Irving rose slowly with a sense of occasion, his aura like the power of gravity. The king lit the candle and said, "I ask the honourable bard to bring you greetings from the far off kingdom from whence he has come." My heart leapt, I hadn't anticipated an impromptu speech.

Irving hesitated, but only for a fraction of a second, and then, as though his entire career as poet had been preparation for this moment, he spoke with passionate eloquence. He began formally by extending thanks to the king, on behalf of the assembled poets, for the feast prepared in their honour, and then extending thanks for himself, for the esteem bestowed upon him by singling him out for the dedication. Then, with the stature and fluency of a great orator, his shoulders wide, his massive silver-black head erect, he launched into a moving address about poetry. He talked about the rich heritage of Irish poetry which gave birth to the poets gathered in the castle. He talked about the important position they occupied in the kingdoms as seers and healers. He quoted poem after poem, never faltering over a single word. He talked about the poet, not only as seer and healer, but as prophet and warrior.

"The poet follows a prophetic path to lead his fellow men toward light and awareness, to expose 'the dark subtleties that plague the human soul'. The poet is a fierce warrior doing battle with man's folly, a warrior like the brave warriors of Ulster and Connacht, who has the courage to use words as his shafts and javelins, to wage war on hypocrisy and repression. The poet is a bard who sings with fullness of feeling, a song so sweet it would fill any person hearing it with peace and music. I propose a toast to Irish poetry and to all the great Irish poets yet to come who will follow in the tradition of Prophet, Warrior and Bard." He ended with Yeats' epitaph.

"Cast a cold eye on life, on death. Horseman pass by."

It was a stunning performance. He received a standing ovation although it was assumed he belonged to the cast. When the clapping and stamping finally ceased, the king signalled for food to be served. Each course was followed by entertainment to allow the guests to rest. Following the lobster bisque one of the girls played the harp and two others sang old Irish ballads. They sang of heroes and of brave warrior kings and they sang of love. After the roast beef and platters of fish a story-teller told tales from the Tain, an ancient Irish epic. Following the cheese and fruit spread on boards, 'The Golden Helmet', a short play based on an Irish legend, was performed. It was a grand evening.

During dinner Irving received a note inviting him and his friends to the cottage in the castle grounds where the cast was lodged. He answered with a resounding 'yea,' and leaving David with a couple we had met earlier, we found ourselves in a thatched cottage with beamed ceilings and an open fireplace. It was one of those rare magical evenings. Irving, elated by wild praise from the cast, was at his charismatic best, dynamic, witty, full of pungent wisdom. "Let us have a poem by the famous bard Irving Layton," Cathleen, one of the players declaimed. He knew many of his poems by heart and spoke them in his rich mellow voice to an enthralled cast. He had everyone sitting at his feet. Cathleen was especially animated, smiling up at him, singing Irish folk tunes, showing him her favourite poems so she could hear him read them. She was a beautiful colleen with burning red-gold hair twisted round her head and fastened by a silver clasp, green-irised eyes with dark lashes casting shadows down her cheeks, and the hands of a princess. Her bright Irish wit sparked Irving to his scintillating best.

"And who do you write your poems for Mr. Layton?" she asked, holding up a phantom microphone and imitating a BBC interviewer.

"For God," he answered, "but you, my dear, are welcome to eavesdrop."

All that Irving required to flourish was an adoring responsive woman, and he was blessed with five, as well as two adoring men. He soared. And we soared with him. It was his night and he filled it with magic. Perhaps we would never meet again - Cathleen, Dierdre, Fergus - but on this night, splendid with poetry, music and Celtic mystery, like lovers, we were joined in perfect union. I felt grateful to be present. Aviva did not. She looked on from a corner of the room, refusing to participate, casting her own special brand of 'cold eye'. I could feel her tightening like a bow, growing increasingly rigid as Irving grew increasingly expansive and embracing. When Cathleen poured her a glass of wine, she took a resentful sip and clenched her lips as though the wine was bitter in her mouth.

It began to grow late. "Where would you be stopping tonight?" Cathleen asked and my heart leapt. I knew she was going to invite us to stay.

"We didn't have time to arrange anything," Irving replied, "we thought we could get rooms in the hotel in town."

"Surely they'll be booked up with guests for the festival."

"We have a car, we'll find somewhere," Aviva snapped like a slap on the hand, "we should leave right now, we have a son to attend to."

Dismissing the sting, Cathleen took her arm, green eyes imploring her to relent. I implored with her. How could she banish us from this Celtic Eden? It was like savaging a blessing.

"Why don't you stay here, in the cottage, bring your son ...we have three guest rooms...and for the next month the castle and the cottage are ours." Aviva's throat swelled with ire. Cathleen turned to me. "Do stay...for as long as you like."

"Do you mean that?" Irving asked, oblivious to the shaft of venom rising in Aviva's throat and spilling on to her tongue. "Won't it be an inconvenience for you?"

"I most certainly do mean it, and it most certainly will not be an inconvenience."

"As a matter of fact we were looking to find a cottage for a few days, somewhere by the sea," I said, resisting Aviva's rancour.

"Look no more. We're not by the sea, but we do have a stream flowing by the door with a family of wee swans that would turn the Wild Swans of Coole green with envy. Will that do?" Cathleen asked.

"Sure now, you are most welcome to be our guests. We would be honoured to have you," Dierdre, the harpist, assured us. "And you'll be wanting for nothing. Lobster bisque for breakfast, roast beef for lunch and mead for the in betweens."

"Stop. I'm convinced," I sang out. This was the answer to our prayers, complete with lobster bisque, swans, and a thatched roof. Surely Aviva would yield. It was just the setting she loved. True, she was also concerned about David, had wanted to check on him hours ago, and furious at Irving's lack of concern, but we could have worked something out even if it meant disrupting David, he had endured worse.

"That's a very generous offer," Irving said warmly blind to Aviva's multiple anxieties.

Then suddenly, precisely, Aviva spat her arrow. "I am not staying. You are welcome to remain, I'll get a room in town."

The silence was so startling we could hear the arrow bite the air. Irving said nothing for a moment, recognising the force of Aviva's attack, familiar with its devastating potential. He tried only one perfunctory, "Come on maidel, let's at least stay the night." He put his arm around her shoulder. "It's late, we'll leave tomorrow." Aviva recoiled as though caressed by a leper.

"Don't maidel me. I'm going now." Irving did not press the issue, gracious enough to give us the evening unspoiled by a scathing scene. I too said nothing, sensing an implacability so fierce it was deaf to any plea. My rational head understood, indeed justified that implacability, knew its source, its anguished history, but my selfish heart wanted to wish it all away. Oh but how I longed to stay.

"Before we depart let us first have a song from that excellent musician, Dierdre," Irving announced, attempting to defuse the explosive.

Aviva icily conceded the song. Dierdre sang a haunting Irish ballad about a Virgin Queen who had a swineherd beheaded because he dared to sing his love for her. A drop of his blood entered her womb 'and there begat a child'. I was grateful for the song. Somehow it soothed the wound inflicted by Aviva's acrimony. Irving proposed a last round of mead and a toast. Our mugs were filled from a choice castle cask. "I toast the fine Irish players from Galway who have made us welcome in their home and who have given me one of the most memorable evenings of my life. Thank you for being our gracious hosts."

"Hear! Hear!" We raised our mugs.

"I also toast the Irish poets who were not here with us tonight but whose spirit we honour."

"Hear! Hear!" We raised our mugs and drank. Aviva did not raise her mug, did not drink.

"My friends it is time for us to leave," he said with a trace of his innate formality.

"I have spread my dreams
under your feet,
Tread softly because
you tread on my dreams."

I went into the night reluctantly, cruelly disappointed - Aviva had wrenched us from a magical encounter - but also elated - Irving had preserved the magic, had even transformed the searing finale into a celebration.

12. The Prince

Casablanca was a city I preferred to avoid. I didn't like its noise, its traffic, its skyscrapers, its shabby modernity. It seemed to cherish the worst of Western influences, it even had a 'new medina', reminiscent of a shopping mall, and that ultimate Westernism – the supermarket. The old medina was squalid - a slum medina – lacking history and antiquity. And although the 'new medina' contained all the right ingredients, archways, cobblestones, alleyways, small shops, bazaars, the final product was a sterile imitation, a stage set injected with charm. Especially after the romantic overtones conjured up by Hollywood, Casablanca was a serious disappointment. But this time I could not avoid it. I needed to see Jos who lived there, to finalise some business arrangements.

Jos was a French Moroccan I had met in Marrakesh during a previous trip and with whom I had developed a warm relationship. It was difficult meeting Moroccan women, they were kept out of the public eye, veiled behind yashmaks and kaftans, not available to Westerners, so spending time with Jos was a privilege. With her English and my French we managed to discuss matters like politics, culture, and current issues, helping me gain some insight into the complexities of Moroccan society. It was from her that I first became aware of the repressive political system and the nasty human rights record hidden from tourist view. She had a Moroccan friend languishing in prison for over six years. He had been abducted by the special branch police and kept in secret detention for nine months, blindfolded, chained to the floor, unable to sit or stand, his head regularly plunged into buckets of excrement. His crime was participating in a peaceful political demonstration.

Jos had a French mother and Moroccan father and combined the warmth, exuberance and spontaneity of the Moroccans with the sophistication and style of the French. Fluent in both Arabic and French she moved easily between the two cultures. With long reddish hair, hazel eyes and fair skin she looked Western, but with hennaed hair threaded with silver and beads, khol outlining her eyes, embroidered babouches on her feet, baggy Arabic trousers and a hand-woven shawl, she looked exquisitely Moroccan. Her bias, too, was Moroccan and I learned much about the fine tuning of Moroccan life through her, directly encountering the heavy influence of black magic which suffused Moroccan living, the fear of magic spells, magic potions, the dread of the evil eye.

Jos had been in Marrakesh to seek out some Western musicians visiting there, in order to induce them to perform at a nightclub her father was opening in Casablanca. Unfortunately they had already departed, leaving her without performers. Her father's cabaret was in one of those fashionable beach strips where expensive hotels, restaurants and nightclubs fringed the sea, internationally manicured with names like Kontiki, Miami and Tahiti. She wanted musicians from the U.S., Canada and England, to endow the club with special status. French and Moroccan musicians normally playing the strip were commonplace, English and American performers would be a prestigious attraction. Since status and prestige was what it was all about for a certain segment of wealthy and aspiring-to-be-wealthy Moroccans who frequented the strip, the formula seemed a winner. The problem was finding the musicians. She couldn't believe her good luck when she discovered I had contact with musicians - during The Finjan days I had developed my affinity with musicians into lifetime relationships - and asked if I would be willing to undertake the booking for her father's club. I agreed, and while the club was being set up Jos and I had been in close contact. The grand opening was now drawing near. I had arranged for two musicians to launch the club, and had to finalise contracts, money matters, etc. Visiting Jos was an important reason for my trip to Morocco.

Although Jos knew I was coming to Casablanca, she didn't know when, and had no way of knowing I would be arriving with four other people. But this was no cause for concern. Unlike Westerners, Moroccans were easy about such matters and visitors were always welcome, expected or otherwise. I remember a Moroccan saying, when my friend Susan and I resisted a dinner invitation because his mother wasn't expecting us, 'if there is enough for three, there is enough for four; and if there is enough for four, there is enough for five; and if there is enough for five, there is enough for six, so please not to worry. Guests are the flowers of Allah, it is written in the Koran.' A favourite Moroccan complaint was that Westerners were too worried, too wound up, too rigid, and took days, if not weeks, to get into the rhythm of Morocco, the slowing down, the letting go, the smoothing of frowns, untying of knots - and some never made it. Once a Moroccan said to me, 'You Westerners come here so speedy, it makes me dizzy just to watch you unwind. Relax, take it easy or you will give us a bad case of your Western Speedy. Here it is not New York. If it does not happen today, why not tomorrow? What for the hurry?' The inability to flow with life was a disrespect for life itself.

For me entering Morocco was shedding a Western skin, layers of obsessiveness, pressures, compulsions were cast off. In my new skin I could allow myself the luxury of just being, instead of always being somewhere or something. I could even forego my endless lists. I had never been to Jos's but I knew she would do everything to make us welcome and comfortable. And we were all due for a little comfort. We needed a break from campsites, from sleeping on the ground, twitching awake to remove a stone pressed into the shoulder blade or lodged in the kidney, eyes seared by flashlight beams. And we could certainly do with real beds. We needed a break from sharing our three tired air mattresses, especially since David usually confiscated one, wheedling Ronit's or Aviva's from them when it was their turn to have one. Ronit would sometimes acquiesce with only the feeble protest, "you know David, you're a spoiled brat." She had a remarkable tenderness for David. "It's easier for me than for him," she once told me. But Aviva would always surrender to David. She functioned with a superstructure of guilts, which David manipulated with a mastery far beyond his years. If the guilt of exposing

David to Morocco was now in the forefront, it dwindled to insignificance in the face of Aviva's massive, all-encompassing guilt - that of denying David a father.

After a concerted effort, she had persuaded Irving to allow her to have his child. Irving was opposed to the idea. He already had two children from a previous wife and now wanted to concentrate his energy on writing poetry rather than on rearing children. Aviva promised to care for David on her own, absolving Irving from all parental responsibility. She kept her promise faithfully. However, each time she saw a father with a child riding his shoulders, or pushing a swing, her eyes filled with tears and she allowed David an extra indulgence. David was nourished on indulgences. Outwardly wiry and taut, the diet of indulgences made him inwardly flaccid.

Morocco accentuated the flabbiness. Accustomed to being served on demand by a compliant mother, he was unwilling to endure physical discomfort or inconvenience. He wanted to be staying at the Hilton, sleeping on snowy sheets, eating steak and chips and drinking coca cola poured over crushed ice. Despite his nagging insistence he was forced to forego. He moaned and sulked because Aviva, embarrassed by his demands, was not as obliging as he had come to expect. Reflected in a new mirror, she was troubled by his image, his inability to share, his arrogance, his abusive treatment of her, and she forced herself to apply some measure of denial. As a result he engaged in a struggle with her to retrieve his position. When a constant barrage of cajoling failed to wear her out, he assumed a suffering posture which Aviva was especially vulnerable to and which always gained him bargaining advantages. He exploited her every weakness and manoeuvred her into positions of acquiescence even when she swore not to yield. Lenient at the best of times, she was hopelessly permissive in a state of emotional fragility and mushrooming guilts. She was no match for David and he scored successive victories. But David enjoyed much more than he let on. He adored being with Ronit, and only her, 'watch it David, the spoiled brat is showing,' could curb his greed for a fifth piece of melon or yet another coca cola from which no one could have a sip. He listened eagerly when we sat up late at night telling jokes and stories, begging me to repeat his favourite ones. He loved the cosiness of our little family around a campfire cooking supper, especially if I was making bean soup. I conducted many an advantageous bargain based on my bean soup. David trusted me, not only because of my stories and bean soup, but because I cured his stomachaches especially one major ache after he had eaten a bag full of figs instead of his allocated five.

But when Aviva was not present David assumed a startling new persona, charming, helpful, considerate, uncomplaining. His grumbles became lively intelligent comment, his sour put-upon expression became sweet, even loveable, his speckled blue eyes reflected humour and enjoyment instead of misery and discontent, and there was not a trace of his 'I want', and 'I want now' attitude. Everything was possible with David except when he was with Aviva and entered into their intense, complex involvement, she tormenting and embarrassing him with her irritating concern, he tormenting and embarrassing her with his whining, his demands, and his domineering behaviour. I knew that at times he resorted to hitting out at Aviva in frustration, something they were both ashamed of. I also knew he didn't like this David, even found him repugnant, but was unable to extricate himself from his dominance, so much was he a victim of the compulsive relationship with his mother. But being in an extended family made it easier for both Aviva and David. My role as surrogate mother was expanded, so was Ronit's as surrogate sister, and Annilee maintained a cheerful neutrality. And so we journeyed onward into Morocco.

It wasn't difficult to find Jos's villa, everyone knew where it was. The villa itself was an unexpected surprise. It overlooked the sea and was set in spacious gardens enclosed by a high picket fence with a heavy wooden gate which only the 'guardian' opened and closed. We hadn't expected anything so grand. Jos beamed welcome, her smile warm with affection, delighted by the invasion of five guests, and began an instant chirping session with the servants. Mattresses were carried from one room to another, rugs and pillows arranged then re-arranged, and beds spread with embroidered cloths. The servants, kerchiefs tied around their heads, hustled back and forth, their Arabian night trousers gathered at the ankles, bagging with yards of bright material.

The moment we arrived at Jos's and the impressive villa gate was opened by Mohammed, the uniformed guardian, David grunted, "this is more like it." During the next hours when he and Ronit were taken on a tour of the grounds, his room prepared and food brought to him, when, contrary to Aviva's instructions, he made it known he was hungry, each subsequent activity reinforced his happy suspicion that this wasn't only 'more like it', this was 'it'. He began making 'I-want-to-stay-here-forever' noises. "Why do we have to go to Marrakesh?" he moaned for the umpteenth time. He loved the idea of a secure haven, protected from an unpredictable and often frightening Morocco, and this one was even fenced in, to say nothing of its film star luxuries.

And who could blame him? Jos's care was exquisite. She insisted we all shower and rest to avoid the afternoon heat. She left me in a room smelling of jasmine, with mosaic walls and an alcove of cushions, with the blessing, "now you must rest." With total compliance, I stretched out on the pillows, submitting to comfort. One of the servants brought a pot of mint tea and partially closed the shutters darkening the room, her bare feet whispering against the stillness. I lay back in the half light, drifting into the long embrace of Morocco, my eyelids caressing my cheeks, my hair caressing my shoulders, my tongue caressing the taste of mint, the scent of jasmine, my body caressed by the warmth, by the coolness, floating in and out of dream-fantasies, languid, sensual, delicious.

Very slowly I became aware of a presence enhancing the sensuality and very slowly my eyes opened to meet it. In the arched doorway, silhouetted by sunlight, was a man who must have emerged from my dreams. He was actually tall, dark and handsome with a startling virility. For a moment I couldn't tell if he was a vision my eyes were actually seeing or some manifestation, raised from the secret depths of my fantasies. I blinked and blinked again, but he remained, tenaciously filling the doorway. Then he smiled, raised one arm, crossed one leather boot over the other, tilted his head into his hand and leaned into the curves. The posture was overwhelming, evoking a thousand images imbedded in my mythology. Clint Eastwood, leaning against a saloon door; Humphrey Bogart leaning against the piano; Lawrence of Arabia, leaning into his horse; images of Finjan musicians leaning into their guitars. Lean, angular, maleness, confident, casual, in control. I became reckless.

"Are you a Cossack?" I said, some subliminal design wildly orchestrating my fantasy.

"No. Why a Cossack?"

He had a delicious Moroccan-French accent. My question conjured up some quiescent memory ready to be awakened.

"It's because of your black leather boots and the way your trousers fall over them below the knee and your satin shirt with the wide sleeves and narrow cuffs and the silver chain around your neck..."

I paused for breath, partially closing my eyes to retain the image, savouring the rush of his masculinity. He stood erect, smiling, leaning into the sunshine.

I considered him carefully - image, man, memory.

"You must be a something." I said finally.

"I am not a Cossack."

"Then what are you? Where are you from?"

"I am Moroccan. I am from Rabat." He seemed amused.

"Rabat. The capital. I was there once but I didn't like it much. It's one of my least favourite cities in Morocco. Do you like it?"

"Not much."

"Then why do you live there?"

"My house is in Rabat."

"Do you have to live where your house is?"

"Yes."

"Why is that?"

"It is that kind of house."

"You mean you're so attached to your house that you can't leave it?

"No, I am not so attached to it, but yes, I cannot leave it."

This was intriguing stuff.

"What kind of a house is it?"

"Would you like to see."

"Yes. I adore houses."

"Then I invite you to see my house."

"When?"

"Now."

"Now? But Rabat is far away."

"But my automobile is very near."

I have a pair of reins in my head which circumstances sometimes force me to apply. I tugged hard. At a reduced speed I said, " I'll tell you what. I'm going to have a little sleep and if you're still real when I wake up, we'll talk about it."

"I will still be real," he laughed. The powerful image receded from the frame. "Have a good rest." He went to meet the sunshine.

I closed my eyes lingering over the contours of the encounter, weaving them in and out of reality, entangling real from surreal. Sleep was no longer possible.After a while Jos and Aviva came into the room. My eyes half opened. "Are you sleeping?" Jos asked.

"No. I was almost sleeping when a tall, dark, handsome Cossack came into the room and tried to carry me off in an automobile to a house he can't leave in Rabat. And what's worse, I almost went."

Puzzle narrowed Aviva's eyes. "What do you mean a Cossack?" she asked, attempting to extract some sanity from my rambling.

"He's not a Cossack." Jos laughed.

"Exactly what he said, but I know a Cossack when I see one."

"That was Bashir Tazi. He came to give me something. He's a prince."

"A prince," I reflected, "I knew he was a something."

"What do you mean a prince?" Aviva asked, her eyes widening.

"He is a member of the Royal family. He lives in the Royal Palace in Rabat, in his own separate palace, Tazi Palace."

Aviva could bear it no longer. "You mean he's a real prince and lives in a real palace, you know, a palacy palace?" She glowed with excitement.

"Yes. Exactly." Jos was enjoying our reactions.

"Is he rich?" I asked predictably. What else could I say, my experience with princes had been seriously neglected.

"His wealth is like a bottomless well, he can never come to the end of it," Jos said with the solemnity befitting a revelation concerning colossal wealth. I respectfully digested this bit of information.

"Tell me Jos, what are you doing hanging out with wealthy princes with bottomless wells?" I asked.

"I met him some years ago in Paris. We cared for each other like sister and brother. Then he travelled in the East and became very sick. He has been in Paris to receive treatment, he just came back to Morocco a few months ago. This villa belongs to him. He is a very good man, he does not act like he is from the Royal family. I love him like a brother."

"A real honest to goodness Prince," Aviva marvelled with little-girl delight. She wrote children's stories about Princes and Palaces and secretly longed to be the Princess in one of her stories - she was devoted to romance. "Tell us about the palace Jos. Were you ever there? What is it like?" She curled up on a pillow folding her legs under her with that child-like wonder I so admired, her blue-green eyes bright with anticipation. She had that same radiant, unguarded, expectant expression I remembered when she was perched on Tom's lap, bewitched by Leonard Cohen. The shine of magic was on her. She was beautiful.

"Bashir will take you to the palace if you like. I have been many times," Jos said.

"I could have been half way there already," I mused.

Aviva ignored my flippancy. "I really want to see a palace. Is it true Jos, can we go?" She was bubbling excitement.

"Of course." Jos reassured.

"But when?" she wailed, sudden agony popping the bubbles, "we're leaving here tomorrow."

"I will ask Bashir," Jos said.

"When will you ask him?" Aviva clung to the palace walls.

"Tonight. He's coming back tonight, later on."

Annilee, Ronit and David went to bed early, exhausted. I had some business to sort out with Jos. Aviva, eager with fantasies, waited for her prince. About nine o'clock Bashir arrived with several magnums of French champagne. Aviva caught a glimpse of him opening a bottle of champagne, expertly withdrawing the cork, bottle between his thighs.

"He even looks like a prince," she whispered, "he's gorgeous."

Graciously, I relinquished all claims. Who was I to tangle with destiny? They made contact quickly, sparkling, easy. They discovered with mutual delight that they had followed each other around the world. They had been to the same places in India, Afghanistan, Nepal. In Bali they were even in the same hospital at the same time, he, no doubt, in a Royal Suite, with an exotic brain fever, she, in a public ward, with the mumps. It was like Cinderella finding the prince. They were fated to meet. I was enthralled as the fairy story unfolded and they became inspired beings, triggered by a special radiance, enchanted, enchanting.

"I invite you to my home in Rabat. We will spend the night there and return tomorrow." Bashir made an extravagant expansive gesture encompassing Aviva, Jos, me, possibly the rest of humanity. He was exhilarated. "We shall leave at once, my automobile and driver are waiting."

I leapt at the idea, believing as Malory the mountain climber did, 'that the greatest danger in life is not taking the adventure.' Besides, I was riding the romance at high speed. But Aviva was not from the Malory school, she needed time to adjust to adventure. As often happened with her, when the moment came, she was hesitant, cautious, unable to embrace it, preferring to postpone it, to relish it in her mind, savour it in the comfortable future.

"We can't go now," she said, terrified by 'now', sudden alarm shattering the spell. Not even her attraction to the Prince, the Palace, the high romance, coupled with the French champagne, could release her.

"Why not?" Bashir asked. He was accustomed to making a wish and having it fulfilled. After all he was a prince. Aviva searched for a reason. She said nothing about David. Having a child to look after was a bit plebeian when one was involved with a prince, it dimmed the glamour.

"We have to meet Cedric in Marrakesh tomorrow night and then take him to Essaouira. He's a good friend and is coming from Canada. He's expecting us." This was true, but could have been arranged otherwise.

"He will wait," Bashir said simply, Moroccan style.

"It's his first time in Morocco. We promised we'd be there. I want to be there." Aviva's voice was terse with resolve - she was prone to sudden obstinacy, even abrasiveness. For whatever the reason, she had made a final decision, determined, irrevocable. Bashir recognised this and made no further attempt at persuasion.

"Today is Thursday," he said unperturbed, "you should have everything arranged in two weeks. I will send my chauffeur to pick you up in Essaouira two Thursdays from today." He calculated the date for us. "Wacha? Be in front of Hotel des Isles at ten in the morning."

A man to be reckoned with this prince. Aviva accepted at once. She could easily handle an invitation two weeks away, and she could cherish it for fourteen whole days.

After this, the brief intrusion of discord vanished, banished to a more mundane realm. We slipped easily into the champagne and the magic. The remainder of the evening flowed like silk, smooth, sensuous, exciting, beautifully meshed, like a perfect waltz. I left them dancing.

13. The Marrakesh Express

Next day Aviva and I took the 'Marrakesh Express' from Casablanca to Marrakesh, a train journey made famous by a Crosby Stills and Nash song. We were not only meeting Cedric but also checking *Poste Restante* for some important mail Aviva was expecting.

When I first suggested that Aviva and I go to Marrakesh on our own, leaving David, Ronit and Annilee at Jos's, David greeted the suggestion with war whoops. Aviva, predictably, objected. She wanted David with her. Ronit and I sided with David but Aviva persisted. After we had exhausted a series of her legless arguments she hit on a valid one, "I don't want David to miss Marrakesh." She gained much satisfaction from exposing David to experiences she considered valuable, even if he did not. She wanted him deprived of nothing, for both their sakes.

"I agree, David shouldn't miss Marrakesh, neither should Ronit and Annilee," I said, improvising a solution. "If David, Ronit and Annilee stay here for a few days and then drive to Marrakesh, instead of going straight to Essaouira, then we can all spend some time in Marrakesh."

This seemed the perfect solution, allowing Aviva time to sort out her mail and for us, time with Cedric. It also had the unspoken advantage of giving Aviva and David a much needed break from each other.

"Only two days at Jos's". Aviva was beginning to relent.

"Only three days," I bargained.

"Promise. Only three."

"I promise."

"I don't care if I never see Marrakesh, I hate it already." David was being his incorrigible best.

"You shut up. Your opinion doesn't count. Besides you're getting to stay here longer, so don't make waves," Ronit said, as she butted David out of the room.

Annilee was quite willing to remain. She wasn't averse to a little luxury and certainly deserved it having done all the driving, since my Canadian licence had expired and Aviva was unable to drive. She wasn't averse to a little night life either, a few Casablanca hot spots, a glittering disco, a glamorous Arab. She was ready for a Western reprieve with Eastern spice.

Ronit didn't mind either. "I can practice my Arabic with Mohammed, if we stay." Ronit had a talent for languages and took to Arabic with a special enthusiasm, she even enjoyed reproducing the impossible guttural sounds. However, since Ketama, her Arabic tuition had been severely neglected. "Mohammed wants to learn English, he speaks a little already, so I can teach him English and he can teach me Arabic," she said, pleased with the possibility. Besides, it had emerged that two young French musicians, whom Jos referred to as *les artistes*, were resident at Jos's and this provided interesting prospects. She swore an oath to 'keep a relentless eye on David' which involved a series of promises Aviva herself would have been unable to keep: 'I'll be sure he doesn't stay in the swimming pool too long'; 'I'll be sure he doesn't gorge himself on sweets'; 'only two cokes a day'; and 'I'll wait by the phone for your call.' She was spared the promise of confining him to the villa grounds - he couldn't even be persuaded to look over the fence. Aviva was still adding to the list through the taxi window with Ronit warning we'd miss the train and David hissing "oh mom" through clenched teeth, fists pressed into his ears.

We reached the platform as the train was about to pull out and scrambled on board with the help of outstretched hands. "Well we made it," Aviva sighed plopping into her seat. I think she had half hoped we wouldn't. "We're actually on board the famous 'Marrakesh Express.'" She looked around excitedly but the train was like any other. Still the idea appealed to her, especially in anticipated retrospect, 'We rode the Marrakesh Express.' It had a nice ring to it. Before we left Jos's she had played the song over and over, committing it to memory.

"All on board that train
Don't you know we're riding on
The Marrakesh Express
Don't you know we're riding on
The Marrakesh Express
They're taking me to Marrakesh
All on board that train
All on board."

Aviva sang happily, feeling herself part of a romanticised journey. I hummed along, not entirely insensitive to the thrill of riding the Marrakesh Express, fragments of the song spinning in my head as we sped past fields with chickens, donkeys and camels, bordering villages and towns pointed with turrets and minarets, and rounded with domes and arched walls.

Eventually we settled into the journey, Aviva reading - she felt undressed without a book - me dreaming and imagining, remembering past adventures, wondering what it would be like this time, assessing Ronit's reactions to Morocco, David's fears, real and imagined, planning our future encounters, watching for the dazzling white of Casablanca, the white city, to become the burnt red of Marrakesh, the red city.

"Do you think he likes me?" Aviva said tentatively, looking up from her book.

"Who?" I asked, startled out of my reveries.

"The prince."

"Oh, the prince, he's hopelessly and passionately and irrevocably in love with you."

"I mean it. Do you think he likes me?"

"Can't you tell?"

"No, I really can't."

"Of course he likes you. How come you don't know?"

"I'm so out of practice, I don't recognise the signals any more."

"You never forget the signals. It's like riding a bicycle. You never forget that."

"I can't ride a bicycle either," she confessed. "It's been such a long time since I indulged in any sort of romantic adventure I've forgotten how to go about it."

"You just relax and enjoy it, like that sick rape joke."

"I've never been raped either. I'm quite serious though, do you think he really likes me or is he going to forget all about me in the next two minutes. I fancy him, and that's unusual for me. Do you know that I haven't been with another man since I began living with Irving?"

"What about Max?"

"That's true, there was Max. What a sad affair that was. What attracted me to Max was his head. I thought his novel was super and I loved the letters he wrote me, so tender and poetic, but when we finally made it to bed, we were like two wet twigs that couldn't make fire. I had a bad case of D.H. Lawrence's 'sex in the head' instead of where it should be. But anyway I only did it because Irving was off somewhere with that Marta, and it was a disaster. No, there really hasn't been anyone since Irving. I don't know if I can still do it."

"My bet is on you."

"I wish I could be so sure. I really loved last night, but today I feel all nervous about Bashir, all girlish and shy, like a virgin teenager."

"Not too many of them left... and you certainly didn't act like one."

"Didn't I? It's true, it was special last night, the full moon, the champagne, and how often do I get to meet a prince, but now I'm all caught up in tangles. Do you think he knows I fancy him? Was I making a fool of myself?"

I knew her distress was genuine, but I found it hard to comprehend her lack of confidence, her self-doubt. She had so much going for her, sparkle, intelligence, looks, humour, warmth, surely any man would find her desirable, and surely she would know that. Outwardly she seemed so confident, so sure of herself, so fearless, yet inwardly she was riddled with insecurity. I had encountered this phenomenon often, especially with women, the lack of objective assessment about themselves, the depleted, fragile, self-image which bore no relation to reality, the inability to believe compliments about their appearance.

I myself was not immune to the syndrome. I remember a lover whispering, as his hands caressed my back, my shoulders, my thighs, 'you have perfect skin'. I panicked. Leaping from the bed, I switched on the lights. "My skin is full of blemishes...look!" I almost shouted as I frantically pointed to several bumps on my legs, barely visible blemishes on my arms, a mole on my left breast.

"My skin is terrible." I couldn't bear him thinking I had perfect skin.

I remember reading that even Cher, the famous singer/actress, considered the world's sexiest woman, revealed that she's never felt beautiful. An extreme example of the syndrome was Susan, Leonard Cohen's lady, who eventually became the mother of his children. When she first saw Ronit she said something to me about Ronit being beautiful.

"Please tell Ronit," I urged, "she needs to know because she doesn't think she's at all good looking, and my telling her isn't convincing."

"I understand what she feels," Susan said, "when I was her age I thought I was ugly although everyone told me I wasn't, and every night I prayed that one day I would be beautiful."

"Well it worked," I said lightly. Susan was exquisite, a startling beauty according to any criteria.

"Oh no, it hasn't," she said sadly, "I'm not beautiful, and I still pray." I was stunned. If she didn't know she was beautiful, what hope was there for the rest of us? I had to reassure Aviva.

"Aviva stop worrying. First of all there was no full moon last night. You're just a natural. You were beautiful and so funny and loveable, Bashir thought so too, how could he help it? Don't tie yourself in knots. You'll see, it will all work out. Just let things happen. Try to allow yourself to be immediately available to whatever is happening, instead of

146

immediately unavailable."

"You're right. I'm going to make an effort. But do you think he really likes me?"

"I know he does."

"Honest?"

"Honest."

"Travelling the train through
clear Moroccan skies
Looking at the world through
the sunset in your eyes.
Don't you know we're riding on
the Marrakesh Express
They're taking me to Marrakesh
All on board that train."

We were both silent, riding the Marrakesh Express, watching Morocco unfold, mulling over our thoughts. Earlier, when Aviva had used the words 'sex in the head', the phrase had struck a responsive chord and I tucked it away with a view to considering it more fully. I explored it now. Wasn't there an element of 'sex in the head' in every sexual encounter? Wasn't imagination paramount in determining physical response? My own life contained several disconcerting sexual encounters I often puzzled over, which seemed relevant in this context.

When I was fifteen, I had a serious crush on a beautiful young man in my dance class, to the point where even today I can still experience the physical sensations, the small tingles, the delightful quivers of excitement leapfrogging over my body when he merely looked at me. Just knowing he was in the same room was physically overwhelming, racing my heart, sweating my palms, goose bumping my arms. I spent hours fantasising, wondering if I would be able to contain the delight should he touch me.

Then one day it happened. I was alone in the office waiting for the secretary, my back to the door, when I heard his voice in the hallway. Next thing I knew he had come up behind me and gently, ever so gently, put his hands on my shoulders. The sensations were formidable. I felt myself dissolving, melting into paradise. Without turning my head I leaned into him. The contact was multiple bliss, bliss upon bliss upon bliss. I could feel it in my head, my neck, down my spine, creeping up to my nipples. I don't know how I survived the ecstasy. I wanted to preserve it forever. Slowly I turned to face him, my eyes half closed, my lips parted, ready. To my utter astonishment and deep disgust, it wasn't him. It was someone else, someone who had been pestering me since the course began, someone I disliked, even found vaguely repulsive. I was in a state of shock.

Another incident occurred some years later, in Israel. I was spending a weekend on a kibbutz, a collective settlement, helping with the harvest, sleeping in a hayloft with ten other people. I was the last one in a row of sleepers. In the middle of the night someone came tiptoeing into the loft and found his way to the end of the line. I half awoke.

"I was told to sleep here", he whispered.

"That's O.K., I mumbled and rolled over to make room. In the darkness he arranged his blankets and lay down. I was hardly conscious. I was almost asleep when I felt fingers moving through my hair, coming to rest in the hollow of my neck. There was something so fine, so tender in the touching that I felt myself moving toward its source, eager for more, wanting to embellish the dream. I soon discovered it was no dream. I was awake and making love. It was wonderful discovering his body - I had no idea what he looked like - I reached for his head, feeling the texture of his hair between my fingers, sketching in his lips, his eyes, his eyebrows, his nose, with the pencil-thin line of my forefinger. Delicately, silently, hardly daring to move lest I disturb someone, we made love, sweetly, deliciously. And in the dark silence, I loved a man I could only imagine. The pleasure was exquisite. When I woke next morning he was gone. I never saw him, never even knew his name, but that sexual encounter remains one of the most exciting, most memorable, I have ever had.

I thought Aviva was dozing when she slashed into my reflections.

"I can't live with him and I can't live without him."

"Who? The prince?"

"No, Irving. I've been sitting here, my mind lulled by the rhythm of the train, feeling peaceful and good for a change, fantasising about the prince, even feeling sexy, and suddenly there's Irving looming up between me and the prince. He doesn't leave me alone, he won't even allow me my fantasies...I must admit, I do miss him. It's a relief being without him, but I miss him...I must be some kind of masochist," she said miserably.

"Hope the days that lie ahead
Bring us back to where they've led.
Don't you know we're riding on
the Marrakesh Express
They're taking me to Marrakesh."

"Yet every time I miss him and want him and feel loving toward him all I have to do is think of him on a Mediterranean island with that Marta, the Mistress from Minsk, and it hurts so much, I hate him. It's so painful...some 'climbing a hill in Italy with a knapsack on his back', he's probably climbing a bed in some Hilton with Marta on his back. So why do I still want him and miss him? You tell me." Her voice was in tatters and she had that little-girl look baffled by adult behaviour, although the adult was herself. She reminded me of that Bob Dylan song,

"She takes just like a woman,
She makes love just like a woman,
And she aches just like a woman,
but she breaks just like a little girl."

"You've been locked into a tiny combat arena with Irving for so long you've forgotten there's a whole world out here with lots of people who aren't Irving...but you can't banish him from your psyche overnight. No matter what happens he's going to be there, probably for the rest of your life. Right now you need a break from each other. And you especially need a break from him to dissipate the pain. You told me yourself, when Shimon and I were separating, that if you've learned one thing it's that pain does pass, it seems like it never will, but it does."

"And he's certainly given me enough pain," she said bitterly. "Right from the beginning he's been treating me to great wads of pain, huge doses, he's fed me on a diet of constant pain...pain, pain and more pain. Even on the day we were supposed to get married all I got was pain." For a moment she gazed mournfully at the orange ball of sun being sucked into the horizon, then continued, her voice subdued, saddened. "I was so excited about marrying him. We decided to have a really private wedding, a small civil ceremony in the court house. Leonard, of course, was the best man and arrived right on time with a huge bunch of roses and the wedding ring. As it turned out he was not only the best man, but the only man. Irving never showed up. That was my wedding day, pain, humiliation and tears, wedding presents from Irving. Thank God for Leonard. He put his arm around me, 'never mind,' he said, 'we don't need him. I'll marry you. I'll put the ring on your finger' and he did. I'll always love him for it." Her voice broke with anger and hurt, and she began twisting her ring, something I hadn't seen her do since Malaga.

"Speaking of Leonard," I said, anxious to spare us both another round of Irving's deceptions and infidelities, "did he ever say anything more about that infamous magic mushroom trip?"

"No. Never."

"Did he or Irving ever write about it?"

"Not that I know of."

"That's strange. I remember Irving saying to Leonard after it was all over, 'I wonder which one of us will immortalise this night in a poem.'"

"He would say that. Irving is only interested in the poem," Aviva said irately, unwilling to allow her anger with Irving to be defused.

"Even when Lillian died and I was devastated, Irving rushed off and wrote a poem about her death. He used my friend's terrible tragic death as inspiration for a poem. I really resented it."

"Maybe that's his way of coping."

"It has nothing to do with coping. He uses experience merely as a subject for his poetry. It's the poem that counts. Lillian died, that's bad, but her death gave him a poem and that's good - my grief was irrelevant, unless he could use it in a poem. Graham Greene said, 'there is a splinter of ice in the heart of a writer,' Irving's heart is a huge icicle made up of experiences he keeps frozen in case he might some day melt one into a poem. He once wrote:

'One miserable human more or less
hardly matters
But the loss of a good poem does,
being irreplaceable.'

He's full of all that bombast about the poet as prophet, as healer, as God. What about the poet as parasite? I should write a book called, 'A Portrait of the Poet as a Young Parasite", or an old parasite for that matter. I certainly have enough material."

She sat quietly for a while, her anger suddenly spent, then said, "yes, it is strange that neither of them ever wrote about that night, that neither of them 'immortalised' that incredible experience. I wonder why."

"Maybe it was too close to the bone, too powerful, even for them."

"Sweeping cobwebs from the edges of my mind
Had to get away to see what I could find.
Don't you know, we're riding on the Marrakesh Express
They're taking us to Marrakesh."

The sun was setting quickly as we spoke and suddenly the sky burst into fire. Tongues of red and crimson and magenta blazed, leaping over streaks of coral, vermilion and seething gold. Date palms silhouetted tall and elegant against the flames, fronds arching fragile into the crimson, slender trunks rising arrow-straight to heads of furled leaves, pointing into incandescence; and the outline of mountains, dark and heavy tipped by flashes of burning snow, embracing the fire. And we, speeding into the sky grew silent, sunset flaring in our eyes, all else irrelevant. The train stopped. We were in Marrakesh.

14. Marrakesh - The Red City

Morocco was a sensual feast, a continuously exotic offering. The colours blazi ng in the souks, the incense hovering in the air, the throb of drums, the music of pipes, twisting, coiling, undulating through the alleyways, and everywhere the country drenched in blues and golds.

The vast blue embrace of the sky, the silver blue of the sea, the startling blue of Tuareg robes - the desert nomads, Blue People. The great golden flood of the desert rippling with darker gold shadows; the pyramids of spices - tangerine gold, saffron gold, lemon gold, cinnamon gold; the amber gold, ebony gold, chocolate gold of smooth Moroccan skins. And most of all the sensuality radiating from the people, palpable, delicious. The flash of dark eyes defying the yashmak; the young men walking arm in arm, hand in hand, graceful, smiling, the effortless flow of their bodies like fine saplings moving in a breeze. I could feel their quiet sexuality, their easy acceptance, their long silky limbs, soft voices, soft smiles, soft eyes, their golden darkness.

If years later Tibet was to become my spiritual home, the home of my spiritual being, Morocco was my sensual home, the home of my flesh, of my physical being. Each time I returned I found the hit as exciting as I had the first time and as deeply enigmatic. For a brief moment the tastes, the sounds, the colours, the smells, the rhythms were unfamiliar, forcing me to pause, to consider, to respond. My senses were refreshed, bathed clean, ready for a new awareness. Yet it was as though I had never left. It was all so vivid, so clear, so ever-present in my psyche, so finely etched on my nervous system, that I slid back into Morocco like sliding into an embrace - with total surrender.

If Morocco was my superb sensual adventure, Marrakesh was its heart beat, its essence. Here everything was heightened. The physical sensations, that edge of sexuality, the colours, textures, sounds, were squeezed together so tight, riot and explosion were always imminent. One walked with the possibility of blazing eruption.

Cedric had always wanted to visit Morocco, but like Aviva suffered from paranoia induced by the terrifying tales he too had heard and by the fact that his Perth County Conspiracy band had to raise money to free one of its members from a Moroccan prison. Unlike political sentences, freedom from drug crimes could be easily bought. However, certain of safety in the embrace of so much female protection, he had agreed to join us. Aviva and I met him at the airport and headed directly to the old section of town. I decided to plunge them into the Marrakesh experience by arranging a room in the C.T.M., a small hotel in the Place Djema el Fna, the central square cum market place. The hotel was on one of the streets which formed the square and its roof-terrace hung directly over it.

The Place Djema el Fna was for me a microcosm of Morocco, the symbol of its enigma, that mystery which struck some deep responsive chord but which remained unknowable, that fascinating plunge from West to East. Aviva loved it immediately, and couldn't be torn away. Cedric, jetlagged and tentative, unable to speak Arabic or French, was more cautious, preferring to immerse himself in that mystery from the safety of the hotel roof. From this vantage point he could be within the buzz and throb of the square - the collage of vendors, jugglers, acrobats, fortune tellers, water sellers, musicians, snake charmers - yet removed from the hassle of the crowd scene.

The crowd was an incongruous mixture of Arabs and foreigners - Moroccans from the cities in modern dress, carrying briefcases; Berbers in long kaftans, turbans and yellow babouches, from remote villages, carrying bundles of belongings, coming to the square to have letters written for them by the scribes, to buy spices and herbs for medicines and potions, to listen to stories told by the story tellers; Western tourists wandering clumsily, clutching inevitable Japanese cameras, intent on reproducing the local colour for home viewing; hippies wearing leather sandals and a tangle of Moroccan and Western clothing. From our roof terrace we could avoid the set smile reaching out from the kiosk, 'for you, student price,' the tireless commercial come-on as, before our eyes, East met West. Later, Cedric would sit undisturbed for hours with his guitar trying, unsuccessfully, to duplicate the Eastern rhythms which throbbed in the square. Although he was a musician - singer, guitarist, song-writer - he was unable to comprehend the cadences, the syncopations, the rhythmic structures of the music which emanated from an unfamiliar assortment of pipes, drums and string instruments.

Devoted to theatricality, Cedric was intrigued by the continuously changing but often predictable scenarios in that vast theatre in the round where, eventually, every scene was enacted before us. A favourite was the unsuspecting tourist ecstatically photographing the boys in white with red sashes somersaulting on to each others shoulders, unaware that with the click of the shutter, one of the tumblers would leap off the pyramid into the expensive camera lens and wait with radiant smile and open palm, until the photographer awkwardly crossed the palm with silver.

But on our first morning in Marrakesh we encountered the Place Djema el Fna head on. I wanted to take Cedric and Aviva to my favourite breakfast café on the far side of the square for coffee and croissants. Crossing the square was no easy matter. As soon as we emerged from our hotel a young Moroccan, who had been waiting by the door with several friends, came toward us. Undoubtedly there was some prescribed order for approaching foreigners because he detached himself from the others as though claiming a right. He wore jeans and a dazzling white shirt.

"Welcome to Morocco," he said smiling brightly, his smile matching his shirt.

"Thank you," I answered, signalling Cedric and Aviva to continue walking.

"Do you wish for me to show you the medina? I am not a guide, I will not charge you, it is only for the pleasure of practising my English." He smiled again.

"No, thank you. I have been to Marrakesh before, we don't need

155

a guide," I said, trying to be firm but polite. This in no way deterred him and he continued to walk with us.

"I am Kebir," he said, "I am from Marrakesh. What is your country?" He had given up on me and was now addressing Cedric, obviously a softer option. His manner was pleasant with just a touch of shyness.

"We are from Canada," Cedric replied.

"Welcome to my country. Is it your first time here?"

"Yes," Cedric answered, glancing toward me to determine whether he should discourage conversation. But I gave him no clues. There were advantages to crossing the square with a Moroccan - it deterred further approaches, a kind of protective escort. Cedric continued talking to Kebir, who leapt at this as a positive signal and quickly began leading us through the myriad of sellers, performers, hustlers, dissuading a shoe shiner from accosting us with a mere glance, stopping someone about to put a monkey on Cedric's shoulder with a flick of the head, negotiating three glasses of freshly squeezed orange juice, and one for himself, from the row of carts with striped canopies, lining the square. With Kebir's strategically uttered warnings, "be careful for your money", calculated to cement his allegiance, we were ushered safely into the café, Kebir now part of the team. "Never mind," I said to Aviva, "he seems O.K., and it will make things easier."

"And he's not bad to look at either," Aviva agreed.

After a leisurely breakfast, I told Kebir we wanted to take a short walk in the medina, which led off the square. "Just to give Cedric and Aviva a little taste. It's Cedric's first day here, we must go easy on him," I explained. "We'll just go as far as the wool market. You are welcome to come with us Kebir, but please don't take us to any shops, we don't want to buy anything."

Guides, official and otherwise, made money by taking visitors into shops, they received a percentage of the sales, and tourists often ended up plodding in and out of the shops owned by the guide's relatives and friends. Kebir was quick to agree. "No shops, only for to see the

156

medina, I am happy just to be with my friends and to speak English."

But it was inevitable that as soon as Cedric saw the shops piled high with jewellery, crafts, carpets, perfumed oils, Moroccan clothing, he wanted to buy. Next to theatre and music, Cedric loved shopping. Shopping was his relaxation, his great pleasure. He was an instinctive shopper with an uncanny flare for finding the ideal gift. He had an enviable talent for anticipating the recipient's taste, be it in clothes, jewellery or even books, and an unerring eye for size, colour and style.

His favourite people, predominantly women, as he was the first to admit, were always present in his imagination and he was constantly discovering some choice item one of them must have. Half my wardrobe – my favourite possessions - including purses, belts, socks and knickers, were given to me by Cedric. Best of all was his commitment to my passion for purple - almost everything I had was some shade of purple – presenting me with purple soaps, purple pillow cases, even a purple hot water bottle. I remember Aviva admiring a purple chemise-style blouse with lace lavender trimming I was wearing and moaning, "I'll scream if you tell me Cedric gave it to you." Of course he had.

Walking along the covered alleyways crammed with shops, Cedric was intrigued by the wide variety of hands of Fatima on display - a symbolic hand of the prophet Mohammed's daughter - especially after Kebir told him that every Moroccan had one to ward off the evil eye. To prove the point he put his hand under his shirt and produced a hand of Fatima with a yellow jewel in its palm, hung against his chest on a silver chain. Cedric had to have one.

"What, you want I should be in Marrakesh without protection – a guy like me needs all the protection he can get. And just to be on the safe side, I'm going to get us all protected, if it can't help, it can't hurt. Speaking like an actor, I always appreciate a good hand."

Those words were music to Kebir's ears and within minutes a shop window materialised heaped with hands of Fatima. Cedric spotted one he especially liked and before we could stop him went in to ask the price, unaware that asking the price of anything was considered the foreplay to purchase. In a few minutes the shopkeeper had about ten hands lying on the counter, and was busy producing more from drawers and off walls.

"How much is that one?" Cedric asked, pointing to the one in the window, in its palm a finely etched dragon with a tiny red eye.

"Ah, monsieur," the man replied, "you have very good taste; that one is a very ancient one, very old silver, very beautiful work."

"And how much does it cost?" Cedric repeated.

The shopkeeper removed it from the window cradling it like a precious jewel. "Ah, monsieur, this one is very special, the silver is very high quality, the eye is a genuine ruby, but because you are a man of good taste, for you I will make a special price...300 dirham (about $60).

At this point, Aviva could contain herself no longer, she leapt into the fray.

"No, thank you, it is much too expensive for us, but thank you very much for showing my husband so many lovely hands of Fatima. Come, we must move on," she said addressing Cedric, in a formidable English accent. Cedric looked confused and somewhat sheepish as he allowed Aviva to usher him toward the door. The shopkeeper knew he was dealing with a professional, Cedric was dropped from the scenario.

"Wait one moment madam, what price do you offer me?" he asked.

"Monsieur, I cannot offer you a price, it will only insult you."

"Please, madam, offer me a price, no price will insult me," the shopkeeper persisted, warming to the challenge.

"Well since you insist, I will offer a price, but I know you will not be happy with it. We do not want to pay more than 10 dirham." Cedric was aghast. Aviva gave him a silencing prod.

The shopkeeper's laugh had just an edge of derision, "10 dirham, that is not a serious offer, I cannot even sell these for 10 dirham," he riffled dismissively through smaller, inferior hands which looked like they were made of tin, "these cost me more than 10 dirham," he said, with obvious distaste both for Aviva's offer and the suspect hands.

"You see," Aviva said, "I knew you would be insulted."

"No, no, madam, I am not insulted, but let us talk business, not 300 dirham, but not 10 dirham, I will go down and you will go up."

Cedric's idea of bargaining was holding out for the January sales. It was one art form he studiously avoided, definitely an acquired taste. Although he observed with fascination, I could sense his cringe, his trying-not-to-notice attitude, and knew he would rather be an unseen spectator than an on-stage actor, even though he had been demoted to a barely visible extra.

"We can offer you 20 dirham, but that is my final price," Aviva said firmly.

"For 20 dirham you can have this one," he dangled a hand made of small pieces of coloured glass at arm's length, as though it gave off a bad odour. "But I will give you the one you wish for 250 dirham, that is a very good price."

"No, no monsieur," Aviva protested, "we are only interested in the one my husband has chosen. I offer you 25 dirham, but no more."

"Look madam how beautiful it is, such fine work, it is a very ancient Berber Hand of Fatima, you will not find another like it in all of Marrakesh." He presented the hand of Fatima to Aviva as though he was offering up the crown jewels.

Suddenly a young boy who had been cleaning the shop arrived with a tray set with four glasses of tea brimming with plump green mint leaves. Kebir waited discreetly outside. Three low stools were placed in a circle and the boy served tea - the shopkeeper drinking his while producing beautiful artifacts. "Not to buy," he assured us, "just for to look, for the pleasure of the eye." There was no further bargaining, no mention of hands of Fatima.

We admired the elaborately carved swords and knives, the beautifully crafted brass bowls, the graceful silver teapots, and then Aviva announced that it was time to go. "Thank you very much monsieur, you have some very beautiful things in your shop."

159

Cedric and I muttered agreement. As we were about to leave the shopkeeper put his hand on Aviva's arm, "for you and your husband who has such excellent taste, 200 dirham."

"50 dirham," Aviva said resolutely.

"100 dirham." Things were happening fast now.

"50 dirham", Aviva stood her ground, and started to leave.

"100 dirham," the man pleaded, "you must allow me some profit."

"I am sorry monsieur, but we can spend only 50 dirham." With that she walked out, Cedric and I tagging behind.

Cedric looked pained, his handsome features compressed into a grimace. "I really liked that hand," he said, "I would have been happy to pay 100 dirham for it. Where did I go wrong?"

"It's not only the money," Aviva explained, by now expert enough to write a manual on 'The Art of Bargaining In and Out of Medinas', "it's the satisfaction, the skill. Without bargaining there's no sales satisfaction. You can't deny the man his sales satisfaction, bargaining is his way of life."

"What about my satisfaction?" Cedric wailed. "I'm here, my hand is there, and the evil eye could be anywhere, there's no satisfaction and there's no sale." With that he broke into song. "I can't get no satisfaction....and he don't get no satisfaction... and we won't get no satisfaction," concluding with, "Oh what a waste. Of my excellent taste."

"Don't worry, you are in Marrakesh," I said, "nobody here foregoes a sale." Kebir smiled.

About fifteen minutes later we were in a small alleyway inside a tiny courtyard, watching a man stitching leather, making a pair of yellow babouches for Cedric, when the shopkeeper appeared. "For you madam I have polished the hand of Fatima so you may see how beautiful it is. He opened his palm and the hand of Fatima glowed, the dragon's eye glinting.

"How did you know where to find us?" Cedric asked in utter amazement.

We had been twisting and winding through the medina, and now

Ronit, that state of the art baby: 3 months

Ronit, performing with Shimon: 7 Years

Brian Stavechney as Cuchulian in At The Hawk's Well by W B Yeats,
London Production

Niema with Irving Layton and Leonard Cohen

Ronit and Leonard Cohen: 11 years

Niema with Gnaoua musicians in a Marrakesh street.
(photo by Jeremy Ornstin)

Ronit and Habib in Essaouira

Ronit making tea in the sands of Morocco

were invisible inside the makeshift shop.

"Telegraph Arab," Kebir smiled again.

The shopkeeper smiled as well. "Whacha madam, 70 dirham and I give you a beautiful small hand as a present. Look how beautiful."

But Aviva was relentless, "two small hands, monsieur, one for myself and one for my friend." She put her arm around my shoulder, "my friend must have a present as well." Cedric winced.

"You are a difficult lady, madam," the shopkeeper said putting his hand into his pocket and producing another hand. "Two presents, one for the madam and one for her lovely friend."

Cedric paid the 70 dirham quickly, with a flourish of finality, as if to ward off any further rounds of bargaining. Just as quickly the shopkeeper pocketed the money. There was much smiling and hand clasping. We all began congratulating each other on the success of the transaction - even the shoemaker joined in - jabbering in French, in English, even in Arabic. Except for Cedric: he was speechless, overwhelmed by the theatre, the script, the acting, the three hands of Fatima, the shopkeeper, the sales satisfaction, Kebir, Aviva, the medina, Marrakesh, all of them together.

By the time we reached the wool market with crimson, purple and orange wool draped over bamboo poles swaying in loops across the narrow streets, drying in the sun, we were all exhausted. Cedric was seriously suffering from too much input - carpets and silver and Tuareg robes and sparkling kaftans blasting at him from all directions and now the fiery wool. He looked about to disintegrate. I suggested we return to the hotel to rest and then have lunch. There was a special event I was saving for the afternoon, and I wanted Aviva and Cedric well rested for maximum appreciation. It was a stunning piece of live theatre and during my previous visits I had been irresistibly drawn to it, unable to grasp its significance, but mesmerised by the power of its drama. I could hardly wait for Cedric and Aviva to witness it. I checked with Kebir to make sure it was still happening, and then asked him to escort us to the C.T.M., promising to meet him again in the late afternoon to continue our medina wandering. Right after lunch, we climbed to our terrace and leaning over the railing, waited for the drama to unfold beneath us.

Every afternoon, at the same hour, in the same part of the square, two Berber men detached themselves from the twisting crowd. One was old, one young, both with faces leathered by the sun, the older one wrinkled cowhide, the younger one smooth calfskin; both with glaring white teeth, the older one flashing black holes between the white; both barefoot, with tough sinewy feet. They dressed alike in bright poncho-like tops and lose cotton trousers, except that the older man wore a white turban wound around his head, the younger a red headband pulling his long black matted hair from his eyes. They exuded a wild energy as though they had plummeted from some tranquil mountain village and were trapped by the frenzy of the square. Each day, without deviation, they enacted the same drama, oblivious of the crowd which separated to receive them and then watched with rapt absorption. Today the spectators included Cedric, Aviva and me, watching from our balcony seats, with that same fascination.

The ritual began with the unrolling of a long strip of opaque plastic, about twenty-five feet long and five feet wide which they stretched tightly on the ground. Then working with the care and concentration of a stage crew preparing for an imminent performance, they set up a bewildering assortment of props. First they placed a checkered red and white plastic table-cloth on either end of the strip, pinning it down with covered wicker baskets, one on each corner. On each table-cloth they arranged, in a crescent, a camping stove, an Arabic teapot and ceramic jars and wooden boxes of various sizes. In the centre of the crescent they carefully placed an ornate hookah, a Moroccan pipe, with a long curved stem.

Next a bizarre garden materialised in the plastic expanse between the hookahs – long, faded, artificial flowers, each one crudely stuck in a can filled with sand. The rusting, dented tins, adorned with colourless blossoms, were interspersed with bouquets of red plastic roses entombed

162

in milk bottles and aerosol spray cans, some with insect repellent labels still intact.

The stage set, the Berbers raised the lids of the wicker baskets and two dozen white doves were released into the lifeless garden. The birds soared, momentarily etched against the bright blue sky, and then swooped to a landing position on the plastic strip. With familiar ease they strolled through the floral arrangement, pausing to peck in the sand, then fluttering on to the milk bottle rims to sit in pairs, snow white among the red roses. The Berbers sat cross-legged on the chequered table-cloths before the hookahs, facing each other, motionless across the landscaped plastic. After a few moments of meditation, as though they were praying in the silence of a mosque instead of surrounded by the din of the square, a note of domesticity was introduced.

Remaining in the lotus position, the two men began preparing mint tea, busily boiling water and opening and closing jars and boxes. Then, slowing their movements to a dance-like precision, they ceremoniously filled the hookahs, and began to smoke, exhaling billows of white smoke which rose above them, enveloping them like mist. The younger man punctuated his inhalations with sharp drum beats. Between inhalations they sang and chanted, wailing to each other across the stretch of plastic, the wails so piercing they penetrated the noise of the square, lashing onto our balcony like the strike of a snake.

All at once, obeying some secret signal, the doves left the garden in a graceful choreography of hops and swoops and divided, an equal number going to each man. They settled symmetrically on arms, shoulders and head, in arc formation. When their perches were secure, the young man rose through the smoky mist, haloed by doves, and began to dance. In slow motion he first opened his doved arms then leapt into the air, twirling and leaping. The old man broke his hypnotic trance with a piercing shout to the young man, waving his arms, the wings of the doves flapping wildly. The young man answered the call by gliding down the plastic sheet, weaving through the sparse foliage toward the old

163

man, stamping his feet and slapping his thighs, his body twisting and writhing in frenetic agony. The doves beat their wings crazily in a frantic attempt to retain their perches, clinging with quivering claws.

In response, the old man wailed a long thin lament, eyes closed, face lifted to the sky, and the young man answered, in explosive dance, then in crazed screams and savage drum beats. As the frenzied dialogue developed they both grew hoarse, and the coarse rasping voices heightened the harsh primeval drama. They seemed to be enacting some fierce ritual, frightening and fascinating, some blood myth linking a prehistoric past with a plastic modernity. We could feel it with them pulsating in our veins, throbbing somewhere in our own history.

The drama climaxed with the old man raising his arms to the heavens, the white wings trembling. Then, crying out in a long sustained moan, like a death rattle, he fell to the ground. The young man's limbs and the doves' wings thrashed wildly together, ending in a convulsive shudder of bird and man. Drained and staggering, the young man zig-zagged through the plastic blossoms, lurching to his table-cloth position and collapsed cross-legged, panting with exhaustion. Silence. The old man slowly opened his eyes and sat up dazed and dumb, spent. The doves fluttered gently from their human perches and resumed their stroll in the garden, stopping to nibble among the flowers. The Berber men quietly sipped the tea they had prepared. Someone collected money in a tin can.

Disturbed and uneasy, we were aware of a profundity just outside our grasp, haunted by a mystery which remained elusive. No one spoke. Aviva and Cedric, who usually had so much to say, were still. After a while, I abandoned the Western attempt to categorise or locate the experience and surrendered to a sense of wonder. Mint tea was brought to us on the roof and we sipped in silence, sitting in the hot sun, gazing at the Atlas mountains covered with snow. The persistent call for prayer pulsated from the tower of the Katoubia mosque, sentinel to Marrakesh, the red city.

15. An Invitation

If I found it easy to understand and respond to the overt sensuality of Morocco, the subtleties of its culture, its society, its moral codes, remained a mystery. Through trial and error I had learned to behave appropriately in a variety of situations, but it was a Pavlovian conditioning without any real comprehension of the ethics, mores, religion, traditions, the deeply rooted values of a people who carefully guarded its secrets, a culture centuries apart.

One aspect of behaviour especially bewildering to me as a Western female was that of relating to the Moroccan male. Arab society was heavily male-dominated - the female barely visible, shielded by clothing, secured by codes of conduct. Western women, however, were thrust into a male arena, exposed, unprotected, vulnerable, ignorant of the rules for sexual survival. It was vital therefore to devise some way of relating to men that was friendly but devoid of unwanted sexual overtones. The balance was precarious. Moroccan men were easily offended by what they considered Western aloofness, but quick to respond to the slightest erotic suggestion, often finding such a suggestion where none was intended. Expectations were different, interpretations different, attitudes regarding male-female relationships millenniums apart. It seemed to me the very language of communication was different, even when that language was English. To prevent disaster it was necessary to walk a sexual tightrope careful not to make a move which would lead to the fall.

During my visits to Morocco I had evolved, through painful research, a code of conduct calculated to foster friendly encounters with men while avoiding an unwelcome bedroom aftermath. The emphasis was on non-provocative behaviour. For example, Moroccans were very much into touching. They resented anyone who pulled away, interpreting this as an insult. It was therefore important to perfect a repertoire of non-provocative touching, like handclasping - especially with the addition of the Moroccan hand-to-heart greeting - back slapping, arm pressing, while scrupulously abstaining from sexual signals or coy manoeuvres. Appended to the code was a guide for non-provocative dress and suggestions for non-provocative verbal exchange. One always had a male friend or husband who was expected soon. One refrained from discussions on drugs. One loved couscous and mint tea but preferred eating in cafes with friends to meals alone in someone's room. The code also included such precepts as looking as though one knew where one was going and strict avoidance of the euphoric, vague look. There is respect for someone who walks with purpose, people step out of the way. But someone wandering aimlessly, expressing a blend of confusion and hesitation, becomes an easy victim. It was precisely this victim condition the code warned against.

During our long hours in the car I had advised the novices, Annilee, Ronit, Aviva, even David, on the rules for staying out of trouble with Moroccan men. They agreed with my sociology but I sensed resistance to following my advice. This was understandable since I didn't always follow my own advice. Moroccan men were not only attractive but possessed that compelling allure of the unknown.

The morning after our Medina adventures, I was seated alone on the terrace of the café next to our hotel. Cedric was paralytically asleep, replenishing an exhausted psyche, recovering from his first day in Morocco. Aviva was at the post office collecting mail. I was sipping my *café au lait,* slightly distanced from the activity of the square which was already beginning to throb.

I was enjoying a quiet reflective moment, mainly thinking about Ronit who was due to arrive next day, pleased with her response to Morocco, her ability to adapt, her ease, her interest, thinking how much she seemed the perfect traveller, the ideal travel companion. I was excited about introducing her to Marrakesh, sharing my favourite places and people, planning where to take her, making notes in my journal, when I

166

looked up to see a young Moroccan approaching my table.

"You speak English?" he asked.

"Yes," I answered.

"May I join you?"

I nodded reluctantly, thinking 'there goes my quiet moment.' I knew he would want to talk. I was right. He told me his name was Mohammed and began with the usual questions.

"What is your country?"

"Canada, but now living in London."

"How do you like my country?"

"I love it."

I knew that neither my quiet moment nor my journal had a chance, and with a mental shrug of resignation abandoned both to talk to yet another Mohammed. Mohammed told me he was a student studying at the University of Rabat and home for the summer holiday. His family lived in a small village in the mountains surrounding Marrakesh. He began telling me about the village and must have noticed my increased attention because he unexpectedly said, "would you like to visit my village? My family would be happy to receive you." I grew even more interested. Cedric and Aviva had been saying how much they wanted to visit one of the villages in the Ourika Valley outside Marrakesh, and how wonderful it would be if a Moroccan family invited us to their home. Both wishes could be fulfilled by accepting Mohammed's invitation.

"I'm not alone," I hastened to explain, "I'm with two friends, my friend Aviva has gone to the post office and my friend Cedric is in the hotel but he will be joining me soon."

My code dictated that Mohammed know there was a man on the scene, a fact which could well modify his invitation or cancel it altogether.

"Then you must all come." He was not put off, on the contrary, he seemed more enthusiastic. "I will have more chances to practice my English. My cousin will come to the cafe to take me in one hour. We will all go to my village in his car," he said proudly - a car was no mean achievement, even knowing someone who owned one conferred status.

"How will we return?" I asked, always on the alert, "we must be back tonight."

"No problem. There is a bus at nine o'clock in the night. It takes only one hour or maybe one hour and a half."

I made one of my on-the-spot-decisions. "Great. I will get my friends and we will meet you here in one hour." We shook hands like old friends. I left him drinking mint tea and rushed off to report the good news to Cedric, who was up and dressed when I got back to the hotel. I thought he'd be delighted. He wasn't. He was suspicious, his paranoia in full swing.

"Who is this guy?"

"I told you, a student at the University of Rabat studying English and visiting his family for the holidays."

"How come he invited me?"

"He didn't, but if he wants me he has to take you. Look, he's studying English and wants the opportunity to practice."

"So what else is new?"

"Do you want to come or don't you? I thought you wanted to go into the mountains and visit a Moroccan family. This can be your lucky day."

Cedric was quiet for a few seconds, and I knew he was wrestling with a lurking suspicion that I was going to get us raped or mutilated or worse. Finally he replied by picking up his guitar and strumming his version of a Spanish Fandango, executing a few Flamenco stamps and shouting "*Olé*!" He paused for correction. "Oops...that's the wrong country..." Then, accompanied by guitar chords, he did an imitation of the young Moroccan boy who had solicited him in the square the previous night, and whose burning glances seething with promises of pleasure, had left him reeling.

"Hey meester, you come with me,

My mother she make you couscous.

168

Then you drink mint tea,

 I no have a seester.

So you sleep with me."

He paused dramatically, rose up on his toes, flicked his head to one side, "Wacha, we go!" he concluded unexpectedly, with a final click of the heel and a strident strum.

"But what if this guy wants me and you and Aviva? There's a lot of blazing sexuality out there. I'll bet that kid last night has many a white queen whimpering." He was already having second thoughts.

"I promise you it won't blaze your way, not with this guy, he's O.K., and he's not into whimpers, maybe bangs, but not whimpers. But you must promise me one thing."

"That I'll disappear if you nod three times and pull your left ear lobe."

"That we won't stay the night even if we're invited. There's a bus returning to Marrakesh at nine this evening. Under no circumstances do I want to stay over."

"Why not?" Cedric asked suspiciously, "you just gave him the good spouse-keeping seal of approval, you've just convinced me he's O.K."

"He may not be so O.K with two Western ladies sleeping in his house, maybe in the same room. The day is one thing, the night another. Why add fuel to the blazing sexuality?"

"Settled. We return tonight...I'm plumb sorry mam, it's my missus here, she likes your couscous and your mint tea just fine, but she thinks your son is too doggone horny." His accent was Texan.

Aviva begged to stay behind. She had urgent mail from her agent to answer and was grateful for some time on her own - to sort things out. She was probably worried we wouldn't get back in time for David, and in any case didn't want to make the trip to the Ourika Valley without him.

In an hour Cedric and I were back at the café. It was hot. I wore a thin, but not see-through lilac blouse with wide elbow-length sleeves and purple tie-dyed trousers, nothing provocative. Cedric was far more provocative in an open gold-coloured Madras cotton shirt held loosely together by ties, made by a lady friend, and brown light corduroy jeans, bronzed, lean, with the energy and stance of a fencer. Mohammed greeted us with a bright-toothed smile and shook hands formally.

"Welcome to Morocco," he said to Cedric.

I had told him it was Cedric's first time in Morocco, a fact which assured a good impression. Cedric returned the smile, less brightly. Mohammed received the news that Aviva wouldn't be coming with a small philosophical shrug. "Perhaps next time," he said.

"Perhaps," I agreed. Although he carried no bags, he had changed completely and was wearing a freshly laundered shirt which matched his teeth.

Mustafa, the cousin, arrived as we were still shaking hands and we commenced another round of hand shaking. Had Aviva cast eyes upon Mustafa her resolve to remain behind would have vanished. He was one of those beautiful young Moroccans with black curly hair, dark shining eyes and a slender body supple with sap, able to bend in any direction. His shirt was unbuttoned on the chest, the fine white cotton opening on smooth olive skin and revealing an exquisite five-pointed star. He wore real levis, another sign of superior connections, hugging his bottom and squeezing his crotch into 'a juicy bunch of fruit, a tempting handful', as Aviva had said about a similar young Moroccan. He was probably unable to cross the Place Djema el Fna or sit in a café without multiple propositions. The international homosexual jet-setters flocking to Marrakesh would find him irresistible and the Club Mediterranee ladies would slip him coy messages. He had a quietly confident manner which assured me of his ability, not only to handle the heavy come-on scene, but to turn it to his advantage.

We stepped from the café into the car. Leaving the red-walled medina with its sentinel Katoubia in the old part of Marrakesh, we drove through the new city, the French section, with wide avenues lined with orange trees and Parisian-style sidewalk cafés. The red city with its houses built from the local terracotta clay soon gave way to a cultivated countryside, green fields blossoming with flowers and crops. Donkeys loaded with farm produce, melons, tomatoes, grapes, passed us on their way to the Marrakesh markets. We stopped to allow a row of camels to cross the road, their fleshy bodies swaying seductively, belying eyes glaring malice out of small hard heads.

Mustafa told us he had a sister living in Mohammed's village and was visiting both families, remaining with the sister for the night and then continuing early next morning, before the sun was up, to the south of Morocco. His father owned a shop in the Marrakesh medina, renowned for its fine Berber jewellery, and antique swords and daggers. Several times a year he toured the desert and Atlas villages searching out the craftsmen who still made rings, necklaces and bracelets in the centuries-old Berber tradition, duplicating ancient Berber designs. He, himself, had apprenticed for several years with some of these masters and had made the delicate star of Arabia he wore. I made sure to get directions to his shop.

Mustafa parked the car, leaving it in a roadside village with mud huts the colour of henna. From there we waded across a cold stream and headed toward the mountains to the tiny cluster of dwellings nestled red among the green and gold foot hills where Mohammed's family lived. It was about a thirty minute walk. The sun was hot and bright, the countryside spectacular with mountains rising behind the hills capped by gleaming snow. The red of the soil and the green of the grass rose from the valley into the white of snow. I walked in hot silence remembering the coolness. As we approached the village Cedric said, "this looks more like an archaeological dig than a village." The houses seemed to grow out of and into the rocky hills. Mustafa left us to visit his sister, promising to rejoin us later.

Mohammed's family house was built into the side of a hill using its stone for walls. It was built in Arabic style with rooms and corridors surrounding a central courtyard and with arched windows and doorways framing the mountains and the valley. Wherever we looked the view was startling. Mohammed's grandmother and two younger sisters were at home to receive us. His mother was away attending an older sister who was about to give birth, his father had gone to join her and his grandfather was working in the fields. Although we had not been expected, in Moroccan tradition, we were warmly welcomed. Tea was brought immediately. We sat on pillows, gazing through arched windows, resting in the contours of the hills.

It was strange to see the women, their faces finally unveiled, smiling their welcome. The grandmother was still beautiful with dark liquid eyes which Cedric pronounced 'very sexy'. A special fuss was made over Cedric. Whether it was because he was male, or film-star handsome, he was served with dedicated adoration, especially by the grandmother, who was much taken by him, intriguing him with her 'sexy eyes'. The girls were just as adoring but not as forward, serving him with equal commitment, but less panache. He had only to lift an elbow to find a pillow under it, he had merely to shift his anatomy to find himself propped by more pillows. The men - Mohammed's grandfather was summoned from the field for the occasion - offered him pipefuls of hashish and the women, honey cakes, tea with mint fresh from the garden, and golden glances. I was served after Cedric, graciously, but without the adoration. Cedric reclined among his pillows, feeling like the Caliph of Baghdad, loving every pampered moment.

We spent the afternoon eating cakes, sipping mint tea and smiling. At one point we were shown some of the fine carpets and cloths the women of the family had woven. The pillows, walls and floors were covered by their work. In the late afternoon Mohammed, Cedric and I went for a walk in the valley. Up until then Mohammed had been generally cordial, paying me no special attention, but as soon as we left the village behind, I could feel him hovering. At one point, when Cedric was out of sight, Mohammed took my hand squeezing it with sudden passion. His eyes fastened on mine. "It's beautiful here," I said, attempting to miss the point. I danced on ahead, a sprite on a Moroccan hillside, not to be confused with a seductress in a Western bordello. Cedric was sitting on a rock gazing into the mountains. I sat beside him. Mohammed brooded on another rock. Nobody spoke. A silent meditation in the Ourika Valley, Mohammed's impure thoughts suspended over my pure ones.

Mohammed recovered from my rejection quickly. On the way back he kept pressing up to me when Cedric wasn't looking. At one point he took my hand and swiftly swung it to his groin. "Just for a minute," he pleaded as I sharply pulled my hand away indicating anger and distaste. Why didn't he try that with Cedric? What about all that Moroccan homosexuality? Where was it when I needed it most? And why was Cedric romping about oblivious to my meaningful glances? "No Mohammed," I said coldly, "don't spoil it." I stalked ahead. Gradually my anger melted into the grandeur of the mountains and I was overcome by compassionate thoughts. Poor bugger, all he wanted was a modest wee feel from someone he knew must be into far heavier things. And a sneaky little thought wiggled through my indignation - what if it had been Mustafa, would I have behaved differently? I wanted to make amends. I wanted things to be the way they were before Mohammed's erection.

"Look at this stone," I called to a sulking Mohammed, and brought him a beautifully marked stone as a peace offering. He accepted with an enthusiasm which far surpassed its cause - perhaps his apology for having offended me. Still, when Cedric emerged from behind a rock, I tried to flash him don't-leave-me-alone-with-Mohammed looks, unwilling to chance a repeat performance. But he was too stoned on the Ourika valley to notice.

When we returned to the house dinner was in an advanced stage of preparation. I wanted to leave immediately before we got involved in invitations.

"Will you take us to the bus stop Mohammed?" I asked.

Mohammed looked as though I had made an obscene utterance.

"But you are invited to eat with my family. My grandmother and my sisters are cooking for you. You cannot leave before eating with us."

"But we'll miss the bus."

"No problem. There is a later bus."

"Are you sure?"

"Yes, for sure, there is a midnight bus and it is a much better bus, much faster."

He had never intended for us to make the nine o'clock bus. Cedric looked relieved, he wanted to stay, he had a natural empathy with people, a congenial ease, a warm sympatico, and was enjoying getting into the family. So was I, but with reservations – I didn't want Mohammed getting into me. When Mustafa returned, he smiled when I told him we were staying for dinner, he had never doubted it for a minute.

Dinner was leisurely and lovely. Mohammed, in the bosom of his family gave off no lustful vibrations. He was friendly and polite, even slightly distant. Cedric and I communicated with the family via Mohammed and Mustafa. We answered questions about Canada and England, asked questions about living in the Moroccan hills. Cedric was interested not only in the people, but in their economics and sociology. We smiled a lot. The couscous was excellent. Tender chunks of lamb cooked in saffron and kamoun, couscous grains immersed in vegetables and covered with a rich tangy sauce, and home made Arabic bread. The grandmother and sisters anticipated our every move. Before we could request a piece of bread it was beside us, before we could reach for a piece of meat it was on the bread. They didn't eat with us, but gave the impression of taking more pleasure in our eating than in their own. The couscous was followed by honey melon and plump purple figs. Then almond cakes and mint tea. It was the meal we had dreamed, served with that special Eastern grace.

After dinner the pipe was brought in. Women did not smoke, but I, as that peculiar brand of woman called 'foreigner', was expected to partake. It was beginning to get dark. The evening poured in through arches open to the hills and sky. Between draws on the pipe, I made signals to Mohammed and Mustafa about our departure, pointing to my watch - Cedric was beyond signalling. They comforted me with smiles.

The pillows embraced us. Cedric's grin had settled in. Gradually my departure signals grew weaker, muted by the taste of almond and mint, dimmed by the pipe, enfeebled by the sight of the lovely Mustafa. I roused myself for one final attempt, "Mohammed, we should go before it gets too dark." As though sensing my attempts at departure and determined to thwart them, the grandmother launched into a flood of Arabic.

"My grandmother says you must not leave. She invites you to stay with my family for tonight. You will be our guests."

I looked at Cedric blissed out on Arabic hospitality, at the family radiant with the excitement of entertaining Western guests, at the ladies enamoured by Cedric. My own better judgement was up in smoke.

"All right, we'll stay the night," I conceded. Mohammed and Mustafa nodded, knowing all along that we would. Cedric grinned still wider. "But we absolutely must leave early tomorrow morning," I added, trying for a tone of urgency, "we have friends to meet in Marrakesh."

"I too must leave early," Mustafa said, I will take you to the bus."

The evening passed between pipefuls of smoke, and a stream of offerings. One of the sisters brought a pot of henna and painted my palm in a traditional Berber design, similar to the one painted on her own hand. We never left our pillows. Mustafa produced a guitar from somewhere and Arabic drums - I had told him Cedric played the guitar. Cedric sang, singing old folk songs and improvising new ones. In the hills of Morocco, accompanied by Moroccan drums, his voice was especially beautiful, his music absorbing an Eastern quality, plaintive and haunting.

"The pulsing throb of Africa
Is heating up my veins,

175

The sun and the kif
And the moon-spilt reef
So delightfully insane
It was all like riding, glory riding,
Riding a horse without the reins."

The family was thrilled. The sisters and grandmother glided in and out with trays of mint tea, pistachio nuts, cakes and fruit, their eyes shining with pleasure, their kaftans swaying, as they knelt to serve us. The grandfather nodded and smiled as he received the pipe. As my anxiety transformed into velvet contentment, I sank deeper into the pillows. I loved Cedric's singing and he was including my favourite songs as a vote of thanks.

At one point Cedric lit the pipe with his lighter, a see-through affair with pink fuel. The grandfather's expression of rapt wonder inspired Cedric to offer it to him. After repeated refusals we finally persuaded him to accept, convincing him that to refuse would be an insult. His eyes alight with admiration, he received the lighter as though it was a gift from the kingdom of heaven.

Eventually Mustafa rose to go. Cedric stretched and yawned. As though this was the awaited signal, preparations were made for sleep. Cedric and I were to sleep in Mohammed's room. Mohammed, to my great relief, in the passageway leading off his room into the courtyard. Once the arrangements were established, the sisters went off to find night clothes, returning arms laden with finery. The night dress chosen for me could have adorned an Arabian bride. Worn over a thin cotton shift, it was made of silver silk, embroidered in various shades of off-white, with wide sleeves inset with lace, and a lace hem which brushed the floor. I thought I was being dressed for my wedding, but Mohammed and Mustafa assured me it was only for bed.

After I was helped into the night gown, my hair was arranged for sleep. Never having experienced a bedtime coiffeur, I was delighted. With exquisite care, my hair was braided into thin plaits and bound with a silk cloth matching the dress. White embroidered babouches were slipped on my feet. Next my eyes were made up with kohl. My only regret was that Aviva and Ronit were missing out. Sharing the experience with them would have made everything perfect. When the sisters were through with me, I felt like Cinderella after the fairy godmother had waved her wand. Would a prince suddenly appear and whisk me off to the ball? Was I being dressed for Lawrence of Arabia, the Sultan of Persia, the Sheik of Araby? Then for a fraction of a terrible moment a twinge of anxiety darkened my illusions: I was being prepared for Cedric, or horror of horrors, for Mohammed. But no! The silver/white of my robe and slippers compounded the story-book quality of the occasion. Ordinarily I wore only purple. Purple was my reality. But now the shimmering of silver and white enhanced the fantasy, sustaining the romance.

Pleased with the results, the girls gave me a mirror to view their handiwork. I was entirely Moroccan. They embraced me laughing with the pleasure of having created an unexpected sister, complete with hennaed hand. Finally I was presented to Cedric. He was overwhelmed by the transformation. "You look like a woman I once knew," he said whimsically. Fortunately we weren't lovers. I would have hated for my finery to be disturbed, my eye makeup smudged, my hair mussed.

Mustafa left after ceremoniously kissing my hand and assuring me I was a Moroccan Princess. Cedric and I sat in the courtyard contemplating the stars and hills and the mysteries of Moroccan life, waiting for the cue which would allow us to retire. Suddenly I realised there was an urgent mystery I had yet to solve. "Cedric, where's the loo? I haven't seen a loo. I went earlier behind a rock but what happens if I want to pee in the night?"

The incongruity of the question coupled with my regal persona had Cedric leaping from his seat. He knelt before me taking my hand. Gazing into my eyes with a flash of mad grin he crooned, "Peeing in the night, with my true love...I'm peeing in the night, with only you love..." Then, improvising a jaunty little tune he jigged back to his seat singing,

"Oh we haven't a clue, about the loo, fa la la la , what can we do."

I burst into laughter while insisting, "It's not funny. Please ask Mohammed," I pleaded, "it's more the kind of question a man would be expected to ask."

As if summoned, Mohammed appeared.

"Mohammed, my good man...there seems to be a question...about the W.C." Cedric cleared his throat, "where precisely is it?" His accent was immaculately English.

"W.C.?"

"Toilet, yes, the *toilet*." The second *toilet* was French. "*Ou est le pissoire?*"

"Toilet?" Mohammed sounded surprised. "The toilet is anywhere." He made a grand inclusive gesture toward the surrounding hills.

"You mean there is no toilet?" I panicked. My extensive travels in Morocco had not prepared me for a house without a toilet. Even in the desert there was some sort of convenience. My code of behaviour contained no advice on this phenomenon.

"You can go anywhere," Mohammed repeated as though I had not understood. Actually I hadn't understood.

"You mean we have to pass through the rooms where your family sleeps and go outside?" That was the only exit.

"No...you just go outside the courtyard."

"But how?" My eyes darted around the enclosure looking for a secret door. A stony hill descended into the courtyard forming one of its walls, the others led into the house. There was no visible exit.

"Just climb up the hill and go anywhere in the fields on top."

Mohammed couldn't understand my worry. I had a sudden vision of myself framed by moonlight, in my silk embroidered gown and white babouches, some kind of mad Ophelia, struggling up the hill to urinate. My bladder was never renowned for its retentive ability, and I had euphorically sipped cup after cup of tea, reckless of consequence.

178

The family came to wish us a good night. We kissed the women, bid Mohammed and his grandfather goodnight and headed for our bedroom. Cedric's bed was on one wall, mine parallel on the opposite wall, between us, on the third wall was an unused bed, and the fourth wall had windows and an open archway leading to the passageway, where a bed had been arranged for Mohammed, and through the passageway to the courtyard.

I climbed into bed, carefully arranging my folds of finery, anxious not to tear or even crumple anything while I slept. I had never been so beautifully dressed. Cedric was already in bed.

"Do you really like the way I look?" I asked.

He sat up for a final viewing. "So how often do I get to sleep with a Moroccan princess who speaks such good English?"

"Listen Cedric...I'm worried about having to pee. I can't believe there's no toilet. What will I do in the middle of the night?"

"My dear, when in Morocco, the world is your toilet." His accent was Shakespearian.

"Actually, I'd prefer a more modest arrangement." I drew the sheet over me, plumped up the pillow and sighed fatalistically. "I might as well get to sleep. I'm exhausted. Goodnight."

"It's been a splendid day. Goodnight and sleep well," Cedric said tenderly.

I closed my eyes, dismissing all toilet thoughts. It had been a splendid day. I fell asleep quickly, aware only of the softness of silk.

I don't know how much later I awoke to the dreaded call of nature. I had to do something fast. From bitter experience I knew these matters never get better, only worse. I reviewed my plan. I had to go through the passageway, where Mohammed was sleeping, to the courtyard, and from there climb the hill to the grand toilet in the sky. O.K. Better get it over with. I fumbled into my babouches. It was very dark. Holding up my dress and underskirt, I tiptoed past the sleeping Mohammed, hardly daring to breathe. I made it to the courtyard and stood for a moment surveying the terrain. The courtyard was lit by erratic patches of moonlight, turning the cushions, low benches and small tables, so colourful and exotic earlier on, into hostile, alien shapes. I shivered, consumed by an urgency to finish my business and split. I began clambering up the rocks on all fours, struggling to keep my dress from getting soiled. I had stupidly removed my knickers, depriving myself of a place to tuck my skirts. The babouches kept failing off. One finally rolled down the hill. I continued the climb with one babouche. The hill was steeper than I thought and covered with stones. Tripping over my dress, stumbling over rocks, grazing my hands and my unshod foot, I paused to re-think my strategy. Why did I have to go all the way to the top and get to the field? Why was up there better than down here? Convincing myself that down here was good enough, I lifted my dresses and stooped, amazed at how much liquid my bladder had retained. Finally I rose, wonderfully relieved, only to discover that the bottom of my dress was sopping wet and gritty, also one foot was wet, fortunately the bare one. Why hadn't I been more careful? I'd better get down and clean up.

Slipping and sliding, I scrambled down the hill and looked for my babouche. Suddenly I gasped in disbelief. A stream of urine had followed me down the slope and was settling into a puddle, right in the middle of the courtyard. The stone floor slanting to the centre formed a perfect base to receive it. I watched in fascinated horror as the puddle grew into a pool reflecting the moon. I froze, mortified. I had urinated in the middle of the family's living room. How would I be able to face them? I had turned their courtyard into a urinal. What a reward for their hospitality. Terrified that Mohammed would hear me and discover my terrible humiliation, I abandoned the lost babouche, thinking only of escaping into bed.

Nervously, in a state of disgrace, I crept into the dark tunnel of passageway. It was imperative not to wake Mohammed. I tried desperately to walk a straight line, but instead stumbled, stubbing my toe, almost falling over the sleeping Mohammed. I stood stark still hoping I hadn't woken him.

"Who is it?...Niema?" He said sleepily. How did he know?

"It's alright Mohammed. It's just me. I had to go out for a minute. Go back to sleep." Somehow I got back into my room. I leapt into bed as though chased by a monster about to grab my foot, and pulled the sheet over my head, drawing my legs safely under me, oblivious of my lovely dress bunched and crumpled and dirty. In the foetus position I squeezed into myself, rigid with shame.

Above all, I wished Mohammed wouldn't go into the courtyard. I was almost glad when I heard him groping in the room. At least he wasn't in the courtyard. I could hear him getting into the bed perpendicular to mine. I pretended I was fast asleep. He knew damn well I wasn't. I'd have to be the fastest sleep in the West. "Niema," he whispered. I breathed evenly, deeply, simulating sleep. "Niema," his whisper was louder. I was overcome by coma. But he wasn't having it. "Niema," I detected an urgency in his voice. Nothing from me except deep, regular breathing. Should I wake Cedric? Hopefully he would wake by himself and nip Mohammed's approach in the bud. "Niema," Mohammed insisted, throwing caution to the wind. But when I sleep, I sleep. Cedric wasn't nipping anything. Why didn't he wake up? (Next day he told me he had heard Mohammed calling but didn't know how to respond. "I wanted to answer in a high-pitched voice, 'Yes Mohammed, I'm over here' - that would have confused him, but then he stopped.")

Mohammed was quiet for a while and I began to think my tactic had worked. It hadn't. Suddenly I felt a hand on my shoulder. He had reached from his bed to mine. I jerked to a sitting position.

"What? What? Who is it? What's happening?" I tried for the appropriate hysterical pitch, my voice shrill, louder that I intended.

Mohammed must have feared that Cedric or even his family would hear, because he said, "sh...sh...it's O.K."

"What? What? Who's there?" I panicked even louder and then flopped down, simulating death. He was probably relieved I was only

181

dead and not going to pursue my hysterics, because he was suddenly still. He lit a cigarette and I watched it glow in the dark. When it was finished, he lit another. He lit cigarette after cigarette and I watched each one glow, afraid to close my eyes. I waited the night out, lying painfully still, fully awake. He remained awake as well, tense, restless. When morning finally came he returned to the passageway. I was exhausted and grubby. The beautiful princess gown had changed back into Cinderella's rags. I felt like the pumpkin.

I dressed and woke Cedric. Fortunately breakfast was simple, strong black coffee and Arabic bread with honey, served without fuss by the grandmother, the sisters already at their weaving, and the grandfather working in the fields. Mustafa arrived. We finished eating, said our goodbyes and thanks, and accompanied by a subdued Mohammed and a chatty Mustafa, headed for the bus. As we passed through the courtyard I grabbed Cedric's hand and pumped it nervously. Sunshine flooded the room, the colours sparkled. I cast a furtive glance at the floor. Not a trace of my puddle. Had the sun rescued me?

When we reached the road, we bid Mustafa goodbye, promising to visit him in Marrakesh. Mohammed waited with us. We hardly spoke. As soon as he heard the bus, he shook our hands, first Cedric's then mine.

"A present for you Niema," he said suddenly, stuffing the pair of white embroidered babouche into my bag. Before I had time to react he was off, returning to celibacy in the hills.

Cedric and I found seats together. The other passengers, mostly men, were Berbers from the mountains. Half way to Marrakesh the bus stopped by the roadside. The men left the bus, the women remained inside. Through the window we could see them heading for a field beside the road. We watched as they entered the field and stood in the bright sun their backs to the road, their long cloaks and hoods silhouetted against the sky - a row of strange birds in a barren patch of land. They seemed to be performing some ritual. I thought they might be responding to the

Muslim call for prayer, their religion requiring them to pray five times a day, facing Mecca, no matter where they found themselves. But when they finally returned to the bus I realised it was a different call they were responding to. I looked at the field. The parched earth and rocks were covered with dark patches. At least there was one mystery I could understand.

16. Feminina

Several days after Annilee, David and Ronit arrived in Marrakesh, we went in search of Mustafa's father's shop. I had told Aviva about the beautiful Mustafa and the Berber jewellery and she was eager to see both. Cedric remained behind playing music on the roof and watching the square.

We found the shop on one of the more affluent Medina streets where dealers negotiated Moroccan artefacts for export. The shop was small but as soon as we entered we could sense it spelled quality. Display cases exhibited necklaces, rings, bracelets, hands of fatima, to exquisite advantage. Jewelled daggers, knives and swords hung on velvet backdrops. It looked more like the inside of a treasure chest than a shop. Mustafa, in attendance on his own, was delighted to see me and to meet the others. He looked even more beautiful than I remembered in a wide-sleeved Tuareg robe, the blue vivid against fragile silver embroidery. Immediately he sent for his father who was visiting a merchant close by.

"My father would enjoy to meet you and to talk with you. He tells many excellent stories," he said, smiling one of his wonderful smiles.

"And we will enjoy meeting him and listening to his stories," Aviva said graciously, returning his smile. She was thrilled with Mustafa and the entire setting. The father arrived minutes later, a tall dignified man in a white kaftan, who welcomed us as though we were part of his family.

"*Je suis enchanté, Madame Niema,*" he said, touching his heart. "My son has spoken of you so often that I feel you are my friend as well, and, of course, your friends are also my friends," he said, greeting the others with hand clasps and embraces. He spoke English with a charming French-Moroccan accent. If anything the father was even more handsome than the son, with the patina of additional years. I couldn't tell if Aviva was more intrigued by Mustafa or his father.

Almost before the introductions were over, we found ourselves seated around a low olivewood table inset with mother-of-pearl and covered by a silver tray, while tea was ceremoniously poured. The father was pleased by our avid appreciation of his jewellery and delighted in talking about it, elaborating on the silver, the stones, the designs, explaining the difference between original and copy, with such enthusiasm, erudition and love that even David was fascinated. Aviva was especially attentive, and her perceptive questions and intelligent interest, inspired the father to enthral us with stories concerning the history of various pieces, and the adventures in procuring them.

He told us about the famous bandit who had owned the dagger encrusted with precious stones, David couldn't put down, and showed us a secret compartment in the handle where he had hidden jewels. The bandit not only robbed travellers but held them prisoner demanding enormous ransoms. Legend had it that he was so charismatic, so elegant, so handsome and that life in his hidden fortress was so fascinating, that even after the ransoms were paid, the prisoners begged not to be freed. Women, it was said, were so enamoured of him that they vied to be robbed and held captive.

Then, from a concealed drawer he produced a jewelled box and from within the box an eye-shaped ruby set in pale gold. It had been worn in the navel of an ancient king's favourite belly dancer who, it was rumoured, could make the eye wink. He told us about salt caravans with jewels imbedded in the salt; about a lost oasis which ran with the waters of eternity, where an ancient silversmith had fashioned a ring which could bring forth the waters and which he now revealed to us; he showed us rare Goulimime beads, buried long ago deep in the desert, which had been used as currency by nomad tribes, and told us that to this day no one knew how to reproduce them, and only fake ones could be bought. He gave us each a bead as a gift and explained that my special square one was a harem bead and would have purchased a harem girl in times past.

We sat transfixed, feeling we were being transported on a magic carpet into the pages of the Arabian nights, and listened imbued with that special sense of experiencing something unique, making some magical discovery, glimpsing something of that mystery which kept eluding us.

When we finally left and returned to the mundane, a spark of magic had been ignited to glow for always. Aviva and David went off to find a leather cowboy hat coveted by David which Aviva had promised to buy for his birthday. I decided to take Annilee and Ronit to Achmad's pipe shop. Cedric had entrusted me with the sacred mission of procuring hashish, after I had forbidden him to accept street offers. Achmad was known as 'the man' in Marrakesh and his shop was a good place to begin. Besides, I wanted Ronit and Annilee to partake in the shop culture and I needed somewhere to reflect, to preserve the fantasy Mustafa's father had evoked.

On previous Marrakesh visits the shop had been my medina refuge. It was a tiny place, crammed with a large variety of chillums and sepsis - kif pipes - with elaborately carved stems like small totem poles, and bowls made from soapstone and red clay. There were invariably several friends sitting on rolls of carpets or small wooden stools, sampling the pipes and playing tam tam drums. The door was always open. Whenever the bustle of the medina became too much, I had headed for the shop. I liked sitting in the cool interior watching the sun move through the waves of wool - golds, oranges, blues and purples - hanging in the street, listening to the rhythm of the tam tams and contemplating the mint leaves crowded in my glass of tea. Achmad was always friendly and I had come to trust him.

But I had difficulty in finding the shop now, remembering only that it was in one of the corridors where the dyed wool hung drying, draped over bamboo rods suspended across alleyways. After getting lost and found and lost again, I finally located it in the maze of narrow passageways, tucked into the wool, barely visible. Achmad greeted me like a long lost sister and introduced me to several friends playing music and smoking. I, in turn, introduced Annilee and Ronit. Foreigners were always welcome, especially females. Annilee and Ronit were a big hit, Ronit with her Arabic and long plait and Annilee with her blond curls, and flowing clothes - she always looked like opening night at the theatre. We joined the others on the carpets and settled down to tea and music.

At some point, one of the boys passed Ronit a drum and with nods and smiles encouraged her to play. She began timidly, but soon became so entranced by the rhythms, so involved in the playing, that forgetting her Western origins, she drummed as though born into it. The boys, inspired by her innovations, allowed her to lead them, and the result was an excitement of rhythms, rising to wild pitches and rippling into soft heart beats, so rousing, so fundamental, that I could feel my blood throbbing with the drums. Only hunger persuaded us to move on. It was way past lunch time. Before leaving I discreetly informed Achmad about my buying mission and he told me to return to the shop next day.

After lunch we wandered through the Place Djema el Fna. We were deeply absorbed, fascinated by a man playing a strange tune on a pipe, while two mesmerised cobras moved their heads as though drugged by the music, coiling and uncoiling their bodies in unison, obeying the will of the piper, when suddenly someone tapped me on the shoulder. It was Achmad.

"I have something very extra. Zero-zero, for export only," he whispered into my ear. "Come for to try." It was customary to sample before buying.

"That was fast," I said, signalling Annilee and Ronit to leave the people knotted around the snake charmer. "Are we going to your shop?" I asked, assuming that we were.

"No, to a café over there", he said, pointing to the other side of the square.

"To a café? Is that cool?" I asked, perturbed. My rule was never to smoke in public places.

"It's O.K. The manager is my friend."

I wasn't satisfied. "It's not a good idea Achmad."

"Believe me. I tell you it's O.K. It's my friend," Achmad said with a trace of annoyance at my lack of trust.

But I remained unconvinced. "I don't like to smoke where anyone can see us."

"No one can see us. It's on the roof. No one will be there."

I followed Achmad reluctantly, trying to persuade myself I was doing right. After all it was his city, he was Moroccan, he lived in Marrakesh, he did this all the time, why should I question his judgement? Besides if I didn't like the looks of the roof we could leave. As we crossed the square, weaving our way through the people gathered around the acrobats, jugglers, fortune-tellers, musicians, Achmad pressed something into my hand. "For you," he said, "a present for you." It was a lump of hashish about the size of a large grape. I reached quickly into my bag, fumbled for a Kleenex, wrapped the lump in the Kleenex and squeezed it into a corner of the bag. I felt uneasy. I didn't like carrying hashish.

We entered the café and climbed a long, narrow flight of stairs to the roof where there were several tables. Two of Achmad's friends, whom I recognised from the shop, were seated in the shade. We joined them. Before sitting down I checked to be sure the roof wasn't visible from the street. Achmad went downstairs and returned with a tray of iced coffee, and an orange juice for Ronit - she avoided caffeine. I moved my chair out of the shade and lifting my face to the sun, satisfied that we couldn't be seen from the street, decided to relax.

We sipped coffee and said little. One of the Moroccans drummed on the table, keeping time with the music coming from the square. Annilee filed her nails. Ronit reviewed a list of Arabic words she always kept handy, checking her pronunciation with one of the boys. Achmad prepared the chillum. He removed a large chunk of hashish, wrapped in plastic, from his sock. I was always impressed by the quantity of hashish Moroccans carried with them, and by the amount they consumed in one sitting, enough to last a month in the West. He softened the hashish by heating it with a match and crumbled great wads into the chillum. The chillum was lit and passed around. Achmad inhaled so long without breathing that I found myself gasping for breath, then exhaled billows of white smoke, like a steam engine. The lung capacity of Moroccans was also impressive. I noticed that between chillums, he kept bending down and the hashish and chillum disappeared. I assumed he was putting them back into his sock and wondered why he bothered.

The smoke was indeed excellent and the chillum recalled the encounter with English Tom and Matthew. Although by now Annilee was an expert, Ronit a competent acolyte and even I, who had difficulty with the mechanics of smoking, was doing remarkably well, we always stopped after two or three rounds, Ronit sometimes sooner, Annilee occasionally adding some extra rounds to her quota. After we had exhausted the second chillum, I had an urge to read an English language newspaper, sitting in the sun, my feet up, sipping iced coffee. *Alesh lo*? Why not?

"I'm going down to get the Herald Tribune before they sell out. I'll be back in a minute. Anybody want anything?" It was as though I hadn't spoken, not an eyelash flickered.

I started to descend the stairs, aware of how dark the narrow staircase was after the roof, noticing how the sunlight blast in at the entrance, far below, forming a sheet of light. I moved slowly, clinging to the banister, intrigued by the approaching light. I was totally absorbed by my journey to the sun, when suddenly the sheet was ripped apart. Two men filled the entrance. I paused, expecting them to ascend. They didn't. I stood still, looking down, waiting for them to move aside allowing me to pass. They remained blocking my exit. What did they want? Were they just being rude? Oh my God, was I going to have a scene with these two guys right here on the steps? Should I turn back and run? I observed them more calmly. They were business types, in dark suits and white shirts. One carried a briefcase. Their hair was cut short, their jowly faces clean shaven, except for a well-trimmed moustache.

They were like twins except that one was taller and heavier. Bank employees or even managers. They looked arrogant rather than lecherous. I decided not to be paranoid. They weren't about to attack me on the stairs. I resumed my descent, assuming they would separate and let me through. *"Excusez-moi,"* I said politely when I reached them.

They didn't budge. We stood facing each other.

"Return upstairs," the heavier one said, "we are from the police."

"What do you want with me?"

"Just return upstairs," he said curtly.

My mind began to spin. Thoughts tumbled like clothes in a dryer. We were done for. They were all up there smoking. Trapped. I had brought disaster upon Annilee and upon my own daughter, an innocent, her first time in Morocco. Why had I listened to Achmad? Oh my God, the piece of hashish in my bag. Should I drop it? No. They're right behind me. How could I warn the others? I couldn't. I climbed the stairs as if going to my own funeral, the policemen pressing me on, an unrelenting wall, sealing my exit.

Everyone turned to see me enter, one man on either side, like heavy book-ends. I could see the anxiety creep into Annilee's and Ronit's faces. The policemen spoke first in Arabic to the Moroccans, then in French to us. They had voices like ice, aloof, superior.

"You have been smoking hashish. Give it to us," the heavier one threatened with cool confidence. My glance took in the table. It was clean except for the empty glasses, and several lumps of sugar. How did he know? "We saw you smoking." He answered my unasked question. Impossible, I thought, I had checked the roof. We could see no one, how could anyone see us?

"We are from the police station," he said, pointing to a squat red building in the distance. But how could anyone see us from so far away? Again my question was answered. The guy must be psychic. "We have been watching you with binoculars." Achmad explained in English, we didn't understand the word for 'binoculars'. Perverted bastards. Lousy peeping toms. They knew everyone smoked dope. It's part of their way of life. It's even grown legally, probably their biggest source of income. I had seen circles of Moroccan men smoking chillums on street corners right in the medina. Why didn't they watch them with binoculars? Fraudulent creeps.

Achmad was talking to the smaller man in Arabic. I decided to say nothing and let him handle matters. I had learned that when dealing with police, customs, or any officialdom, not to volunteer anything, to speak only when spoken to, and to answer questions giving a minimum of information.

"I told him we have no hashish," Achmad said, giving us our cue. But he is going to search us."

Search us? The coffee soured in my stomach. How could Achmad conceal that massive chunk of dope, and what about my piece? The heavier police officer opened his briefcase, obviously in charge, and took out a clean sheet of paper and a freshly sharpened pencil. He cleared a space on the table with a display of efficiency, and sat down, the paper and pencil arranged before him. He was loving this. I was first. "Name?" he asked in a disinterested official tone. I told him. He wrote it down. "Address?" I told him. He wrote it down. "Age?" I told him. "Country of origin?" He wrote everything down, slowly, carefully, with a sense of infinite purpose, his gold ring glinting on his pudgy finger. "Do you smoke hashish?" His tone did not change.

"No." He wrote 'No' without looking up. Ronit and Annilee went through the same interrogation. Thank goodness they were clean. I had warned them against carrying dope in the street, instilling in them the fear of God. They had listened. Why hadn't I? I was good at giving advice, not so good at taking it.

When he finished with the questions, the policemen frisked the Moroccans. Achmad was last. My body was rigid against the impending disaster, bracing myself as though for a crash. But miraculously they found nothing. I knew Annilee, Ronit and I wouldn't be touched. A male policeman could not touch a female suspect. At least there were a few Moroccan rules one could count on.

"Empty your pockets," the policeman instructed us. There were two pockets between the three of us, one belonging to me. Nothing.

"Empty your bags." Ronit had a small bag containing her English-Arabic notebook, pencil, and an empty change purse. He opened the notebook. Achmad translated the English, word by word, "market", "camel", "hotel", then her party piece. "Money? I have no money. But I have one friend, very crazy." The policeman looked at Ronit as though she came from Mars and put the notebook in his briefcase to decode later.

He signalled Annilee to follow the thinner policeman to another table. I dumped the contents of my bag, trying to appear calm, even bored. I was terrified. Nothing could save me now. Shimon had been right all along. What kind of mother would expose her child to this? And what about Aviva and Cedric, they were finally beginning to trust Morocco and me. At least Ronit and Annilee wouldn't be incriminated. Aviva would look after Ronit. Ronit would be happy living with David, and she adored Aviva. Cedric would have to do another benefit concert. Then panic emptied my mind. I obeyed as though hypnotised, like the snakes in the square, the policeman playing the tune.

A multiple of sundries fell on the table. A map of Marrakesh, a plastic container of contraceptive pills, two crushed tampons, a small purse, a wallet, some old letters I kept intending to answer, pen and paper, a few candied almonds stuck with fluff, a purple velvet ribbon, a portable douche bag - shit why was I carrying that - a cosmetic case, and the dreaded Kleenex bunched up tight like white knuckles. He shook the bag, examining it for hidden pockets then checked the seams. His dedication was admirable.

"Open that," he commanded pointing to the small purse. I complied, sliding the zip, spilling the coins on the table. "And that." He indicated the cosmetic case with a flick of the head. Obediently, in a neat row, I lined up a vial of perfumed Moroccan oil, an eye-liner pencil and a tube of 'erase', pimple cover-up. Pathetic. He pointed to the wallet. I extracted a jumble of miscellany, a bankers card, expired driving license, some photos, a few American dollars, and something scribbled on a scrap of paper. He picked up the paper scrutinising it as though discovering some vital bit of information, and held it away from me in case I would grab the evidence and swallow it.

"What is this?" he glowered accusingly.

"My boyfriend's name," I answered passively. The previous night I had been in a disco dancing with a Dutch guy. At the end of the evening I asked him his name. He wrote it on a shred of newspaper and I had shoved it in my wallet. I hadn't looked at it until now. The policeman held the paper for me to read. I made out the words , "33 M.D." I shrugged. After all I wasn't responsible for Dutch names. Grudgingly, he accepted, but the scrap of paper went into his decoding bag.

"What is that?" He picked up a tampon, regarding it with suspicion.

"*Feminina!*" I lashed out like a slap on the hand. Somehow violated, my mesmerised state of passivity was suddenly replaced by a desire to hit back. The tampon dropped. He picked up the contraceptive pills. "*Feminina,*" I barked the magic word. He put the packet down like a disease. Feminina strikes again.

But my small victory collapsed as I scanned the battlefield. Little else remained to be inspected. The sword was hovering. I could feel the lump of hashish in its white shroud like an insidious growth, pulsating, spreading, malignant. It was drawing me, powerful, like gravity, to my doom. I forced my eyes away from it, willing the policeman's attention elsewhere. He picked up the douche bag.

"*Feminina!*" I snapped. Either he wasn't buying yet another feminina, or else thought he was on to something big. With an air of supreme superiority, as though confident of delivering the fatal blow, he unhooked the clasp. But his high and mightiness suffered a serious set-back as he peered inside. For a confused moment he hesitated, then gingerly withdrew the folded rubber bag from the case. The rubber was thin, almost transparent and slightly clammy. He held it between his manicured thumb and forefinger, like a used condom - it was a similar colour - and laid it aside with distaste, wiping his fingers with a handkerchief. With severely diminished assurance he fumbled in the case and removed several pieces of hard plastic tubing, regarding them uncomfortably. Perhaps he was big with the binoculars but he wasn't too good with the douche bag.

"Permetez-moi monsieur," I gallantly offered, expertly snapping the bits together, producing a device resembling an enema nozzle and displaying it with satisfaction. He became visibly embarrassed, perhaps fearing I would attempt a demonstration. Deciding not to probe further into the mysteries of foreign femininity, he began to reassemble the intimidating apparatus. The soft rubber bag and the parts forming the nozzle would fit into the compact container only if placed a specific way. Having no experience with douche bag assembly, he was trying to jam the contents into the case, becoming increasingly rattled as the parts seemed greater than the whole. His cool was crumbling.

I don't know if it's my inherent criminal nature, or the flush of health in the dying, or just my perversity when confronted by the law, but as he grew more flustered, I became increasingly calm. With a sense of the kill I was aware of his disadvantage. I struck. Very casually, I reached across the table, picked up the Kleenex, blew my nose, and slipped the whole lot into my pocket. Nothing happened. The policeman had somehow forced all the bits into the container and was trying not to show his relief. His ordeal was over. He signalled me to put my things back, femininas and all. Then pretending to write some dignified notes on his paper, he spoke with authority in Arabic to the other policeman and gathered up his belongings.

The policemen left, taking the two Moroccan boys with them. Achmad remained behind. I felt a rush of elation but sat very still not even daring to embrace Ronit, in case big binoculared brother was watching.

194

"They found nothing," Achmad said proudly.

"How come? What happened to your dope?" I asked, with a blend of bewilderment and relief.

"I kept it under the table on the floor. When I saw them coming I kicked it off the roof," Achmad said as though stating some obvious.

So he hadn't returned it to his sock after all. Too close.

"What will happen to the other boys and to my note book?" Ronit asked, surprising me with her calm.

"To the two boys, nothing. In the tourist season they have plenty foreigners with money, they do not bother with Moroccans. They will just ask some questions and let them go. And I will get the book back from them, no problem."

"No problem? Listen Achmad, I almost ended up in jail and Ronit almost ended up without a mother," I said with an attempt at castigation, although the elation persisted, and the relief was overwhelming.

"You had such a small piece, I would have got you out, no problem."

I'm glad I didn't have to put that particular 'no problem' to the test.

Annilee and Ronit celebrated with a visit to the loo. Achmad went to retrieve the hashish. I celebrated with a stricter set of dope resolutions. I promised myself I would never risk anything like that again, never, never, never. Achmad returned with more iced coffee, orange juice, and a Herald Tribune. I sat in the sun with my feet up, sipped my iced coffee and read the Herald Tribune, giving the 'up yours' signal, just in case the binoculars were in focus. But inside I was trembling.

17. Guest Appearance

In discussing the police incident later that day with Ronit, I was impressed by her easy acceptance, her lack of upset or agitation, as though it was simply another experience in the vast Moroccan happening.

"Weren't you scared when you saw me suddenly appear with those two heavies?" I asked, attempting to probe her reactions.

"I knew something was wrong and I was worried at first because I didn't know what was happening and why they were there, but as soon as I saw it was a dope bust I wasn't worried any more."

"Why?" I asked somewhat incredulous, I would have thought a drug bust would be a major worry for her, a sinister encounter.

"Well, we didn't have any dope on us and we weren't smoking, so what could they do? I knew you could get us out of that one." She had more confidence in me than I had.

"But I didn't know you had a piece of hash in your pocket." she admitted, "Had I known that I would have been scared stiff."

"I'm really sorry Ronit. Achmad just shoved it into my hand and I couldn't make a scene in the middle of the Place Djema el Fna, the safest thing was to hide it in my bag. I feel terrible about that."

I must have looked utterly miserable because she said. "It's not your fault, don't feel bad, you're usually so careful." She paused thoughtfully then said, "do you think Achmad was setting us up?"

"I thought about that too, but I honestly don't think he was. Word would get out fast among the Westerners, he's so high profile, he's the recommendation in Marrakesh, he depends on Westerners for his business, besides I trust him, he's an O.K. guy."

"I guess you're right. Just a thought."

"I'll have to be a lot more careful in future."

"But don't blame yourself, it wasn't your fault, anyway it all worked out, nothing bad happened," she put her arm around my shoulder to compound her reassurance.

It was strange the way our roles often reversed and Ronit looked after me, protected me, was concerned about my well-being. I remembered an incident in London before we left for Morocco. Shimon had cut his small allowance for Ronit and I was having difficulty getting extra teaching work. We were very hard up. Ronit had outgrown her clothes but I couldn't afford new ones. She made do by adding borders to her jeans to lengthen them, embroidering flowers over holes in her blouses and mending everything mendable. The few clothes she did buy came from jumble sales, even her shoes were second-hand. And, to my great regret, I could never afford to let her go horseback riding, the activity she loved most and had so looked forward to enjoying in England.

Then my brother came to London, and we went to visit him in his posh hotel suite. He knew I was short of money and had offered to help. But I had refused. Long ago I had made a point of not accepting money from anyone, feeling I had no right to it. When I was Ronit's age I left home to finish high school and to study dance in New York, working after school to support myself. I remember being so poor that I couldn't afford underwear but I never let on, never accepted money from my parents. I never have since. Financial independence gave me the freedom I craved, more important to me than all else. It was my contention that if I had chosen a life style of travel, adventure, avoidance of career and commitment, I had to be able to sustain it, I had no right to expect others to sustain it for me. They were probably doing work I would hate to do, taking risks I refused to take. If I chose to, I could easily make my own sacrifices for financial gain, I had no right to exploit theirs.

That night my brother was treating Ronit and me to dinner in a superb seafood restaurant where we could eat lobster, my absolute favourite. In our enthusiasm we had arrived early and had to wait while he showered and dressed. Before getting into the shower he called from the bedroom.

"I just emptied my pockets on the dressing table. I have no idea how much money I have, so I won't know if you've taken any. You might as well help yourself. I promise you I won't know the difference, and I won't miss it."

I knew his European business was doing extremely well. When we heard the water hitting the glass shower compartment we went into the bedroom. Heaped on the small table was a profusion of notes, English pounds, American dollars, Spanish pesetas, Italian lira, German marks, - it looked like the King's Counting Table.

"How can he get all that into his pockets?" Ronit asked, gaping in disbelief.

"He must have big pockets," I answered, marvelling at the colourful global spectrum spread before us.

Ronit was impressed and excited. "I've never seen so much money. Mummy this is wonderful. I'm so happy. He's so great. How much are we going to take?" She could hardly contain herself.

"We're not going to take any."

She was stunned. "Not any? But he wants us to have it; he's being generous to us, you must take some."

She observed my resolute expression and said, "just take a little, he said he won't know the difference, so even if you don't take any he won't know."

"But I'll know the difference."

"But mummy please," she begged, "you'll be able to fix your tooth." I had broken my tooth and couldn't spare the money to fix it. "Just take thirty pounds to fix your tooth, he must have hundreds there, not for anything else, just for your tooth." She was almost in tears.

I didn't take the money but I was deeply moved by Ronit's compassion. She hadn't requested anything for herself, no clothes, no horseback riding, nothing, her concern was for me. More the selflessness of a mother for her child. However, in my heart of hearts I knew that if push came to shove and the broken tooth had been hers, I would have adjusted my principles as part of a continuous effort to balance my needs with hers. (Years later when Ronit had finished college and went on to make money, 'tired of being poor', her first splash out was in the Harrod's Ladieswear Department, where the Queen shopped. She abruptly abandoned the ethnic/hippy look we both favoured and opted for a more classical look - tempered by a punk hairdo sporting pink and green spikes.) But now, although she didn't fully comprehend my axiom that one had to finance one's chosen life style on one's own, she accepted it without recrimination.

That concern for me was especially evident when we were travelling. In Morocco it expressed itself in many ways. One of the most endearing exhibited itself at meal times. Our group meals were frequently served, Moroccan style, in one central tagine dish. Because I ate very slowly, Ronit, anxious that I wasn't getting my fair share, would set aside choice bits. "I have to be sure my little mom is getting enough to eat," she would explain. I loved her for it.

Our most spectacular Marrakesh surprise occurred the day before we were leaving for Essaouira. We were all lazily finishing lunch in a café facing the square, stilled by the intense heat, looking forward to a siesta in a cool room, or perhaps a swim in the pool Cedric had discovered, when suddenly Aviva emitted a piercing wail, "Oh no....I don't believe it," and clamped her hands over her eyes to shut out some horror. I peered through the decreased high noon activity of the square to see a powerful figure stomping toward us, like a buffalo bulldozing a path through a tangle of bush, causing the gazelles and deer to leap out of its way. He was wearing a brown felt hat pulled over his forehead, baggy khaki shorts and was mopping his face with a red kerchief. It was Irving. He appeared before us, grinning. I viewed him through the harsh sunlight, an apparition, an alien descended from space. Finally Aviva dared to uncover her eyes and moaned, "what the hell are you doing here?"

"I came to see my maidel and my son," Irving said matter of factly, as if it was the most natural thing in the world.

Cedric was the only one with any presence of mind, he brought a chair for Irving and set it at our table. Irving sat down beside Aviva.

"Isn't anybody glad to see me? A welcome like this I could get if I was coming from a leper colony."

David went up to him. "Hi dad. You sure look kooky in that hat."

"Hello son." Irving put his arm around David's shoulder. "You look well. I think you've grown," he boomed.

"How the hell did you find me?" Aviva groaned in exasperation, "and why are you wearing those awful shorts?"

He ignored the shorts question. "I used my noodle. I phoned Toronto several times from Italy and when I couldn't reach you I phoned your agent, he always knows where you are. He gave me Marrakesh *poste restante* as your forwarding address. So I got on a plane and headed for Marrakesh. The post office gave me your hotel address and the concierge obligingly told me you were in the square having lunch."

That elusive Telegraph Arab again, I thought. Somehow the Moroccans always knew where we were. Another one of the mysteries.

"You see I used my noodle," Irving said proudly, tapping his head with his forefinger.

"Well you almost didn't use it good enough because we're leaving here tomorrow and you never would have found us."

"Ah, but I arrived today. Like I always say, 'poets make lucky things happen'. Come on friends, let's celebrate my arrival with a bottle of wine."

"You can't get wine here," Aviva grunted.

"Well let's celebrate with something."

"Let's have brown cows, that's coca cola with ice cream," David said eagerly, quick to play the advantage.

"Fine. Seven brown cows." Irving signalled the waiter. "It's really good to see all of you here," he said glancing around the table with satisfaction, his eyes coming to rest on Aviva. "Let's have a kiss maidel," he said softly, taking her hand.

Aviva was unable to resist. They embraced.

"Irving, I just don't believe you," she sighed. "I don't think I'll ever understand the things you do."

"As long as you keep trying, that's all I ask," he replied, good-humouredly. "Well, have you been having a good time in Morocco?" he asked, brimming with good will, and an almost fatherly interest.

As though Aviva's embrace was a signal, we all burst into animated conversation recounting our Moroccan adventures. David was especially voluble, having much to relate.

"Dad, I met this Moroccan boy in the market place and we became friends, you know we horsed around together, and yesterday he came with mom and me to a shop and a policeman grabbed him and took him away...he wasn't even doing anything wrong, was he mom?" Mom shook her head in agreement.

"I've never seen David so upset," she said. Even the retelling agitated him and he continued breathlessly.

"Well how would you like it if some crummy cop suddenly came and took you away, just like that. It was scary. Mom and I went to the police station to see what was happening. Mohammed, that's my friend's name, but I call him Mo Mo, well anyway he was arrested because Moroccan boys are not supposed to pester tourists. I couldn't believe it dad." David paled remembering. "He has no parents, nobody to help him, so the police said he had to stay in jail. Mom talked her head off to all the policemen, she told them Mo Mo wasn't bothering us, she said we asked him to come with us. We spent the whole afternoon in the police station, mom said we wouldn't go away until Mo Mo came with us and you know how mom can talk. In the end she had to sign some papers for them to release Mo Mo. Poor Mo Mo was crying. I was so glad to see him get out of jail that I gave him my new cowboy hat mom bought me for my birthday. And when we get back to Canada I'm going to send him half my allowance every week. Honest dad." Ronit put her arm

201

around David's shoulder. He reached for his brown cow and sipped with unusual restraint.

We chatted over several rounds of brown cows, Irving encouraging us to tell more, intrigued by our experiences.

"Cedric, what are you doing here?" he asked.

"Just being one of the girls," Cedric lisped. Throughout the talk, the banter, the recounting of stories, Aviva said little, her eyelids alternately lowered, gazing into her undrunk brown cow, then suddenly raised, staring at Irving as though to confirm his reality.

Aviva was bewildered, caught completely off-guard by Irving's crash landing. "Just when I was feeling so good," she confided to me later that evening, "just when I was letting go of him, just when I was enjoying my visits with Mustafa, looking forward to seeing Bashir, turning on to other guys, turning on to myself, getting sex out of my head and putting it where it belongs, Irving falls from the sky to ruin everything."

"Don't let him. It's your choice."

"How can I help it? He has this insidious way of sneaking back into my life like a bad odour. It's like the time I kicked him out, you remember. We had that big scene after the Governor General awards fiasco. I said I couldn't take any more humiliation, he said he couldn't take any more jealous tantrums and that he was leaving. I told him to go to hell. He packed a bag and left. I slammed the door so hard I broke the stain glass window. I was frothing at the mouth like a mad dog. I changed the locks and told everyone we had separated, something I'd never done before. This was it. The final break. Several nights later I was having some people over, John, my publisher, his wife and a friend of theirs. Irving must have found out because when the doorbell rang and I opened the door to let them in, suddenly there was Irving. He had crept in behind them, hunched over so I wouldn't see him. He simply proceeded to make himself at home, like nothing had happened, took everyone's coat, played the perfect host. What gall. He was counting on the fact that I wouldn't make a fuss in front of John. In the end I had to laugh. What else could I do? There he was, in like Flynn, and it all felt so familiar. It was his home as well as mine. It seemed silly to throw him out at that point. We both laughed, and he stayed."

"But what will you do now?"

"I wish I knew," she said fingering a silver bracelet Mustafa had made for her. "I didn't tell him I knew he was with Marta. When he asked me how come I was in Morocco and not in Toronto, I said I'd explain some other time. I guess he sensed something was terribly amiss because he left it at that. When I asked him how come he wasn't in Italy, he said, 'too many tourists and I missed my maidel too much'. I just let that pass which, as you know, is not my style. Ordinarily I'd be rubbing my hands in sinister glee, like an old witch, while I'd set the trap for him. I'd bait it with his lies, allowing him to tell me lie after lie, pretending to believe him, drawing him further into the trap, and then bang, I'd spring the catch with something delicious like, 'as a matter of fact, I was at the airport to see you off, and I just happened to see you board the plane. You looked very happy, but why not, you were wearing your favourite whore on your arm, showing her off for all the world to see, and now you're here because she gave you a rotten time.' I'd derive great satisfaction from trapping him like that with his pants down. Then we'd have one of our scenes and I'd cry and shout and rave and rant and go through the list of his unforgivable sins, wallowing in every infidelity. And finally he'd make me all sorts of promises and we'd make love, and everything would be fine... until the next time. I never realised how predictable it all was," she sighed.

"But this time I couldn't get into that scenario. The actors were there, the script was all too familiar, I knew most of the lines by heart, mine and his, but I couldn't strut and fret my hour upon the stage. Perhaps it's the set that's so different, the lighting, the props, the backdrop, the entire staging. Ours is the kind of theatre that doesn't travel well. I'm feeling so relaxed, so good, so not uptight about anything, for a change. I'm enjoying myself. Remember how shattered I was when we first arrived, what a mess I was? I'm healthier now, stronger in the head, more confident about myself as a woman - I'm enjoying being female. I feel a new strain of something developing in me, something important, and I like it, I don't want to lose it, to stunt its growth. I resent Irving bursting into my trip, uninvited and taking over. It's inevitable that he'll take over and I'll end up catering for him, running with pillows to cushion things for him, doing his laundry, making sure he doesn't wear those awful shorts, arranging his good times. I don't want it. I've been on his trip too long. This is my trip. I want to keep it mine."

I knew exactly what she meant. If it was anyone's trip, it was hers. As she allowed herself to enjoy the sensuality of Morocco, she in turn, radiated a sensuousness, an appeal which drew the Moroccans to her like bees around the honey flower. When we were all together it was she who received most of the male attention, despite Annilee's prettiness, Ronit's youth and my experience, it was Aviva who exuded that indefinable touch of magic. She finally came not only to accept it and to trust it, but to flourish on it. She blossomed visibly, opening like a flower, petal by petal.

"Then tell him to put his knapsack on his back and go climb a mountain, like he's always wanted to do," I suggested.

But Aviva's heart wasn't in it. When it came to the crunch, the only time she could hit back at Irving was when she was enraged by something in the present, usually some woman. Her fury had to be urgent, immediate. The incident at the airport and her violent reaction to it, her need to savage, seemed long ago, dimmed, in the past. Desire for revenge, desire to wound Irving had been sunned away in Morocco. Now she simply wanted to 'do her thing', travel with her knapsack on her back, far away from Irving's influence without the desire to breathe vengeance, inflict pain. In the end the best she could do was tell him she needed some time on her own, and that she would let him know when she was ready to be with him. For whatever the reason, guilt, compassion, love, or lack of choice, Irving was compliant. He agreed to stay on in

Marrakesh. Our journey would proceed, for the time being, as planned, without Irving. Cedric too decided to remain in Marrakesh for a week or so before joining us in Essaouira. He loved Marrakesh and was glad of a companion to share it with. Aviva's maternal soul was secretly comforted knowing that Irving would not be alone during his first time in Morocco. She could leave for Essaouira with an easy mind. However, it was no longer the same; just knowing Irving was somewhere in Morocco was an invasion of her privacy. He would be an invisible concern.

As it turned out, Cedric did remain in Marrakesh for another week, but Irving could not maintain his distance from Aviva. After the second day he grew restless, uneasy. He needed Aviva's presence, if only as a scent in his periphery, to enable him to relax into an unfamiliar setting. Morocco exaggerated this tendency. It was a country so alien to him that Aviva's anchorage was indispensable before he could master any of its overwhelming foreignness and enjoy its exotic offerings. Besides, he hadn't come to Morocco to see Marrakesh, he had come to reclaim Aviva.

On the third day he made another guest appearance, this time in Essaouira. Aviva was almost pleased to see him. So was I, with reservations. For my own selfish reasons I was glad Irving was in Morocco, that is if it wouldn't interfere with my time with Aviva or Aviva's time with herself, if somehow they could manage the quiescence between them I had seen them enjoy on the Greek Islands - a tall order in present circumstances.

Irving's sensibility was unique. He experienced events on such a different level that he would add a philosophical sub-text, another dimension, to our Moroccan adventure. He had a special talent for penetrating to the soul of an experience, an ability to reveal the essence of a person or a place, which he seemed able to absorb by osmosis. I remember an exasperated Aviva complaining as we drove through a spectacular Greek landscape with Irving's head buried in a book.

"Irving you're not even looking - for god's sake, look!" To which

Irving casually replied, "You look...I'll tell you what you see."

This was no idle boast. He had a special gift for comprehension be it of life or of literature, like an extra sense able to probe subtleties, nuances, and a way of extrapolating from that comprehension which produced a new awareness, even a sense of revelation. It was that same talent which had me taking every course he gave in my university days. He had the power of seeing coupled with the power of communication. His presence, if he could give Aviva the space she required, if she could take that space and keep the trip her own, could be an unexpected bonus.

18. The Tattoo

Next morning we were waved goodbye by a forlorn and incongruous farewell committee - Irving, a solid robust figure accustomed to battling the Canadian north, displaced on to an exotic, Arabian Nights setting; Cedric, a Canadian actor with the agility of a gymnast and a deftness with words, grinning through a worried grimace, with only a Hand of Fatima to sustain him in a land whose foreign tongues prevented him from juggling language and forced him into a cultural straight jacket; Mo Mo, a normally invisible Marrakesh street urchin, flamboyant in a Western cowboy hat, several sizes too large.

David bravely fought the tears as he shook Mo Mo's hand, awkwardly covering his heart with his hand in a touching attempt to express special significance, although the gesture was one of greeting rather than leave taking.

"I will come back to see you very soon, don't worry." David consoled both himself and Mo Mo. Aviva had promised he would return to Marrakesh the instant she could arrange the trip.

I watched the faces of dear friends recede with an acute sense of loss, as though not only leaving a vital part of myself, but leaving the good times, the Moroccan adventure itself, momentarily forgetting that we were going on to new adventures, perhaps even better times. With unusual quiet we settled into the journey submerged in a bitter-sweet sadness, grieving for a Marrakesh slipping from the vibrancy of reality into the quiescence of memory, the further we travelled. Driving through a deserty landscape, strewn with stray camels, echoed the aridity in my heart.

After several hours, a road sign pointed to Essaouira, the countryside turned green and I knew we would soon be there. I closed my eyes for the final stretch of contemplation, my thoughts abruptly abandoning the ache of Marrakesh and with a fickle surge of anticipation I remembered Essaouira and Salim. I hoped Salim was still in Essaouira so that Ronit, Aviva and Annilee could meet him - especially Aviva.

He was the kind of enigma she couldn't resist, the perfect remedy to expunge debilitating preoccupations with Irving.

Essaouira, one of my favourite places, was a small town cradled in a bay of the Atlantic. White houses reaching to the sea were enclosed by an ancient wall built by the Portuguese, its ramparts silhouetted against the sky. Stone archways curved over the narrow streets and led through the wall to the sea. At one end of the wall the waves crashed black and fierce against a ruined castle rising out of the fortifications, at the other end they lapped against the beach, gently rippling the white sand. On previous visits I had come to the wall often, fascinated by the contrasts it revealed. It was here that I had first met Salim. He fascinated me like the wall itself.

With me Salim was always charming, the perfect gentleman, but I had been warned against him by the Moroccans I knew who cautioned me in guarded tones to keep away from him, telling me he was a bad man, not to be trusted. "He's from Algeria," one of them whispered, shrugging his shoulders in a what-can-you-expect attitude.

"Algerians are thieves, they carry knifes, be careful of them." Salim did carry a knife. It was a switch-blade, classified as a dangerous weapon and illegal to possess. Though it was usually concealed, I had been witness to its sudden flick and the flash of its sinister blade as he smilingly peeled an orange, teeth gleaming, green eyes flashing, hair glinting blue-black in the sun. There was something polished and shining hard about Salim, like the steel blade of his knife. At night he prowled the streets with his half-grown Siamese cat coiled on his shoulder. Like his cat, he was always watchful, tensed for the pounce, his body sinewy, taut, on the hunt. I liked him with an uneasy liking, unsure when the handshake would become a vice. He never trusted anyone, myself included, and I maintained a careful friendship, never getting within pouncing range. I knew instinctively that I didn't dare risk losing his friendship. Walking that wary tight-rope with Salim intrigued me.

Each time I came to Essaouira I brought him a gift, always jewellery. He adored jewellery. A silver snake embraced his wrist, heavy silver rings twisted through his fingers and a jade earing shone in one ear like a third eye. "Did you bring anything for Salim?" was his first question whenever we met. He was delighted by presents, glowing like a child on Christmas day, reassured he was remembered. Later when I'd meet him on the street he'd proudly show me he was wearing the gift I had brought him. This time I outdid myself, unable to resist a silver hawk with a green emerald eye, its talons extended, hung on a chain.

He moved house frequently, but his rooms always looked the same, elaborately arranged in Arabic style with wall hangings, low seats covered with woven materials and surrounded by pillows, small round tables, thick Moroccan rugs, bowls of fruit, silver trays, and always a view of the sea and the wall. He would invariably invite me to remain as his guest, and I would invariably refuse. "Then come for dinner. I will make fish tagine." He knew my weakness for his fish tagine, made with that day's catch from the port. Other friends were invited and he would prepare an excellent tagine, spiced by live Arabic music. He played the Moroccan tam-tam drums. He was the perfect host, aware of everyone's needs, supplying an endless stream of grapes, melons, cakes and hashish. By dawn most of the guests would be draped over the rugs and pillows, asleep.

It was mid-summer when our beat-up Vera rolled into Essaouira bearing her cargo of ladies and David. We headed directly to my favourite pension only to discover it was full. I hadn't counted on that. This was my first time in Morocco during the summer months; I preferred lapping up the sunshine in winter when it was scarce in England and Canada. I wasn't prepared for the influx of people into Essaouira, mainly Moroccans from Marrakesh, trying to escape the desperate heat there. Aviva and David managed to get a room in a less appealing, more expensive hotel, and Annilee, being mobile, moved in temporarily with Azdine, a Moroccan I knew who lived on a farm several kilometres from town, but Ronit and I could find nothing. Wandering around town, looking for someone who could help us, we ran into Salim. He was delighted to see me and welcomed Ronit warmly. Upon hearing our problem, he immediately invited us to stay with him until a room became available in the pension. This time I agreed. We had no choice. I was pleased I had brought him a special gift.

That evening, sipping mint tea, leaning into the pillows and the candlelight, Salim, Ronit and I listened to music. The room was warm and Salim rolled up his shirt sleeves. I noticed the edge of a tattoo peeping under the sleeve of his upper arm. I hadn't seen it before and inspected it more closely. It said, 'love', a message I would not have suspected Salim of harbouring.

"I never knew you were tattooed, Salim. Do you have any more?" I asked, idly wondering what other unusual messages he concealed.

He didn't answer at once and I glanced at him to see if he had heard. His expression was surprisingly stern. "I have one tattoo, very special."

"Can I see it?" I asked, only casually interested.

He was suddenly formal, withdrawing into an erect posture.

"No!" He seemed unnecessarily sharp. Now I was genuinely interested.

"Why not?" He remained silent. The question penetrated the layers of stillness and hung uncomfortably. I looked at him, waiting.

"Because it is on my sex," he said finally, meeting my eyes head on.

"What?" Ronit squealed. She had been browsing through Salim's tapes only half listening, but was suddenly alert. "On your sex?" she repeated, looking at me for verification.

"Yes," he said curtly.

"What do you have tattooed there?" she asked, perplexed.

I could tell that Salim was not anxious to continue the discussion, but I persisted. "Come on Salim, tell us," I urged, aware that I must not press too hard, but spurred on by an unrelenting curiosity.

Again silence. Then, as though forced into a decision, he said, with a combination of pride and arrogance, "I have my name, 'Salim', tattooed on my sex and an arrow pointing to the head. On the head I have a flower."

We both stared at him, unable to believe this incredibly vital statistic. But there was something about his manner which convinced me he was telling the truth. It was too outrageous a lie.

"It's not true Salim," Ronit protested, unable to compute the information, "you can't have a tattoo there."

His spine stiffened, his voice verged on irritation, "I do not lie."

"But it's not possible," I said, trying to visualise the tattooing process. Then on a sudden impulse, "would you show it to us?" He hesitated for a fraction of a second aware that his integrity, his honour was being challenged.

"No." he said, decisively, his eyes narrow and cold. His tone eliminated the possibility of further debate.

"Why did you want your name tattooed there?" Ronit asked puzzled, "where no one can see it?"

He regained his bravado. "Because when I am in a woman I want her to know Salim is there."

Salim's secret was suddenly exposed. Normally I have great respect for a secret and pride myself with being entirely able to keep one, but this secret was too splendid to hoard. I couldn't wait to tell Aviva, which I did at the first opportunity. She and Annilee were still unpacking Vera.

"Did you see it?" Annilee asked excited.

"No. He's not into showing.

"I must get to see it," Aviva decided.

As I predicted, she had been attracted to Salim from the first moment she laid eyes on him. "What a gorgeous, wild, sexy thing," she had said, closing her eyes and tasting her lips. "I'll think of a way."

Salim was Arabic hospitality incarnate. He insisted on giving Ronit and me his bed with its embroidered pillow cases, obtained by an undisclosed method from a bride's dowry. He played soft music to put us sweetly to sleep. He made coffee in the morning and served it to us in bed with fresh bread and honey. Only once did we catch a glimpse of the dark side of Salim. A Moroccan came to see him. Salim greeted the man with a smile of steel. They spoke Arabic which I couldn't understand, but I could see the venom poisoning Salim's face, distorting it with rage, although his voice remained calm, even pleasant. All at once his elbow shot out, like the sudden flick of the switch-blade, and he jabbed it, dagger hard, into the man's ribs. It happened so fast that the threatening stab of fear I experienced had no time to materialize. Salim continued talking without a pause or change of tone. The man said nothing and soon left. "Business," he explained. I didn't dare question him. However, with us he was considerate, generous and always entertaining. We didn't mention his special tattoo again, but were acutely aware of its presence.

On our third day in Essaouira Irving put in his second surprise appearance. I think Aviva was half expecting it, besides the second crime is no longer a sin. She decided not to challenge Irving's presence until she could examine her reactions to it and sort out her priorities. If he would allow her the space to do this, the space to pursue her own agenda she would maintain a civil geniality. Irving, thankful to be in Essaouira without the anticipated traumatic reunion, was quick to agree. He had his own agenda, he wanted sun and sea, he wanted to write and he wanted to contact Scott Symons, a fellow Canadian writer and friend living outside Essaouira. He was content to slip into our scene and enjoy whatever he could of it, delighted to explore Morocco and the potential for poetry it afforded in the embrace of family and friends.

News of Salim's tattoo reached Irving quickly and he related to it with profound connection. Irving was known as 'the man who took the pants off Canadian poetry'. His intense preoccupation with masculinity was evident both in his poetry and in his life. He bucked convention and battled a 'castrated morality' armed with curses, bombast and a bronco energy. Physically he gave the impression of an armoured warrior, with his massive head of iron-gray hair, heavy neck, fortress-like chest, arms and legs like clubs and a charging energy. Salim's tattoo was significantly relevant to him.

When I introduced Irving to Salim there was an instant flash of recognition between them. Salim boasted to Irving that he never worked, preferring to live off whatever and whoever he could. "Only fools work. Work is for the slaves. Me, I am no slave." He flashed Irving one of his radiant smiles.

"Good man," Irving clapped him on the back, "kick them in the balls." Salim became a potential poem.

His eyes shone, flattered by Irving's approval.

"I invite you all to my home for tagine," he announced expansively. "I will make fish tagine to celebrate my friend Irving."

Indifferent to the reason for the invitation, my mouth watered in the best Pavlovian tradition.

Before going to Salim's we all met at a café. While drinking tea Aviva announced, "I've thought of a way to see Salim's tattoo." I was sure she'd come through. Irving applauded. By this time his poet's imagination was inflamed by the idea, with the added respect one male must have for another who possesses such a remarkable tattoo.

For Irving, experience was potential poetry. I could feel the poem shaping in his head. I listened to Aviva's plan with keen interest and a large measure of apprehension, somewhat sceptical about its wisdom. Knowing more about Salim and Arabic attitudes to sexuality, I was worried that it could backfire and turn ugly. But in the end I agreed that if it worked we would be witness to a feat belonging in the *Guinness Book of Records*. It was worth the risk.

Salim's room looked enchanting that night, soft with candlelight and warm colours. Bowls of fruit and nuts were arranged on tables with a circle of little glasses for mint tea. We removed our sandals and sat cross-legged on pillows around the small low tables. Salim had invited no other guests. There were only the four ladies and Irving. David had gone to bed early, to dream of Mo Mo. He was leaving for Marrakesh next morning with Rosy, Andrew and their two children, close London friends who had recently joined us and who were meeting Cedric in Marrakesh

The houseboy brought warm water and towels to wash our hands. We opened the wine we had brought. Then ceramic dishes were set before us filled with succulent spicy fish and vegetables. Salim broke chunks out of flat Arabic breads and passed them around. He removed the bones from the fish, placing pieces in front of each of us, making sure we all tasted the choice morsels. We dipped our bread into the rich tangy sauce and scooped bits of fish and vegetables from the tagine dish. Irving's chin shone saffron gold. Aviva's fingers dripped as she plunged them into her mouth, sucking through pursed lips. I closed my eyes among the pillows savouring the splendid sauce and the chunks of firm white fish with the delicacy of lobster.

Salim was at his best, pouring wine, breaking bread, bringing more food. After the tagine there were large purple figs, Moroccan cakes and mint tea. Pipes were passed with smoke from Salim's finest collection. We leaned back suffused with that special sense of well-being which comes from abandoning oneself to the pleasures of an exquisite meal.

"Let's play a game," Aviva's voice was deceptively casual. A nervous twitch fluttered in my stomach, disturbing the placidly digesting tagine. I had almost forgotten.

"I know a good one. Only two people can play at a time," Aviva continued, then half turning to Salim, "do you want to play with me?"

I could feel a wave of excitement pull each of us into a new posture, a flick of energy stabbing the aftermath of content. Irving stood up.

"Yes, why not?" Salim said. "What is the game?"

"It's called strip."

No reaction from Salim, and I wondered if he understood the

214

word 'strip'. Aviva produced a deck of cards.

"I deal one card at a time to each of us," she explained. "The first person to get two of the same cards, wins. After each round the loser has to take off one item, one piece of clothing."

Salim said nothing for a dangerous moment. We waited uneasily. Then he smiled wickedly, "Wacha! OK."

I couldn't tell if he understood our game and was playing his own and grew more excited.

One round was played. Salim won. Aviva rolled off one of her socks. She waved it above her head. We all cheered. Salim won again. Aviva took off the other sock. We cheered more enthusiastically. Salim's involvement in the game increased visibly, his eyes glistening, his features sharp. He won a third time. Aviva took off her blouse and threw it to Irving on the other side of the room.

"*Olé! Olé!*" Irving shouted, stamping his heels and flaring the blouse like a toreador provoking a bull. Should he title the poem 'The Tattoo' or simply 'Salim'? Aviva was wearing a red bra. I never knew she owned one. Salim's muscles tensed in a ready-to-spring posture. Exhilaration mounted. But I was seized by niggling doubts. Were we going too far? Was he able to cope with our game? I knew he was exceedingly modest, he never undressed in front of Ronit and me, never even appeared in an undershirt. Were we tempting disaster?

Salim lost. He wore few clothes. He ripped off his shirt and flung it to Ronit. His chest was smooth and bare except for my silver hawk glistening on his breast, its green eye watching. Dancing around in a little circle, he beat several slow strong beats on a tam-tam he held above his head. Shouting some words in Arabic he crouched like a dice-thrower, eager for the next round, tam-tam between his thighs, green eyes gleaming. A strand of hair fell over Aviva's eyes. Salim leapt toward her and brushed it away with a lingering finger.

Salim lost again. He sprung out of his trousers and stood naked except for a pair of black briefs and the silver hawk, talons extended.

Slowly he lifted the tam-tam overhead and raising his other arm he beat on the drum, legs astride, muscles flexed. His body glowed bronze in the candlelight, the curve of muscles rising and falling into each other, twisting and flowing from neck to arms to chest to stomach to thighs to calves, like a coil of copper snakes coming together in slow writhing movements. "Dance!" he commanded. Aviva wearing a long full skirt began to dance around him. He stood rooted, his body watching her, his hips undulating, his torso snaking in place to follow Aviva's movements. She came close to him, her skirt brushing his legs. The hawk flashed. Then she moved away winding around him in a slow figure eight. I glanced at Irving and knew he was lusting after the poem.

Salim continued to beat the drum, weaving strange rhythmic patterns with syncopated moments of silence. Suddenly he leapt into the air and landed in the card-playing crouch, accompanied by a throb of the drum. "Play!" he hissed. Aviva dropped to her knees and dealt another round. She lost. We were silent now. No one cheered. Aviva rose to her feet, put her hands behind her back and slowly undid the hooks holding her skirt. As each hook was released her skirt slid further along her body, pausing at her hips and finally falling to the floor. It gathered in a pool of colour around her feet. She stepped over the pool and began to dance wearing only a red bra and red bikini. Her body was tanned from weeks in the sun and firm from swimming in the sea. She was at her best, her legs beautifully shaped, her blond hair flecked with sunshine falling in soft waves around her neck. Feeling powerfully female in the spell of Salim's unmitigated maleness, she began to move, circling her hips, arching her back, curving her hands over her body, intent upon Salim. He rose and moved toward her. Again I glanced at Irving. He was motionless, gripped by Aviva and the dance, the poem abandoning him. Their bodies entwined without touching, only their heads leaned together, her blond hair laying with his black. Their arms and legs twisted in and out of each other in long writhing movements without making contact, the hawk swooping between them, their eyes held, magnetised.

Unexpectedly she drew away from him and moved her hands behind her back. Her bra dropped to the floor. She extended her arms, opening them slowly as though against a great weight, revealing breasts full and brown. She continued to dance, her arms raised, moving her hips, simple, fundamental. Salim's rhythm on the tam-tam grew faster, more compelling. She rotated her hips and torso, twirling, twisting, gyrating, in spirals of shoulders, torso, hips and belly, her breasts spreading and flowing to their own fluid rhythm. Abruptly, in the midst of the driving turbulent drumming, she stopped, head turned to Salim, legs apart. Her dance continued motionless, pulsating, frozen still, as the drum beats continued wild and mounting. With a sudden crash the drumming ceased. Silence held the wild rhythms. Gradually, like a flower unfolding, she opened her arms to Salim. Salim stood facing her, hard and taut, the hawk black in the shadows, poised for the kill. They remained still, drawn by gravity, sculpting the space between them. Then, with slow deliberation, his eyes fastened on hers, he drew the hawk over his head and lowered its chain around Aviva's neck. The hawk shivered, its green eye fixed on him. Then in slow motion, like a Samurai unsheathing a sword, Salim slid out of his briefs. The letters forming his name were clear and strong. The red arrow pointed toward Aviva. The flower glistened.

19. The Silver Teapot

Even before arriving in Essaouira, I had decided that we would spend only a few nights in a pension, jut until we could find a house. I wanted a base for the rest of the summer from where we could reach out into Morocco and then withdraw into the reassurance of our own company, the solace of our own space. Essaouira was the perfect place to make us a home. It was virtually hassle-free, low-keyed, with a bustling old medina, a port, a beach, and it was visually beautiful. I planned on buying a terracotta tagine dish - a centre to draw us together, while we scooped sauce and shared adventures - like The Finjan, the Arabic coffee pot around which people told stories and sang songs. I had brought various pieces of material to drape over things to make them pretty, and small touches like candle holders, to create cosiness. Morocco made me feel like a mother hen with the need to spread wings over her befuddled chicks, gathering them into a haven of well-being. After all they were in Morocco because of me - I owed them some measure of comfort.

On my previous visits to Essaouira, finding a house would have presented no problem but, because we were in the thick of summer when every inch of accommodation was let, our initial inquiries brought little joy. Then Irving managed to make contact with Scott Symons, the Canadian writer friend who lived several miles outside Essaouira. Scott sent word that the man to see about a house was Karim who owned the antique shop on the alleyway leading into the small square. Excited by our unexpected arrival in Essaouira, Scott was planning a special welcome dinner. He was working hard on a novel set in Morocco and was eager to read us - especially Irving - parts of the manuscript.

The day after Salim's tattoo event, we managed to get two rooms at my favourite pension, Hotel Tourisme. The pension was outside the town walls, facing the sea, with a courtyard and landings hung with plants and birdcages. Aviva, Irving and David got a triple room, Ronit and I a double with a small balcony overlooking the pale gold beach and a large windowsill on which we could sit and watch the sun set. There was also a roof where we could read, sunbathe or just listen to the sea.

Annilee was still at Azdine's farmhouse, loathe to leave, surrounded by a clutch of beautiful Moroccan men, who soon appeared in town wearing various items of her clothing. She was so taken by Azdine's striking appearance, his sharply defined features, his fiery eyes outlined with kol, his earrings, bracelets, beads, head dress, his robes sewn and embroidered by his mother and sisters - he had the exciting beauty of a bird of paradise poised for flight - that she began to fantasise about taking him back to London. "Just to wear him on my arm to theatre parties. Imagine what a sensation he would be." I couldn't imagine. My contention was that Moroccans looked wonderful in Morocco, but the exotic glow, the flare, the proud swagger, didn't stand up to the English climate, they faded to insignificance in the damp grey. Much like the lovely young palm tree I had once brought from Morocco and planted in my garden. It mourned its homeland with such pathos that, timid and estranged, it slowly folded into itself. Consumed by a creeping malaise, its romantic appeal withered and finally expired.

Despite our good luck in getting rooms at Hotel Tourisme, Aviva and I were determined to find a house and set about pursuing Scott's contact with serious intent. We found the small antique shop easily and were immediately fascinated by it. It was piled high with beautiful shapes and colours, amber, coral and silver crafted into Berber necklaces, earrings, serving dishes, teapots, all coming to life as the layers of dust were wiped away. It reminded me of Mustafa's father's shop in Marrakesh, but Karim's shop was more cave-like, hidden, less available, much like Karim himself. He fascinated me even more than his shop. He was a Berber, born and raised in the Rif Mountains. Young - not yet thirty - with an abundance of thick, tangled, black hair and sullen, smoky eyes dark behind drooping lashes. His lips, half concealed in a heavy moustache, were full, his skin brown. Not browned by the sun, for he gave the impression of avoiding the sun, of watching from dark places. Lean and agile, he moved with a feline caution. He was always wrapped in a jellaba, despite the heat, intense, mysterious, suspicious, yet inviting, like a caress not given. He reminded me of a line from my friend Jesse Winchester's song, *'he knows magic he won't show me.'* I was drawn to him by some inevitable magnet, pulled to that magic.

Aviva and I spent many hours in Karim's shop, waiting for a man who never came, a key which never came, waiting for Karim who seldom came. Aviva would grow tired of waiting, but I never did. I could remain for hours. I loved the shop, the dark retreat where I would sit on pillows amidst ancient carpets of many colours and designs, and listen to Arabic music, reading, writing in my journal or remaining still, while sipping mint tea served to me by the young men who took turns working there. I liked waiting for Karim, waiting for his silent greeting when he finally appeared. He didn't speak much, although his English was good. He just watched and brooded and sometimes a smile would slowly creep up through his jellaba and for a moment the darkness would light. I became attached to some of the antiques in the shop, and would have my tea poured from a particular silver teapot with a long curved spout and a delicately chiselled butterfly etched into the silver. I liked watching the thin stream of amber gold flow from the raised spout, then returned steaming into the teapot and poured out again, in the traditional Moroccan manner. Waiting for Karim became a ritual shaping my day.

When Scott came to Essaouira, he was sent to the antique shop to look for me. He found me reclining in my usual corner, waiting for the mythical house to materialise. He told me he would be staying in town that night and had arranged for all of us to have dinner together at a restaurant he liked. It was one of the rare times Karim was in the shop and he embraced Scott warmly, kissing him on both cheeks and touching his heart in the customary Moroccan way. I was pleased when Scott suggested that he come to dinner with us, although I hardly expected that he would. Karim shrugged his shoulders non-committally.

That night, seated at a long table in one of the few stylish restaurants in town, which meant the provision of paper napkins and salt shakers, I was surprised to see Karim slip into the restaurant, and even more surprised when he set his chair beside mine. *"Bon appetit,"* he said softly. I smiled. He ordered tea, saying he had already eaten. His attention was directed to Scott. Scott and I had been talking noisily but Karim's voice was subdued. I tried to hear what he was saying, but couldn't. I watched and said nothing. He hardly looked at me. When he got up to greet friends at another table, I said to Scott, "he intrigues me, what do you think?" I wasn't sure exactly what I was asking, but Scott was.

"Forget it. He's a committed homosexual. Not a heterosexual bone in his body. As a matter of fact, he has the biggest male harem in town, all the most beautiful boys." I hadn't considered that possibility. He gave no homosexual signals that I could recognise. However, I trusted Scott's judgement implicitly. He claimed he was bi-sexual, but admitted to preferring males, and I was sure that this preference was largely responsible for his being in Morocco. He would say, "I'm homosexual, not gay," a difference he considered crucial. He was never thrusting about his homosexuality but it was a persistent fact of his existence and had caused him much grief in Canada. I needed to digest Scott's revelation about Karim and I wasn't sure why. Homosexuality in Morocco was hardly surprising, although it was supposedly contrary to Muslim religion. Besides, my Moroccan code advised against relationships with Moroccan men. Those I had witnessed between Western females and Moroccan males usually ended in tears. Was some tiny part of me leaning in an uncharted direction, yearning for the forbidden. Was that why I spent so much time in the antique shop? If so, Karim's unavailability was a good thing, my principals would remain intact.

Karim returned to our table unobtrusively. Scott was deep in conversation with Irving and didn't notice his return. Karim had come to bid us goodnight and as he was about to leave, he turned toward me and in a low intense voice said, "would you like to come to my shop later tonight? There will be music and tea... it will be good."

"Yes," I replied, surprise flicking my eyelids.

"Good. I would like that." He shook hands with the others and left.

"How about that?" I said to Scott as soon as I could get his attention. "Karim has invited me to his shop tonight." Scott was not impressed.

"Oh, he always has people in his shop at night. They listen to music...smoke. He does it all the time. I used to go often when I lived in town."

So it was nothing special. Never mind. I was glad to go anyway, pleased I had been included.

I got to the shop late because Rosy and Andrew had returned from Marrakesh and I had helped them get settled. I also had a word with Ronit who was being courted by Habib, another beautiful young Moroccan with dark curly hair, radiant smile, and a charm that could melt the iciest of resolutions. She had agreed to go to a film with him and two of his friends, and I could see that she was very much taken by him. It's not that I worried about her going out with Habib and his friends, her judgement was impeccable and the boys would be careful, but I wanted to reinforce my warning about becoming involved with a Moroccan, even one who spoke poetry. I also wanted to tell her where I would be later that night.

Karim was waiting, leaning against the open door, watching down the narrow street. He was alone. I thought the others had already left, that I was too late.

"Where are the others?" I asked, disappointed.

"I didn't ask any others." He paused, "I thought maybe you were not coming."

"Oh no...I wanted to come, I just had some things to do." I was confused. Just me and Karim?

He pulled in the large wooden shutters on the outside of the doorway, then closed and locked the heavy door. I stood watching him, perturbed. I wasn't prepared for this. I didn't even know what 'this' was. "Come, sit down," he said, sensing my hesitation, indicating an alcove at one end of the shop arranged with carpets and pillows. I lowered myself into a pool of pillows. He placed a cushion behind my back. "Be comfortable, take off your shoes." It was customary to remove one's shoes when treading on these ancient carpets. In my state of confusion, I had forgotten. He settled beside me, leaning back comfortably. Arabic music throbbed, gradually slowing my heart beat to a soothing serenity. He lit several tall candles, placed in old silver candle holders. Sandalwood incense glowed amber. An ancient hookah waited beside him. He lit it. It was a scene from the Arabian Nights, a banquet of the senses and served up just for me. I didn't understand what it was all about, but soon it didn't seem to matter. I melted into the pillows, lost in the contours and shadows of the shop, caressing the muted colours, absorbed by the flicker of silver and amber, breathing sandalwood and musk. The magic was being revealed.

"Your shop comes alive in the candlelight. Everything starts to hum, all the shapes glow," I mused. Karim smiled, his face lighting in the soft flames. I had never seen it so alive before. "In your shop everything sleeps in the day and rejoices at night...like yourself." He smiled again. I could see he was pleased. Beside us a kettle sang on a small camping stove. Slowly, he began to prepare tea in the silver teapot, handling it with great care, his movements like a ritual dance.

"Where does that teapot come from?" I asked, carefully embroidering my question into the ritual. "I've been admiring it since I first saw it in your shop. It moves so gracefully, like a ballerina." I curved my neck, following the line of the spout, slowly extending my arms, like the wings of the butterfly. "I love watching the butterfly. In the candlelight it seems as though its wings quiver."

"It comes from Fez. It is very special for me." He spoke softly, with affection. "Before many years there was a man who worked in silver in Fez. Everyone in the country knew about him. The king heard about his work and brought him to live in the palace. He continued to work in silver but now only for the Royal family. He made a door of silver for the palace. They say it has the moon and the sun in it. It was this man who made the teapot. It is very old. I will never sell it." He regarded it tenderly. I had never heard him speak this much.

The tea was exquisite. I sipped it slowly inhaling the fragrance of mint, engulfed by waves of well-being. I was completely content. We listened to music, smoked from the bubbling pipe, and said little. My mind wandered over the objects crammed into the shop - hanging, standing, squatting, lying - each aware of its beauty. I could feel the smoothness of old amber, the cool of silver, the light of jewels, the edge of swords, the flutter of butterfly wings. The touch of Karim's hand on mine did not startle me. Instinctively my body moved to meet him as he slowly ran his fingers along my arm, his touch part of the glow, the colours, the curves. I sank deeper into the pillows succumbing to the medley of sensations, delicate, delicious, my Moroccan policy receding in swells of pleasure.

Suddenly my spine clenched, tight with anxiety. This man is a committed homosexual, 'not a heterosexual bone in his body'. What was I supposed to do, to feel? My erotic experiences with homosexuals had been vastly neglected. A moment of alarm, bewilderment, then a sigh of resignation. Well...if he's a homosexual, he'll have to work that out. Meanwhile...my eyes closed. Karin's fingers moved along my arm, stopping to trace little spirals on my shoulder and coming to rest on the back of my neck. Slowly he spread his fingers, cradling my neck, exploring its contours, filling the curves and hollows with his fingertips. The delicate pressures spread through me with exquisite delight, my body languid, like a cat purring with small raptures. Homosexuals sure do things right, I thought as I folded into the sensations, feeling every nuance, every texture. My neck became a tapestry, a symphony, a fairy gossamer. Then gently, very gently, almost in slow motion, he drew me toward him, held me against him and began to run his hand along the bare skin under my dress, his fingers soaring like the wings of the butterfly. I felt myself opening to him in celebration. The surprise of the encounter, the unresolved homosexual question, compounding the pleasure.

He placed a purple satin cloth over the thick carpets we were lying on, so I would not feel the rough wool. Under the jellaba his skin was like the satin beneath me. "You feel so good," I said, slowly sliding against him. I raised my arms like an offering and reached into the tangle of his hair. And amidst the embroidery and pillows and satin, in an alcove of exotica, we made love. I felt like Mustafa's Moroccan princess grand on her bridal bed.

Later, he covered us with a velvet hanging. So much for Scott's information, I reflected, or was Karim a closet heterosexual? And what did it matter? I fell asleep entwined in him, feeling very splendid.

It was still dark when I felt Karim separate himself from me. "Don't wake up," he said softly. "It is only six o'clock. I must go to an early market but I will be back before nine. Sleep well," he said kissing me on the forehead. I heard him shut the door and closed my eyes. A grey glint of dawn was creeping in under the window. I didn't want to see it. I stretched against the satin and velvet, trying to recapture the romance, trying to hold it in sleep. But in vain. I couldn't return to sleep. A persistent discomfort kept me surfacing, waking me each time I was almost there. The discomfort materialised into a desire to urinate. No wonder. I had recklessly consumed about fourteen cups of tea the night before. Mundane reality strikes again. I tried to ignore it, turning in various positions in an attempt to relax, to mind-over-matter it away. It was no use. I was fully awake and knew I wouldn't be able to sleep until the matter was settled. But how could I settle it? Where would I go? There wasn't even a sink in the shop.

Then I remembered the alleyway behind the shop. No one would be about this early. I could go there. It was worse when I stood up. All at once it became urgent. Somehow I managed to get some clothes on despite the aching. I ran to the door and pulled hard. It wouldn't open. I fumbled with the lock, hopping about in desperation. It wouldn't budge. Suddenly I realised with horror that Karim had locked the door with the key. I was locked in. Oh my god! What could I do? This was worse than the Ourika Valley scenario, with the toilet in the sky. The pain was becoming unbearable. I had to do something fast. I looked about frantically, clutching my groin. In the half-light, sitting majestically, shone the silver teapot. Yes! I hardly made it to open the lid.

The relief was exquisite. I remained absolutely still, luxuriating in it. Only gradually did I became aware of the teapot in my hand. I starred at it, holding it away from me. A sick feeling replaced the relief. What was I to do now? I couldn't leave it there. Karim's treasure, made by the Royal artisan. I must hide it. No. He would miss it, think I had stolen it. I must get rid of its contents. But how? Where? Again my eyes darted anxiously about the shop. They were held by a faint ray of light coming in under the door. The light indicated a gap between the door and the street. Eagerly I inspected it. Yes, it was large enough. On my knees I poured, very carefully, the yellow liquid streaming gracefully from the spout and disappearing gratefully under the door - my own unique ceremony. When it was done I remained on my knees waiting for the panic to subside. "Thank you," I muttered, kissing the still warm butterfly. I rinsed the teapot with the water used for making tea, wiped it with a tissue, and placing it reverently on the low table, crawled into bed, my eyes riveted on the butterfly as though it was some icon that had miraculously saved my life.

When Karim returned at nine I was dressed and waiting for him to release me.

"I must go," I said, eager to escape from the scene of my shame.

"Won't you have some tea first?"

"Tea?" I almost screamed, but forced a controlled voice. "No...no thank you...not now...I must get back to Ronit...she may worry...no tea now...perhaps later."

"I'll be here in the afternoon, will you come back then?"

"Yes, I will, I'll come in the afternoon," I said, my eyes making nervous darts to the door.

Karim opened the door and led me across the threshold. I stopped abruptly. Directly in front of the shop was a hollow in the pavement. In the hollow was a rather large puddle. We looked at each other. Oh my god! Another puddle. I leapt over the puddle and fled.

20. A Gift From The Prince

As the day of Bashir's Palace invitation approached, Aviva and I grew increasingly excited, an excitement not to be daunted by the assurances of those with deeper insights into Moroccan protocol, that nothing would come of it. "Moroccans make grand promises but no one expects them to be kept. The grander the promise the less likely its fulfilment. It's just the way here," Scott cautioned, drawing on his superior store of Moroccan experience. Perhaps that's why he agreed so readily to Aviva's request that he supervise the looking after of David while we were away. Aviva had resolved to go. Nothing would come between her and the Prince. Not David, certainly not Irving.

She had already discussed the invitation with Irving who, to my surprise, was enthusiastic about it. Rather than resenting the rendezvous, Irving had turned it into a celebration, an event of poetic proportions. When Aviva and I had first met Bashir, he'd confessed, upon discovering we were Canadian, that the Canadian he most admired was Leonard Cohen. He was enamoured by his music and poetry. "Leonard Cohen and Bob Dylan are the two great poets of Western Civilisation. Not only the poets but the prophets," he had proclaimed. When Aviva told him Leonard Cohen was a close friend of hers and that I knew Bob Dylan, he turned groupie right before our eyes. Aviva had reported the incident to Irving as a way of making her tryst with the Prince more acceptable. Irving's imagination flared, it leapt over the petty hurdles of jealousy and resentment landing in the arms of opportunity and occasion. "How about a pan-cultural event, bringing together Arab and Jewish poets and musicians on the same platform, the stage to be erected in the Royal Palace and hosted by Prince Bashir Tazi. From what you tell me he's just the man, open-minded, unconventional, daring, you say he was even married to a Jewess. Wonderful!" Then, with typical Irving bravado, "let poets dance where politicians fear to tread."

Leonard Cohen and even Bob Dylan, Bashir's idols, would be used as offerings to tempt him. How could they refuse being the catalysts of such a historical occasion? The event would be a grand first, to be recorded in the annals of history, with the world media in attendance. His enthusiasm was infectious. "What a great idea. Irving, you're a genius," Aviva said with genuine admiration. "That's what I keep telling you," Irving smiled. He couldn't wait for her to present the project to Bashir.

As it turned out Irving had made his own plans. He was returning to Marrakesh to attend a traditional Moroccan music and dance festival. Cedric had written to us about the festival and was staying on in Marrakesh because of it. Unfortunately, it clashed with our Palace date, but Irving was eager to go. Morocco was by now steadier ground, Marrakesh was familiar territory, and Cedric was making all the arrangements. Besides, with the new project in mind, he could talent scout for his pan-cultural event, enriching the experience with impresario dimensions.

Aviva preferred to keep the peace rather then remind Irving that he was, after all, David's father and it wouldn't be entirely out of order for him to look after David. Instead, we arranged for David to stay with Scott and Aaron on their farm outside Essaouira, both of whom were convinced that the plan would never leave the drawing board. Annilee would bring David into town to spend evenings with Ronit, then he had the choice of staying over at the pension with Ronit or returning to Scott and Aaron's for the night. We thought we had provided beautifully for David. David did not. He felt we had scarred him for life.

Years later, when David was an adult and a dear friend, whenever we would meet, no matter what part of the world we were in, no matter what the occasion, almost before the hugs and kisses, he would launch into an unstoppable tirade, which had to run its course, like a fever, before healing was possible.

"In Morocco you left me with those two weirdos in that dump of a

229

place. I was only eleven. I trusted you. You told me you were taking me to a farm, then you abandoned me miles from nowhere. Farm? What farm? I had visions of a cosy farm with green meadows and cows and sheep and little lambs grazing. That place was full of stones and sand and great big prickly things stabbing my ass. The only green thing was slime washed up from the sea, the only animals were scrawny chickens pecking at the sand. I had visions of friendly farmers in overalls and straw hats riding on tractors. All I saw were straggly rows of hunchback camels, appearing from nowhere like bad dreams, with those spooky guys on their backs covered in dark hoods and robes, like some goddamned Klu Klux Klan. I was scared to death of them. I'd run into that derelict room I was allowed to use at the end of that long string of derelict rooms and hide so those creepy camel guys wouldn't see me. I was terrified of the place and I felt deserted by everyone."

At this point I would usually interrupt to protest. "Come on David, don't exaggerate. It wasn't exactly life-threatening. First of all, we left you with two responsible adults. Second of all, you had Annilee and Ronit looking after you."

"They were adult all right. I don't think they ever saw a kid. They certainly never smiled at one. They treated me like I was from another planet, one they didn't want to know anything about. They didn't even speak to me in words I understood. And they expected me to act like a privileged guest visiting royalty. And about Annilee and Ronit looking after me," he'd laugh a bitter little laugh, "you must be joking. Annilee was up to her boobs in Moroccan male bimbos and Ronit would take me to see murder movies - just what I needed - and hold hands with Habib. Then they'd speak in French all night. I trudged after them like some miserable puppy. Face it. You guys didn't give a damn about me. My father was off with his muses, my mother was getting off on her prince, and my auntie Niems left me to perish in some god- forsaken hole."

"Please David, give me a break, it wasn't anything like that.

Besides it was only for a few days."

"What did I know from a few days. For me it was an eternity. I thought you and Aviva were never coming back. Remember I was just a kid. I didn't know where I was. I didn't know where you were. I had nightmares of you stoned on drugs, forgetting about me, leaving me in that hell hole forever. Niems, you and Aviva have a lot to answer for."

David adored exaggerating, remembering scenes in bold colours, grand gestures, torn by searing emotions, enhanced by larger-than-life people. He had a talent for squeezing the drama out of a situation, then intensifying it, heightening it, wringing out every nuance of theatre. His account of events was driven by a sense of theatre to which reality was appropriately adjusted. But, in this case, I had to concede he had a point. Aviva's total focus on David's well-being, her devotion to his whims and pleasures, her indulgences and guilts could, in select circumstances, utterly vanish, to the point where they ceased to matter, they were entirely redundant, and no amount of imploring could move her. This was such a circumstance. Aviva was so entranced by her Prince and the possibilities of the palace, and I along with her, hooked on adventure, feeding the fantasies, that we would have left David with a mother wolf. As it turned out, a mother wolf would have been preferable.

"David, I'm truly sorry. I humbly beg your forgiveness." I'd say contritely. However, unwilling to grant total concession, I'd add, "but at least you got some wonderful stories from the experience." However, it was like Maude Gonne telling Yeats he should be grateful for her rejection of him because it gave him material for his passionate poems of unrequited love. It didn't console Yeats and it didn't console David.

Just as Bashir promised, a green chauffeured limousine arrived in front of the appointed hotel, and although we were assured that Moroccans had no regard for time, it arrived not only on the right day, but the right hour. Aviva and I approached it obliquely, unable to comprehend that the chauffeur, complete with cap and uniform, was waiting to receive us.

231

"Prince Bashir Tazi has sent for me to take you to the Royal Palace in Rabat," the chauffeur announced formally in French, standing at attention, cap in hand. We waited, unsure of our next move. Would the limousine turn into a chariot, the chauffeur into a coachman, or we into pumpkins? "Thank you," Aviva managed. The chauffeur opened the door, waited while we climbed inside, then, with the hint of a bow, pressed the door shut. We leaned back, submitting to the velvet-leather seats, luxurious with arm rests and foot stools. By some miracle we were on our way to a royal palace, invited by a Moroccan prince. Two plebeians whose closest contact with royalty was peering into the face of the Queen on a penny coin.

It was a long ride to Rabat and we savoured every minute of it. We smiled benevolently at people sitting by the road, waiting for buses. We stopped often to appreciate how hot it was outside, so we could better enjoy the air-conditioned inside. We were like kids, playing lords and ladies, taking turns ordering the chauffeur to stop, first tentatively, then with increased confidence, delighting in his immediate response. Aviva even experimented with a 'home James' tone, but quickly abandoned it, her Patois French lacking the necessary style. Our efforts to prolong the ride, however, were finally exhausted. Despite ourselves we arrived in Rabat. Minutes later the palace approached like a fortress, protected by high turreted walls, its massive gates, studded with bolts and iron fittings, forbiddingly shut. Armed guards stood like arrows before them. At the approach of our car, rows of uniformed Moroccans suddenly appeared and, with incredible speed, flung the gates wide open. We didn't even have to slow down. They sprang to attention on either side of the portal, as we slid through the entrance, the gates silently closing behind us.

It was as if some genie had uttered 'open sesame'. All at once we found ourselves in the pages of *A Thousand And One Nights*. We had been transported into a perfumed Moorish garden with fountains climbing through trees heavy with fruit and flowers, out of which rose domes and minarets, like secrets half revealed. We watched Bashir approach with awe, a prince from the Arabian Nights, as though viewing a fantasy. He was entirely splendid. He moved with princely grace, his silk kaftan rippling over his body, its pearly whiteness accentuating his cinnamon skin. His eyes were darker and more penetrating outlined by kohl. His jewellery glowed and sparkled, catching the sun as he moved, earrings with sapphire five-pointed stars, silver and amber bracelets, and the silver chain he had worn the first time we met, with a filigreed Hand of Fatima resting in the hollow of his neck where the ivory silk parted. The white babouches on his feet shone with the same sapphire stars he wore in his ears. The jewellery and eye make-up enhanced his masculinity. And I thought that Western men with their careful avoidance of adornment seemed insipid and graceless in comparison.

Aviva and I, life-of-the-party ladies, equipped with vast resources of wit, charm and scintillating vitality, able to rise to any occasion, remained seated in the car, stunned and helpless. The palace had rendered us dumb. An ancient Moorish landscape had metamorphosed two twentieth century sophisticates into dim-witted incompetents. I felt suddenly awkward, misplaced. Our presence seemed alien to the romance, our Western energy at odds with the Eastern mystery.

Bashir graciously helped us out of the car and kissed us on both cheeks. "Welcome to my home," he said, and taking Aviva by one arm and me by the other, led us toward the palace. Usually strong-willed, we responded submissively, silently obeying, grateful for direction. After ten trance-like steps, I became aware that we were walking along a tree-shaded avenue, paved with marble flagstones, the branches of the trees leaning together, forming an archway. The sun lit the entwined leaves, weaving lacy patterns of dappled greens. The lace revealed glimpses of the palace, its elegant curves silhouetted against the sky. The air, heavy with oranges and jasmine, parted to receive us. Aviva looked up at Bashir, the wonder of the garden reflected in her face, and put her hand in his.

I felt graceless in my purple jeans and tie-dyed blouse. I longed to be a Scheherazade in flowing silks. We passed under an archway carved with honeycomb intricacy, and were suddenly in the palace courtyard. I remained still, dropping Bashir's arm, forgetting my pedestrian clothes, my eyes blinking innumerable photographs, unable to encompass the whole.

The courtyard opened to the sky. In the centre was a fountain, the water gurgling like a natural spring and flowing into a pool, limpid and still. Sunshine fell into the pool like diamonds. Creeping vines and plants bright with flowers were everywhere. The garden had entered the palace. They had become one. Surrounding the fountain, slender marble pillars reached upwards curving into stone arches so delicately carved they looked like lace. Around the fountain, a ceramic pathway formed an arcade between the arched pillars and palace walls. The walls were elaborate arabesques of entwined flowers and ancient Arabic script, giving the impression of rich tapestry. The ceiling was made of carved wood and chiselled stucco, formed into patterns of crowns, stars, and interlaced foliage. My panning, clicking eyes tried desperately to capture the stunning picture.

I felt Bashir easing me out of my locked position. "We can return later," he said, taking my arm. "Tea is prepared for you upstairs, you must be thirsty." But I was transfixed, unable to leave the magic courtyard. Aviva's eyes had turned glassy. As if the courtyard wasn't sufficiently overwhelming, she had to contend with the potent cocktail of desire for Bashir the man, and awe for Bashir the Prince. We remained motionless. Bashir attempted a more subtle approach. "Come, I have a surprise for you," and I wondered what further miracle he could conjure up.

He escorted us through the arcade in silent slow motion. I was enthralled by the sheer poetry of the architecture, by the way heavy materials like plaster, stucco and stone had been transformed to produce an ephemeral quality, light and transparent. Several rooms opened onto the courtyard, their open doorways exploding a rush of opulence, a fantasy of Moorish carvings, vividly coloured mosaics, sumptuous carpets, latticed windows, filigreed ivory, gold, jade, mother-of-pearl. The splendour was dazzling, like the overflow of a pirate's treasure chest.

In one of the rooms women with coloured turbans wound round their heads, wearing embroidered robes and slippers, were incongruously doubled over sweeping floors with handleless straw brooms. I tried to imagine Bashir as a child playing in the courtyard with friends. The idea was inconceivable. The palatial dimension precluded ordinary human activity. We followed Bashir up a wide marble staircase, and entered a corridor tiled with delicate gold and blue geometric patterns. "These are my rooms," Bashir said, leading us through a doorway curtained with beads. We removed our sandals. "Please sit, you must be tired after the long journey. I will arrange for the tea." He led us to an alcove with silk embroidered cushioned seats. I sat down reverently, averting my eyes, over-amped, unable to expose myself to further stimuli.

Bashir disappeared through the beaded doorway. I moved as far back into the alcove as I could, retreating from the reeling wonder in my head. Leaning back I closed my eyes and watched as the profusion of images developed into pictures. My eyes opened into a dome of aromatic wood inlaid with tiny pieces of silver, mother-of-pearl and ivory. I found myself in an Arabian bower of bliss, inhaling the perfume of cedar. Aviva and I who always had so much to say to each other were silent. When I was able to lower my eyes I discovered that a small table with an engraved tray had been set before us. On the tray was a teapot with the same engraving, slender glasses containing pine nuts and set in silver holders, and plates of small round cakes. Bashir appeared smiling, and sitting cross-legged on a cushion before the table, poured the tea from the arched spout, presenting us each with a glass. I held the glass in my hand, gazing into the pale gold and breathing the scent of jasmine and mint. The cakes were dipped in rose-water and slivered almonds - exquisite.

"I have invited several friends. They will be arriving very soon." Bashir's voice pierced the magic spell. Aviva looked up blankly. I stared at him as though he had said something obscene. He seemed disconcerted. No wonder. He had invited two chatty witty ladies to visit, and found himself with two mutes. We had turned into frogs. Aviva must have resolved to awaken from the spell, the frog image alien to her style but without a kiss from the prince, the transition was graceless. She croaked a pathetic, "oh yes".

I tried an ineffective "when are they coming?"

"Very soon." He had already said that.

Another "oh yes" croak from Aviva.

"I must go to receive them. Is there anything you wish?"

"No, thank you Bashir...this is beautiful..really beautiful...it's so amazingly beautiful here...the tea and cakes are delicious...you've been beautiful...we couldn't ask for more...thank you Bashir...thank you." A rush of inarticulate exuberance from Aviva broke the spell.

"You have no need to thank me. You are my guests. It gives me great pleasure to please you."

"You are pleasing us, Bashir. This is a super treat." Aviva's voice was washed with emotion, on the edge of tears.

"That makes me very happy," Bashir said, taking her hand. We were redeemed by Aviva's quick-silver tongue.

When Bashir left, Aviva and I crept out of the alcove, our sense of adventure rekindled by the not-to-be-missed opportunity of exploring the private chambers of a prince. We emerged into a large rectangular room with carved doorways arched with fretwork leading to other rooms. Although similar in style to the rest of the palace, the room did not possess the same aloofness, it felt warm and friendly. This was due in part to the hand-woven Moroccan rugs covering the floor and partially covering the walls, and the profusion of pillows heaped on the rugs, promising comfort. Enormous vases filled with flowers scented the air. At the far end of the room a heavy brocaded material fell like a curtain from ceiling to floor. Against the walls were low benches strewn with pillows and tiled with Arabic letters lazily coiling and uncoiling into embroidered embraces. The room was lit with sunshine, the windows so low that the gardens seemed within the room. Several small tables formed silver circles on the rugs. Byzantine brass lanterns hung from the ceiling. The perfection was intoxicating. We caressed the smoothness of the tiles; rubbed our fingers over the mosaics; inhaled the fragrance of rose and honeysuckle; buried our cheeks in the satins and velvets; squeezed the embossed sections of brocade; inspected the embroidery stitches, examining the silver and gold threads; hung out of the windows to sample different views of the gardens, longing to imprint every nuance of the experience on to our senses, drunk on fulfilling a fantasy.

Kneeling on a pillow, my back resting against the wall, my head submerged in flowers, I reluctantly became aware of a flaw nagging at the perfection. Something was jabbing into the small of my back. I turned to look. The mosaic tiles of the benches extended to the skirting boards, forming a frieze around the room. Just behind my back a dislocated pillow exposed some smashed tiles opening like a wound into the delicate artwork. With a sense of shock I realised that the exquisite tiles had been destroyed in order to fit electric sockets into the walls. The wired connections cut like a bolt of electricity through the romance of the palace. Aviva and I contemplated the violation, and with a sense of loss, rose from the pillows.

Further discoveries were interrupted by a confusion of voices. Bashir entered with a group of Moroccans, two of them female. They all wore traditional dress, the men in light summer jellabas, the women exotic in long embroidered kaftans, their faces veiled by yashmaks. We were greeted in the traditional Moroccan manner. "My friend Mohammed." Mohammed clasped my hand in his, held it for a few seconds then touched the fingertips of that hand, still warm with mine, to his heart, creating a connection between us. The ladies retired almost immediately to one of the adjoining rooms and in minutes reappeared, miraculously transformed from Ancient East to Modern West, by lipstick, hairspray, nylons and short skirts.

We sat on the floor among the pillows. The servants brought bowls of oranges, melons, figs and grapes. Trays were set before us bearing silver teapots studded with Coca-cola bottles pointing like dirty

237

fingers through the curves of silver. The conversation was a lively mixture of French and English. Then Bashir said something in Arabic which prompted several of the men to leave the room with him. The conversation ceased abruptly, replaced by hushed expectancy. All eyes were fixed on the brocaded curtain at the end of the room from which our surprise was to appear. Although the curtain stubbornly withheld its secret from us, we kept our gaze respectfully riveted on it.

Suddenly the curtain parted revealing a stage undulating with a miracle of electronic equipment. Moog synthesisers zapped into view, Hi Watt amplifiers with echo chambers, speakers with glittering disks and vibrating cones, Shure microphones, guitars with fuz pedals, a transparent drum kit, all the latest gear. My psyche quivered under the electronic onslaught. Bashir entered from a door backstage, wearing a tee shirt shimmering with sequins and skintight faded jeans, carrying a guitar with a transistorised pick-up. The others filed in behind him, still wearing jelabas, tripping over the tangle of wires, and arranged themselves on stage. A tuning session followed with piercing electronic shrieks, instrumental moans, buzzes and beeps, the sound man plugging in units, pressing buttons, flicking switches, turning knobs, checking levels. Somehow the magic carpet had flown us to the Electric Circus in New York, or The Rainbow in London. Had some mad Aladdin rubbed the lamp in the wrong direction? My speculations were jolted by a blasting shiver on the drums, a 'one-two-three' from Bashir, and an explosion of *'I Can't Get No Satisfaction'*.

My instinctive reaction was to cover my ears, followed by an intense desire to laugh. I fiercely subdued both impulses. I didn't dare look at Aviva. The others were watching us, anticipating enthusiastic reactions. I smiled weakly and tried to look pleased. The music was painful. If I was no Scheherazade, Bashir was no Mick Jagger. The other members of the audience settled into rapt admiration. Finally, Aviva and I dared to sneak each other what-the-hell-is-happening glances, our palace fantasy exploding in a clash of dissonance. "And for this those beautiful tiles

238

were smashed," I thought. The music was relentless.

"I can't get no satisfaction
Tho' I try and I try and I try..."

Bashir's surprise was certainly electrifying. A twentieth century technological phenomenon had metamorphosed a Moroccan Prince into a Western pop star. The absurd climax came when lead singer Bashir Tazi stepped centre stage and announced, "and now a special song which I dedicate to my Canadian friends," and burst into Leonard Cohen's '*Suzanne*', his delicious Moroccan-French accent suddenly ludicrous.

"Suzanne takes you down
To her place by the river
You can hear the boats go by
You can spend the night beside her
And you know that she's half crazy
But that's why you want to be there
And she feeds you tea and oranges
That come all the way from China."

I sucked hard on my tea and oranges and wondered about Suzanne being half crazy. I could see Aviva staring at Bashir with horror. Cast in the image of super star, he seemed suddenly to have shrunk to less than ordinary proportions.

Then, just as suddenly, the mad genie retreated into the bottle, stunned by the deluge he had loosened upon us. The brocaded curtain dropped, the band vanished and the electric nightmare was over. The Coca-Cola bottles were removed, the lipsticked ladies disappeared, and we had only to erase the memory of the broken tiles to be whisked back to the palace romance. Bashir returned by himself in his white silk kaftan changed back into a prince. "Just a little amusement," he shrugged his shoulders, casually disowning the misadventure. He must have sensed our dismay because no further reference was made to it. The incident was banished from consciousness, a subliminal bolt of horror dispelled by a brilliant reality - and we were most eager to dispel.

Bashir proceeded to attend to his guests in a manner befitting a prince. He conducted us on a leisurely tour of the palace grounds, arranged for our refreshment with bowls of chilled rose-water which we dabbed on our temples and wrists, and pitchers of iced melon juice served in the garden. He picked fresh purple flowers for my hair and a bouquet of jasmine for Aviva which he pinned on her blouse. I could see the flame in Aviva's eyes, brutally quenched by the illusion of Bashir the pop star, rekindled by the reality of Bashir the Prince.

After a superb couscous dinner in Bashir's quarters, served by candlelight, with Bashir, the perfect host, assuring that the palace ambience was at its best, it was as if the black bolt had never struck.

As soon as dinner was over, as though on cue, the chauffeur made an appearance. Immediately Bashir excused himself, returning minutes later still wearing white silk but now fashioned into a western style jacket and trousers. "The night is just beginning," he announced, "we will celebrate it in Casablanca." Although loathe to leave the palace, we submitted to Bashir's wishes. We departed in the green limousine, straining to catch a last glimpse of the palace as the gates closed behind us. Outside Rabat we stopped to collect Sammy, Bashir's Moroccan-Jewish friend, introduced by Bashir as 'my official roller of joints'. Sammy was slight, wiry and full of fun, a kind of adult street urchin. It was immediately evident that he and Bashir had shared many celebrations.

With the closing of the palace gates, Bashir shed all vestiges of Arabic formality. Palace protocol was totally abandoned. "*Sammy faites un jwoint,*" he sighed, leaning deep into the soft leather, one arm around Aviva, the other around me. Sammy not only made the joint but played a Bob Dylan tape to accompany it. We cruised along the Rabat to Casablanca highway laughing and singing, while Sammy rolled the joints.

Bashir opened the celebration by popping a bottle of champagne, which Sammy materialised from some secret place, together with silver cups. The ride was smooth as silk, so was the champagne, and soon Aviva and I couldn't tell if we were driving, floating, flying or all three.

The Casablanca celebration consisted of a round of exclusive night clubs with names like 'Le Balcon', 'Witchita' and 'Zoom Zoom'. They must have posted look-outs to spot the royal limousine because, even before the engine was switched off, we were surrounded by uniformed staff opening doors, offering assistance, showering attention. Proprietors waited to welcome Bashir personally, waiters danced attendance. In each club a number of friends, or friends of friends, or would-be friends, greeted Bashir as though waiting expectantly for his arrival. Some he embraced warmly, others he hardly seemed to know, but all joined our table. Bashir seated Aviva and me, guests of honour, on either side of himself. As if in response to some standing arrangement, plates of caviar, lobster, crabs, shrimp, Moroccan salads, appeared together with bottles of champagne. The food varied from club to club but the champagne was consistent. The music was loud, the conversation louder, the friends obsequious, the service impeccable, the food delicious.

After an hour or two Bashir signed the bill, said his goodbyes, and leading Aviva and me by the arm, left for the next club, where another group and much the same agenda awaited us. Between clubs Sammy was ready with the joints. After the fourth or fifth club, Bashir announced that it was morning and time for breakfast. Incredibly, dawn was beginning to break. The champagned excitement of the night, the glitter of the clubs, the privileged treatment afforded the prestigious guests of a prince, the glamour of being part of a royal entourage of four had acted as a stimulant, heightening response, supplying great surges of energy, overriding instinctive resistance to night clubs. But now that the pale streaks of morning had forced themselves into my consciousness, smearing the velvety darkness with grey smudges, I suddenly wilted. Aviva was flagging as well, her radiant expression dimming. Bashir, however, showed no signs of wear.

"I will take you to my favourite place for breakfast, by the sea, we can watch the sun rise, then we can go swimming." His stamina was enviable.

"It's been a long day for us," Aviva ventured, reluctant to spoil the party and disappoint Bashir. "I'm really exhausted," she added softly. I nodded agreement.

"Yes, of course," Bashir apologised, "you must have some rest...but some breakfast first," he added with that sureness of touch we couldn't resist.

With difficulty we made it through the fresh orange juice, special breakfast cakes and excellent coffee, trying to be bright and responsive, but too weary even to appreciate the exquisite setting, a sumptuous grotto-like structure with waves lapping against the windows.

Jos was asleep when the chauffeur drove us to her villa, but Bashir had his own rooms. He led us to one, kissed me on both cheeks and bade me goodnight.

"Did you enjoy your day?" he asked.

"It was wonderful. Thank you so much," I replied.

"Tomorrow will be wonderful as well," he said, ushering Aviva out of the room and closing the door behind them. I collapsed on to a heap of pillows, too tired to consider Aviva's destiny.

When I awoke around mid-afternoon, Aviva was having tea with Jos, who was pleased to see us and accepted our presence without questions. As soon as we were alone Aviva said, "I think I had a super night with Bashir, but I was too exhausted to really know. I fell asleep quickly and when I woke up he was gone." We spent most of the day chatting with Jos, showering, walking in the garden, sifting impressions, and waiting for Bashir's next move. About six o'clock Buchta, a close friend Bashir had told us about, who lived in Casablanca, came to collect us. Buchta was to take us to his home where Bashir would join us. I liked Buchta immediately. He was intelligent, had travelled a lot and was good to look at. While we waited for Bashir he served us mint tea and almond cakes.

I was enjoying myself, but after the first hour Aviva began to grow edgy.

"Are you sure Bashir is coming?" she asked anxiously.

"Yes, for sure he will be here," Buchta answered.

"When?" Aviva persisted.

"Soon. I am sure it will be soon," he assured her. But when another hour went by and Bashir did not come, Aviva became irritable.

Her insecurities took hold. Were we being stood up? "Why doesn't he phone if he's late?"

"He will come soon. Please do not be worried," Buchta consoled. But when half past nine came and Bashir still hadn't arrived, Aviva's disappointment and hurt turned to anger.

"Buchta would you please take us back to Jos's, I don't want to wait any longer," she said, close to tears, her voice thick with a combination of pique, accusation and humiliation.

"No...please..." Buchta protested, "he will come soon...for sure...he has many things to do...he knows you are with me and that I will take care of you...please be patient...I will make more tea."

"I don't want more tea. I want to leave now." Aviva was assuming that determined iciness upon which reason could not prevail - I knew it well.

"Let's wait half an hour and if he doesn't come we'll get Buchta to take us to Jos's," I tried. To my surprise Aviva agreed. She really wanted to see Bashir but was feeling slighted, rebuffed - feelings she knew all too well - and she didn't want to submit passively, she wanted to register protest, mainly for her own self-esteem.

Ten minutes later Bashir arrived, handsome, smiling, Sammy by his side bearing the champagne. Aviva's greeting was like steel. He was taken aback. "Have you had some problem?" he asked her, concerned.

"Yes, we've had some problem. You. We've been here three and a half hours waiting for you," the words fell like poisoned darts.

"But I did not say when I would come. You had the company of my friend Buchta. I knew he would care for you well. I do not understand the problem."

"Let's go into the other room," Aviva said dryly, "perhaps I can explain the problem."

When they emerged fifteen minutes later, Aviva was smiling, entirely appeased. I was delighted. I couldn't bear a repeat of the Irish saga.

Later, when we were alone, she told me that Bashir had made her feel ridiculous when she accused him of insulting behaviour. He refused the notion that he had offended her. On the contrary, he had carefully provided for us. "I am an Arab," he had protested. "Do not try to change me. I am a Moroccan man. I am not a Western man. Please do not try to make me into a Western man."

"He was right," Aviva said, "what did I want from him? I wanted him to conform to my rules, to force him to fulfil my expectations in the precise way I wanted them fulfilled. He was being an Arab, doing things the way he does them, being a Moroccan Prince. Why couldn't I accept that, even enjoy it? I had to laugh at myself. I don't even know the difference between being humiliated and being well cared for. It was a good lesson for me."

The rest of the night was spent much like the previous one - night clubs, champagne, delicious food - punctuated by Sammy's joints. Only this time we suspended all disbelief and allowed ourselves to enjoy whatever was on offer without expectations. Buchta came with us and this added extra spice to my evening. We danced together, Buchta and I. He was an excellent dancer. One of the clubs had a good dance band and I requested a tango. I rarely had the opportunity of dancing a tango and it was a great pleasure dancing one with Buchta. Bashir danced several dances with Aviva, all eyes focussed on them, but mostly they talked and laughed. Aviva was perfect, animated, exuding her irresistible charm, warm, sparkling, especially delighted that she had salvaged a precious experience she had so nearly let slip away. The combination of Buchta, champagne, dancing, Sammy's joints, Bashir and Aviva, had worked their magic on me. I was wonderfully happy. We returned to Jos's just as dawn was breaking. I spent the night with Buchta. And this time Aviva knew she'd have a super night with Bashir.

Next day Bashir arrived in a Mercedez Benz to take us for a late lunch. We dined in a private alcove, surrounded by pillows, windows facing the sea. Plates of grilled shrimp, lobster, chicken with pine nuts, tagine and excellent couscous were beautifully presented in a symphony of colour, texture and taste delights. During the long, leisurely meal, which was a kind of love making, slow, sensuous, delicious, the pleasure of the food making us more responsive, opening us up to each other, we came to know more about Bashir. Our talk flew from music to travel to politics to jokes and stories. We laughed and sighed and grew pensive and then laughed again. Bashir gradually unfolded, revealing a surprising sensitivity - a beautiful soul. Despite the great diversity of our backgrounds - geography, class, culture, upbringing - I felt so at one with him, our viewpoints so compatible, that I was tempted to discuss delicate matters, like human rights issues, but in the end thought better of it. Aviva broached the pan-Semitic conference and Bashir welcomed the idea, growing increasingly enthusiastic as we developed its potential. A firm believer in peace between Arabs and Jews, he was delighted by the possibility of contributing to it, and the possibility of meeting Bob Dylan and Leonard Cohen was an intoxicating bonus. "I will speak to King Hassan next week when he returns to Rabat," he promised. "He is a very brave man and this can be the kind of occasion he will take to his heart. Of course he will have to discuss it with other Arab leaders. In such matters the king cannot act on his own. I will telephone you in Essaouira to tell you how he receives the idea."

Bashir was in an expansive mood, warmed toward Aviva, toward me, embracing us with affection, prolonging the meal with mint tea, cakes, fruit and more mint tea, as if he wanted to keep us with him indefinitely. At one point he said he would introduce us to the king's sister, she was his favourite and, besides, she looked like me. I felt he wanted to include us in his life, keep us close. At another point he told us he had to go to London for a few days on business and suggested we go with him. I would help him find a guitar teacher to bring to Morocco for some intensive teaching, Aviva would help him select books for the palace's English collection. It was as though he couldn't bear parting from us. It was beautifully touching. I felt engulfed by waves of love. It was as if I had swallowed some wonderful love drug. I loved Bashir and I loved Aviva and I knew we all loved each other. We left the restaurant wrapped in love.

The night was like the others - Zoom Zoom, Le Balcon, Witchita - Bashir, Buchta, Sammy, Aviva and I - dancing, more excellent food, champagne, joints. But by now we adored the dawn breakfast and the sun rise. And there was a different quality to our connection, a superb joyousness, a blossoming of that love seeded in the day.

During our time with Bashir Aviva hadn't once thought about Irving. The obsessive merry-go-round had stopped. She could no longer hear its incessant music. The prince and the palace had worked their magic. And by the time the green limousine arrived to return us to Essaouira, several days later, she felt healed - a fantasy had been realised. We had entered another dimension, and in that dimension Aviva had been reminded of her worth. She knew that the memory would return with her, would stay - a gift from the prince.

21. Essaouira

Returning to Essaouira was like coming home. Everyone was back in town and we received a hero's welcome. Ronit was waiting, eager with reports of adventures and new developments in her relationship with Habib. David was so overjoyed to see us, terrified that this time we had really been sold into white slavery and would languish forever in some distant opium den, that he postponed his censure and complaints. Cedric, who had returned with Irving from Marrakesh the previous day, welcomed us with a song he had composed for the occasion, *'Palace Punks'*. Even Mohammed seemed pleased to see us and asked me to tea at his shop. And Irving invited everyone to the best restaurant in town to celebrate our return. They all wanted a detailed account of our adventure and we spent our celebration dinner filling them in. Irving was delighted to hear of Bashir's enthusiastic response to his pan-Semitic conference idea and thrilled that he would discuss the plan with King Hassan. Aviva explained that since the issue was a political one the king would have to consult with other Arab leaders. But the wheels were in motion and Bashir would inform us of the King's reactions as soon as possible. Meanwhile he asked Irving to set out a more specific plan for the conference.

Much had happened in the short time we were away. Annilee had become increasingly involved with Azdine. "I can't keep my eyes or hands off him," she confessed. "I've been talking about taking him to London with me. He prefers Canada. I'm able to work in Canada. We can both work and save money." Meanwhile I noticed that all her clothes were on Azdine's back and her rings on his fingers. Ronit had become increasingly involved with Habib. She was fascinated not only by his Moroccan charm and good looks, but also by all the differences between them, his intensity, his romanticism, his poetic utterings. They had been spending more and more time together and he was gradually allowing her to enter his life. She had even been invited to join in activities with his friends, sit at their table in a café, an unusual admission of attachment. Although it was prestigious for a Moroccan male to have a Western girlfriend, it was vital that she be kept separate from the all-important male grouping, not exhibited in public, kept on the side as an insignificant other. It was somewhat shameful to admit female connection and disgraceful to display it, it reflected weakness and was punishable by a lowering of status. Annilee complained bitterly that although she and Azdine made passionate love at night, in the day when he was with friends, he gave her the most perfunctory of nods, as though denying any involvement with her and she was never invited to sit with him. It was acceptable for a Moroccan male to sit with a group of Western females but not with a single one unless he was acting as guide - but Essaouira was too small for the guise of guide. Yet, when Azdine wanted a chauffeur for himself or his friends, he would snap his fingers for Annilee. Demonstrating affection for her would be a sign of weakness, using her as a chauffeur, a sign of strength.

Cedric had met several Gnaoua musicians in Marrakesh and had become especially friendly with two brothers. The Gnaoua were a spiritual brotherhood, descendants of Negro slaves brought from West Africa by the Arabs. Marrakesh was their stronghold. Their music, played with drums, long-necked flutes called gimbri, and metal castanets which beat out a trance-like rhythm, had a distinct African flavour. He was fascinated not only by their music, but by their life-style, their supposed occult powers, their spiritual approach to life, their healing ability, partially achieved through music, and planned on more visits to Marrakesh to spend time with them.

Rosy and Andrew had been touring the coast and were back in Essaouira to stay. I was delighted. They were two of my favourite people: Rosy, with her impish face, little-girl blond hair falling over her eyes and agile gymnast's body; Andrew with his fine looks, tall and blond and aristocratic, his unshakeable dignity, his quiet competence that could always be relied upon to steady the boat. He was both the base from which Rosy could launch into space and the net to ensure her safe return. His body was like his presence, strong, comforting. I'd watch him lift Jason or Tammy into his arms, secure and loving, and his tenderness would spill through me. I'd be reminded of my father's arms, when I was a child - nothing bad could happen in those arms.

I loved Rosy's wild unpredictability, her outrageous daring, her desire to ride experience to the limit; I loved her brazen boldness coupled with a heart-breaking vulnerability and deep compassion for suffering that in an instant could turn her boisterous fun-seeking into poignant sorrow, her wide eyes filling with tears, her mobile features riddled with anguish at the sight of an old man struggling to cross a road. She hurt with the pain of every living being. It was always Rosy who insisted on helping. Like the night in Essaouira when a group of us were cheerfully on our way to dinner and someone noticed a cat lying in a ditch. We were all willing to pass it by, ban it from our vision, not allow it to interfere with our good time, all except Rosy. She was compelled to go to it. Discovering it had been seriously injured and unable to bear its piteous condition, she insisted on killing it. Most of us had gone on ahead by then, but Rosy, who could not hurt a spider, summoning Andrew for assistance, ended the cat's suffering. I would never forget that selfless act of compassion.

Our time in Essaouira settled into its own unique rhythm enhanced by the daily rituals which shaped each day - morning coffee and croissants at Café de France; lunch of grilled sardines, tomatoes and sweet onions at the port; dinner at a favourite restaurant or around my tagine dish. Dinner was the focal point of the day, an unpredictable occasion, more a happening than the meal, that took off in directions so full of event, so unforgettable, that no one would dare miss it. After the main course, Tammy and Jason would be put to sleep on a blanket under the table, more wine would be ordered, and the evening would take off into flights of hilarity superimposed with fragments of advice, social comment, political comment, people comment and who got what bargain. Conversation was always a delight spiked by Irving's eloquence, Cedric's wit (when he wasn't in Marrakesh with the Ganoua), Rosy's unruly behaviour - she once danced on the table to emphasise a point - Andrew's dependable graciousness and Aviva's humorous perspectives. I was always lamenting the fact that I had no tape recorder.

A favourite activity was to elicit reports from Ronit and Annilee on the progress of their liaisons and offer agony aunt advice to which they submitted under duress. Sometimes Scott would join us and the evening was transformed into a literary occasion, with gem-like offerings ranging from literary criticism to creative writing. Once Rosy, an avid student of literature, asked Irving what he considered good writing. Irving replied, 'all writing is a recycling of garbage but it has to come out smelling good.' Rosy pulled out a notebook and took notes. Another time, after a tagine dinner I had made, Irving was persuaded to read some poems he was working on. Scott was especially impressed, "all your poems emanate from one central vision," he said, "they are not one-night-stands...they are an apocalyptic vision read between the lines, there's the sense of being the last Jew in them." Rosy reached for her notebook. After another at-home dinner, sprawled over the beds, with Tammy and Jason asleep under them, Scott read the last part of the novel *Helmet of Flesh* he was writing - we had already heard an earlier chapter on Marrakesh. The ensuing discussion was one any creative writing seminar would have envied. First we agreed that the writing was exciting, Irving adding that it was 'finely observed', then we went on to compare it with the Marrakesh chapter. Aviva was especially critical of that chapter; she found the narrator confusing, too close to Scott and therefore lacking objectivity. Irving found it 'too religiously orientated' in its 'sex equals religion' attitude. This time Scott took notes.

It was hard to believe that half an hour before Rosy had had us all screaming with laughter, with her review of Salim's tattoo procedure, an illustrated account of his unique method for withstanding the agony of having his penis tattooed, which he had confided to her. "I take with me a young girl...very beautiful," she said, imitating Salim's heavy accent, "tight she was, *comme un poulet*...like a chicken." She smacked her lips in appreciation. "Me and the girl we make uh...uh...uh," she moved her hips in sharp ecstatic thrusts. "When Salim hard like a stone," she made a tight fist, "the man make tac..tac..tac..with the needle." She mimed a phantom penis set upon by rapid needle pricks, her body contorting with anguish. "Then Salim soft...caput...Salim make uh...uh...uh...with the beautiful girl." Again the thrusts. "Salim hard like stone," again the fist, "and tac..tac..tac..with the needle." More staccato needle work, Rosy's face collapsing with mock torment. "Uh...uh...uh..; tac..tac..tac..; uh..uh..uh; tac..tac..tac, and then my tattoo finished...no problem." Rosy pranced round the room, hips tilted forward, displaying the now legendary tattoo, already immortalised by Irving in a poem.

Although I often met Scott in town, I seldom ran into Aaron. He rarely accompanied Scott into Essaouira and never participated in our dinners. When Scott first introduced me to him, I was reminded of Michaelangelo's statue of David. His face had that same youthful, chiselled beauty. I was struck by how much his appearance and ambience contrasted with Scott's. There was something vulnerable about Aaron, while Scott exuded solidity. Aaron's blond curly hair, fair skin and tall slender body were in stark contrast to Scott's dark robust good looks. Whereas Scott was forceful, decisive, charismatic, Aaron had an ethereal, meditative quality, as though he had spent too long in an ashram. While Scott had the sexual pull of a magnetic field, drawing both male and female into its orbit, with a twist of decadence submerged in his raunchy masculinity, Aaron was pure, chaste, uncorrupted. Scott called him 'my invisible angel'. Scott, on the other hand, was decidedly visible. They were the perfect counterparts of innocence and experience. After exchanging the briefest of pleasantries with me, Aaron seemed anxious to flee, to avoid conversation and didn't join us for coffee. But I felt an immediate affinity with him.

On the few subsequent occasions that I met Aaron he was withdrawn, his step without spring, his features shrouded in hurt as though suffering some debilitating wound. I was destined to find out more about that wound. One afternoon I was sipping orange juice in a cafe, watching the sea, updating my journal and waiting to join Ronit for a late lunch at the port, when Aaron entered the cafe. To my surprise he asked if he could join me. I had never been with him on his own and was slightly apprehensive. However, without Scott he was easier, more open, almost relaxed and conversation was not the difficulty I had anticipated; on the contrary, he seemed anxious to talk. When I asked him how he came to be living in Essaouira it was as though I'd inadvertently opened a flood gate. He began an unstoppable deluge, pouring out the extraordinary events which had brought him to Morocco, and which kept him there.

He told me that the previous year, in Canada, he had married the woman he loved. After a beautiful romantic wedding, which was everything he had desired, his bride, Caroline, and he left for Morocco on their honeymoon, happy and in love. "All was perfection," he said, "I was deeply committed to Caroline in a way I had never been committed to anyone else, deeply in love with her." Caroline knew about Scott, the Canadian writer living in Essaouira, had read his books, and was eager to meet him. The meeting proved disastrous. From the first moment Caroline laid eyes on Scott she was not only smitten, she was possessed. It was as though some uncontrollable force impelled her toward him. She desired him with a passion she had never before experienced. Scott, aware of the impact he had on her, all the while focussed on Aaron, desiring him with that same intensity, played her like a maestro. He seduced her with poetry, with romance, with charisma, until she was completely under his spell. Aaron became a burden to her, an interference. She knew only Scott. He was her Morocco, her magic. As the drama unfolded before Aaron, some part of him died with each episode until finally he was annihilated. "I was unable to cope," he said, "I was destroyed." When Caroline confessed to him that she was in love with Scott, Aaron entered a state of shock.

Right after Caroline's confession to Aaron, Scott confessed to Caroline that, although he was very fond of her, it was really Aaron he wanted. He told her that as soon as he met them he knew Aaron was homosexual and could never make her happy, that she needed a stronger, more dominant male as evidenced by her attraction to him, that the marriage was doomed from the start being based on falsehood and lack of self knowledge. To prove his thesis he lured a traumatised Aaron into bed. "He told me," said Aaron, "that it's not unusual, that it often happens in Morocco like that, couples come here together and leave apart. In the clear light of Morocco they gain new insight into themselves, into each other and see their relationship for what it really is. Morocco has that effect on people."

Before she knew what was happening to her, Caroline was whisked out of Morocco by Scott, persuaded by him that her marriage never would have worked and that it was actually her good fortune she had made the discovery sooner rather than later. She left Morocco in a state of acute bewilderment, having lost all - her lover, her husband, her marriage and above all her self-respect.

"I remained in Essaouira," Aaron said. "Scott was very good to me. Besides where was I to go? I was comatose." Scott, however, was in his stride. He proceeded to console Aaron with affection, with tenderness, with kindness, with reason, persuading him that Caroline was wrong for him, that anyone who could fall in love with someone else on her honeymoon would never be a committed partner, that Aaron would never have been happy in a heterosexual role. But Aaron could not be consoled. His life had shrunk to a spear of pain imbedded in his heart. He could feel nothing else. "For the first three months I was unable even to think of Caroline; the pain was so unbearable, it was impossible to read her letters, let alone answer them....you see, I loved her so much...I still love her, but I could never go back to her...she destroyed too much of me."

"And now?" I asked.

"And now," he answered, "I feel like a fox with a wounded paw who must bury his paw in the sand or climb into a hole and wait for it to heal. Essaouira is that sand, that hole." Then he repeated, "Scott is very good to me." His voice attempted cheerfulness, "we have a good life together." But his eyes were bruised with hurt.

Immediately after returning from Casablanca Ronit introduced me to Richard the Stripper. "You'll really like him, mum," she said. She was right. He had the confident good looks of a Californian life-guard - blond hair streaked by the sun, blue/green eyes, a trim muscular body beautifully tanned, combined with an endearing waif-like little-boy charm. Ronit had met him on the beach and within half an hour was intimately involved in his life. He was English and worked as a stripper in Raymond's Revue Bar, an up-market male strip club in London. He had come to Marrakesh for a two week holiday, but six weeks later found himself still in Morocco. In Marrakesh he had met Torvald and his wife Anna, two Scandinavians who lived in a mini palace outside Essaouira. Torvald, a sullenly good looking Swede, had invited Richard the Stripper to visit and Richard the Stripper had accepted. In Essaouira he was greeted by a harem of Torvald's Moroccan boys and welcomed into a scene of rampant sexuality into which he slipped with such ease that Torvald extended the invitation indefinitely. Richard the Stripper, believing he had reached nirvana, phoned the Revue Bar saying he wouldn't be back for the rest of the summer.

For the first few weeks Richard the Stripper rarely left the splendid grounds. Everything was supplied in abundance, fruit from the trees, food cooked to perfection and served day and night, cool courtyards, archways leading into fragrant gardens, excellent music - some of the boys were chosen specifically for their musical talent – and, of course, hashish and sex. He revelled in indulgences. Initially Richard the Stripper's blond Englishness was especially attractive to Torvald who was surrounded by dark Moroccaness, and although his conversational prowess wasn't the reason for Torvald's invitation, it pleased Torvald to have the occasional discussion in English on a topic not limited to food, sex or drugs.

Ronit wasn't sure how Anna fitted into the equation; neither was Richard the Stripper. In the midst of the raging sexuality, she was busy conducting a thriving business. She had designed an original range of women's clothes, which not only combined the ethnic and the sophisticated, but were graceful and flattering. They were made in soft flowing Moroccan cotton specially woven for her, and dyed in sun-drenched shades of blues, pinks and lavenders. Her clothes were so popular that she was not only selling to Moroccan shops, but exporting to America, England, Italy and France.

Although Richard the Stripper was securely ensconced in Torvald's household he gradually began to notice that his favourite-nation status was being eroded. He was becoming an object of familiarity. Torvald became dismissive of him, treating him with a carelessness verging on insult. Richard the Stripper decided to become unavailable, to disappear for a while, sensing this would whet Torvald's appetite, refresh his jaded palette. Besides, he was becoming somewhat unbalanced by the debauchery, by the orgiastic proportions of the nightly entertainment and he needed a break to restore his equilibrium. One night he moved into a hotel in Essaouira. The problem was that he was running out of money, the only available hotels being expensive, and he risked being forced to return to Torvald's or to London, both undesirable alternatives.

Ronit took to him immediately, his frank open manner, his athletic good looks, his humour appealed to her; besides he elicited her concern. She was touched by his story. At all costs she wanted to prevent him from returning to the arrogant Torvald, to save him from a life of vice and debauchery. She invited him to stay in our room while I was away and hoped to make some alternative arrangement when I returned.

Richard the Stripper was welcomed into our scene probably with equal, if not more, enthusiasm than he had been welcomed into Torvald's. He became everyone's darling, especially everyone female. Cedric was back in Marrakesh, Irving busy writing and hardly aware of his existence, and Andrew accepted him with his usual generosity but with a whiff of reservation. We adored his unpredatory attention to women, and Annilee, who was especially partial to his exuberant, theatrical manner, immediately invited him to drive back with her to London, momentarily abandoning the Azdine agenda. He fussed over us, cut our hair, massaged our aches, accompanied us on shopping trips, and we allowed ourselves to flirt with him, even inviting a seductive, risk-free, physical contact. He added a different dimension to our being together, interacting with each of us, with all of us, evoking feelings we had not considered. I ended up sharing my bed with him. There was never an attempt at sexual contact, which both pleased and disappointed, but it did uncomplicate our friendship. He became the catalyst for an intense emotional encounter between Rosy and Andrew and a disturbing one between Aviva and David.

One afternoon several of us were sunbathing on the roof - Richard the Stripper, Aviva, David, Ronit, Annilee and Mike, a likeable man staying in our pension who seemed interested in Richard the Stripper. There was a good deal of massage happening, Richard the Stripper and Mike performing the role of masseurs. At one point Richard the Stripper was massaging Aviva, enhancing his long slow movements with a generous sprinkling of erotic suggestion, perhaps as a provocation to Mike, his practised fingers stroking, then lingering, manipulating every inch of her body to pleasure. Aviva was enjoying the contact, playing into it, glowing, looking sixteen. Suddenly David leapt up. "You leave my mother alone," he shouted, "take your hands off her!" Pale with fury he ran from the roof. We could hear his door slam with a terrible shudder.

Another day, returning to my room after breakfast, I found Rosy and Andrew there with Richard the Stripper. Rosy, Andrew and the kids slept in their van and used my room for washing, laundry, etc. They had come up for water and found Richard the Stripper still in bed. On impulse Rosy, who was prone to extravagant bouts of spontaneity, jumped into bed with him, provoking him into a wrestling match. So engrossed were they in the wrestling they hardly noticed my arrival. Writhing about, almost naked, they thrashed in and out of wrestling holds, with Rosy, who was wiry and athletic, often in the dominant position, emitting exuberant groans and grunts, while Richard the Stripper was silent and constrained, his movements abrupt, his rhythms broken as he struggled to contain Rosy's wild entwining.

Suddenly Andrew leapt on to the bed, his eyes unusually fierce, and tearing off his tee shirt, jumped Richard the Stripper. I was struck by how similar they were physically. Although raised in the grey and chill of England, they both had the beauty of those born to the beach, bred on sun and sea and surf. But Andrew's looks were somehow dependable, they would endure, while Richard the Stripper's seemed applied, like a woman's make-up and would fade, become undefined and, despite constant attention, would blur as his contours softened and swelled. His were the good looks of a boy, Andrew's of a man.

With uncanny swiftness, Andrew forced Richard the Stripper into a relentless hold, twisting his arms, his legs, limbs forcing limbs into subjection, while Rosy crept to the edge of the bed, irrelevant. Richard the Stripper's response was electric and total. Rolling on top of Andrew, he strained every muscle to hold him down, his face flushed with power, his eyes shining like a cat's before the conquest. But with the strength of a trapped animal fighting for survival, Andrew toppled Richard the Stripper, flesh sucking flesh, pouncing on him, legs astride, slowly pinning his arms open, panting and heaving with the effort, his body gleaming with heat. I was reminded of the wrestling scene from D.H. Lawrence's *Women in Love* as I watched two perfect male bodies sculpt into each other, countour moulded into contour, muscle crushing into muscle, pelvis grinding into pelvis, blood pounding in wild exhilaration, merging into a oneness and suddenly, with a flash of bronzed limb, breaking apart into a swift new posture, in a powerful all-male ballet.

Shouts and groans and growls, turning into roars, filled the room as the victor became the vanquished and the vanquished the victor. Pillows flew spewing clouds of feathers, sheets ripped and, with a splintering crash, like the sound of a tree being axed, the bed collapsed. But they were mindless, consumed by some primal trance. They heard nothing except the sound of hearts thudding on hearts, they saw nothing except flesh knotting and bending and twisting into submission. Then, amid the chaos of breaking furniture, tearing bed clothes and great billows of sound, Andrew shouted, "take me, you bastard!" And Rosy, looking suddenly intense and bewildered, whimpered, "I'm going to do a Caroline." All at once the room was quiet. And in the silence Andrew rolled toward Rosy and took her in his arms, tears mingling with sweat. They lay together like that until his heaving and panting and her wracking sobs were finally stilled.

One evening our dinner ritual was seriously interrupted. Scott asked Irving, Aviva and me to dinner and invited us to spend the night at his place. He had been planning this 'major event' for some time. A great admirer of Irving, this evening was to be Scott's special tribute to him.

We were to be there punctually at seven-thirty so that the evening could commence with the drama of the sunset. Rosy and Andrew dropped us off at precisely seven-thirty, disappearing immediately, not daring to make their presence felt. Scott had made it clear that he couldn't deal with more than three guests at one time and specified that David and Ronit were not to be included. "This is just between ourselves," he winked at Aviva.

Scott looked especially handsome that night with a dark Mephistophelian glow, contrasting with Aaron's blond chasteness. The evening was beautifully orchestrated. Scott had gone to much trouble fine-tuning it to perfection. It was his 'major event par excellence' and he assumed the role of host with style and ease. After a warm, if slightly formal welcome, we were seated on the terrace, facing the sea, our chairs carefully positioned for maximum viewing enjoyment. Nibbling spicy, marinated vegetables and sipping champagne, which I knew Scott could ill afford, we watched the sun sink in a rainbow of reds, pinks and purples, like streams of fuchsias cascading into the sea, staining the water scarlet, while camels filed by silhouetted against golds and blues.

As the last rays dipped into the sea we were ushered into the dining area, a somewhat shabby kitchen transformed by candlelight into an intimate, even romantic, dining room. We took our allocated places around a table set with tablecloth, flowers and bamboo napkin holders made for the occasion by Aaron, and laid with cutlery which gleamed in the candlelight like silver. Dinner began with goat's cheese sprinkled with olive oil and coriander, preserved by Scott in lemon slices, herbs and garlic, and chilled white wine, served on Scott's fine, if somewhat chipped, dinnerware. Scott was no stranger to the art of grand entertaining having been subjected to it in the closest thing Canada had to an aristocratic family life. The highlight of the meal was camel couscous prepared by Scott. Although I balked at the idea of eating camel, I found it surprisingly good, with an excellent sauce, Scott's own recipe. Dinner was a great success, served not only with style and panache but with great attention to detail and to our particular pleasures. By the time Arabic coffee and fig liqueur were served we were suffused with an extraordinary sense of well-being, held in an embrace overflowing with affection and camaraderie.

After the table was cleared, Scott announced that he had planned 'great after-dinner conversation'. And so it was. Irving was at his best. In a moment brimming with generosity he turned to Scott proclaiming, "Scott, you're a should-be poet," Irving's highest compliment, and went on to classify him in the category of Faulkner, Hemingway and Leonard Cohen, writers he considered true poets. With that precedent Irving could do no wrong, and anything he said about Scott or his writing was accepted by him as gospel, without even the mildest rebuttal or offence.

Even when, in comparing Scott and Leonard, both of whom Irving considered 'children of privilege', he said, "you and Leonard think of God as an extension of the fine silverwear, a refined comfort," Scott merely smiled. And later, when Irving said, "you know, Scott, you're a Horatio Alger in reverse, from riches to rags, only you're convinced that your life is a spiritual pilgrimage as significant as the life of Christ..." Scott nodded philosophically. And when Irving went even further, pronouncing sentence on Scott's writing, saying it contained no self-criticism, Scott emitted not a murmur of chagrin. Instead he radiated an air of saint-like acceptance, as though he'd just been blessed.

The conversation veered from the sober to the intoxicated. Scott was serious and intense one moment, funny and mad the next. Irving provoked and quoted, declaiming wisdom after wisdom. Aviva teased and refuted, one moment heightening the rhetoric, the next reducing it to nonsense, interjecting humour into the serious and seriousness into the humour. I chimed in occasionally, mainly to plump up an attitude Aviva was striking. Aaron hardly spoke but the hurt in his eyes was expunged, replaced by rapt attention, the wound stilled. We were all brilliant, if only by association, but Scott and Irving excelled.

It wasn't long before Aviva had steered the conversation to Scott's sexual preferences and bedroom practices, a subject which Scott, who jealously guarded the privacy of his sex life, diligently avoided. But she could sense that, expansive with success, mellowed with celebration, turned on to Aviva, to Irving, to me, to himself, he would deny her nothing, and she could probe deep, teasing out salient details.

Scott was very fanciable that evening, his manner a powerful combination of control and wantonness, and Aviva's flirtation with him, begun years before in Toronto, was rekindled with an even brighter flame. For Irving, immortaliser of the sexual delights offered by women, singer of the wonder and joy of woman's sexuality, Scott's homosexuality was an enigma, as foreign a practice as eating snake. Irving, the macho heterosexual, challenged Scott, the macho homosexual, to a verbal duel in defence of their chosen sexual preferences. Scott pressed his advantage, having experienced both inclinations, while Irving, disadvantaged, being limited to one, had to compensate with hyperbole, metaphor, symbolism and all manner of quotations in praise of female sexuality.

At one point, when Scott was countering Irving's eloquent arguments, holding forth on the superior pleasures to be had in bed with a man, extolling the virtues of the anus, I was compelled to interject, "but women have asses too." Scott stopped short, stunned by my remarkable pronouncement. "You know, you're the only woman who has ever said that." My mundane observation was heralded as a sensation. Scott kept referring to it in tones appropriate to a great revelation. It became the by word of the evening. We sang to it, drank to it, toasted it and Irving vowed to immortalise it in a poem. It paid my way.

We had breakfast on the terrace overlooking the sea - omelettes, fruit, Moroccan bread, fresh butter, honey and tea, and contemplated the windmill turning relentlessly and the camels passing slowly in long elegant rows. Scott said the evening was the most memorable of his life.

Aviva and I left Scott and Irving where they were happiest, deep in discussion about writing and literature, and hitch-hiked back to town. As we were standing on the road, waiting for a ride, the sea-breeze cool on my cheek, Aviva bent down to inspect a flower and I was suddenly exquisitely happy, just like that, for no apparent reason. And I wondered at the way a shaft of happiness sometimes comes to earth and finds a heart to caress, to fill, just like that, for no apparent reason.

One morning Richard the Stripper and I were shopping in the medina for a fish and vegetable tagine I was making for dinner when we encountered an excited Ronit. She had heard that her London boyfriend, Jonathan, was in town but didn't know where and was combing the medina looking for him. Jonathan was her first significant boyfriend. They had a close, warm, relationship, had much in common, similar backgrounds, separated 'hip' parents, liked the same things - music, hiking, travelling, making things with their hands - and enjoyed being together. Jonathan was attractive, dark, wirey, agile. Scott commented, when he later met him, "he looks Moroccan...he moves like a Moroccan, not an Englishman...he's like a cat."

When Jonathan and Ronit parted in London he hoped to get a summer job, save money and come to Morocco to see her. Ronit only half believed that would happen. At first she missed Jonathan, but in the immediacy of Morocco he quickly faded into a distant London. She sent him postcards but didn't really expect him to turn up. But now that she knew he was in Essaouira, vivid and real, she couldn't wait to see him.

"I'm so excited about seeing him. He really did it. He came to Morocco like he promised and he found us. Isn't that great?" Her enthusiasm was dampened by a sudden thought. "But what about Habib? What am I to do about Habib? Habib doesn't even know about Jonathan."

"Don't worry. Something will work out," I said reassuringly, a great believer in something always working out.

"I'll be glad to take care of Habib," Richard the Stripper volunteered.

"Yes, wouldn't you just. Thanks a lot but no thanks. He's my boyfriend, not your's," Ronit said.

"Greedy...greedy..." Richard the Stripper taunted.

Suddenly Jonathan himself appeared walking down the road, looking for Ronit. Ronit rushed toward him, Habib eclipsed by her delight in seeing Jonathan. I too was happy to see him and we headed for a tea room to hear about his adventures in finding us. He told us he had fallen asleep in the train from Tangier to Casablanca and someone had cut the leather thong which secured his money pouch around his neck, and stolen the pouch from under his shirt. He was left penniless and forced to hitch-hike from Casablanca, spending the night in a field under a tree, his knapsack tied to his waist, willing away potential thieves. He would phone London for money, meanwhile we were glad to lend him some. Fortunately his passport and return ticket were in his back pocket, the thief hadn't managed to get them. Despite losing all the money he had saved for the trip, he was cheerful, philosophical about the loss, relieved that he had found us and even expressed admiration for the thief's dexterity - although a light sleeper, he hadn't felt a thing.

My fish tagine that night turned into a welcome dinner for Jonathan, providing the others with the opportunity of hearing his travel tales. Although he was just seventeen he had done much travelling, had even been to India, but he found Morocco tricky to negotiate and somewhat frightening. "I'm glad I made it in one piece," he confessed. After dinner Jonathan and Ronit went to a small, inexpensive hotel where Jonathan had booked a room. However, the night clerk wouldn't allow Ronit in - Ronit wondered if he was a friend of Habib's making a macho solidarity statement - so after a walk by the sea, Ronit returned to our hotel, wonderfully happy. I envied the way she was able to deal with one emotion at a time, keeping the others on hold until she was ready for them.

Next evening, everyone, including Ronit and Jonathan came to Aviva's for a poetry reading. Ronit had managed to avoid Habib all day, but was aware that he knew about Jonathan. 'Telegraph Arab' was especially effective in Essaouira. She was also aware that, although she hadn't known in advance that Jonathan was coming and therefore couldn't be blamed for not preparing Habib, and although Jonathan was staying for only ten days, Habib would feel insulted, as though she had purposely humiliated him, and would react badly. However, no one was prepared for the intensity of that reaction. In the middle of the reading Habib crashed into the room, electric with rage and despair. Normally proud, polite and soft-spoken, he was oblivious to everything except his pain.

"I cannot support seeing you and Jonathan together," he shouted at Ronit, his voice driven through clenched teeth, his eyes bulging with menace and anguish. Then addressing Jonathan directly, his face a black glare, his voice low and threatening, he warned, "Disappear from Essaouira." And, addressing no one in particular, he wailed, "I'm like the goat in the mountain who was free and celebrating, but all for nothing, because he

263

was brought to the town and to the tannery. I am that goat, beaten in the tannery." With that he left the room. The poetry reading was over.

Next evening we gathered again in Aviva's room, hoping to continue the interrupted reading, when Habib stormed into the room, his eyes bloodshot, his movements erratic, uncoordinated, as though bolts of electricity were being shot through him. He stood stiff and menacing before Jonathan. "You are still here. I said for you to disappear. If you do not disappear I will break you. I will plant dope on you and tell the police. Then you will disappear for a long time." He glowered at Jonathan, his eyes dangerous with wild fury. Then picking up an empty wine bottle, he flung it out the window with such force that he fell against the wall as it smashed to the ground. "You cannot understand a Moroccan heart," he said to Ronit, and I could hear the tear in his voice. Suddenly depleted, he lurched from the room, Scott, who had come in minutes before, rushing after him.

We were left stunned by the violence, by the raw, naked passion, the pathos. It was as though we'd all been struck by that bottle. An amiable Habib had turned on us, fierce and unpredictable. There was no telling what he might do. Most of all we were frightened for Ronit and Jonathan. Irving suggested we call the police. But Scott, returning minutes later, assured us there was no cause for alarm. "Don't worry, Jonathan, I've spoken to Habib, he won't plant dope on you, he won't report you to the police and he won't harm you or Ronit. It's Moroccan dramatics. He's been hurt and he has to hit back, he has to save face, tell his friends that he accosted you, drove you out of town. It's the Moroccan way. There's nothing to it, just sound and fury. But it would be an act of consideration if you and Ronit went somewhere else for a few days and gave him a chance to cool down."

Next morning Ronit and Jonathan left for a trip down the coast. Ronit wasn't taking chances.

Our time in Essaouira continued to wind through days filled with event, and hardly a moment for contemplation. Aviva had a vast collage of experiences and thoughts she wanted to reflect upon - Mustafa, Bashir, Irving, herself. I needed to understand my relationship with Mohammed which was becoming increasingly confusing and opaque. Ronit was equally confused about her relationships with Jonathan and Habib. But it was difficult to be reflective through the startling impact of occurrences, like short, sharp vignettes, which continuously bombarded our senses. There was always some new consideration which took precedence, which had to be digested and filed.

Like the afternoon Aviva and I went to Mohammed's shop to pick up some amber beads he had left for us. We were surprised to see a pretty, young, Moroccan girl in the shop chatting playfully with the boys working there. She had a bright eager face, was barelegged and wore a thin clinging dress and sandals, not quite a school girl's uniform. It was unusual to see a Moroccan girl on her own in the shop and I assumed she was the sister of one of the boys. As we entered the shop she smiled sweetly at us. We smiled back. Then as we sat down she continued to smile at Aviva, alternating from shy to bold, trying to catch Aviva's eye, while at the same time talking and giggling with the boys. This went on for several minutes before one of the boys said to Aviva, "her name is Nura." Then with a significance I couldn't interpret, he added, "she likes you."

"Tell her I like her too," Aviva said casually.

"But she wants to make love to you. She likes women," the boy said as nonchalantly as if Nura was requesting a pencil. Unnerved silence.

"How old is she?" Aviva asked.

"Twelve."

"Isn't that young?"

"Not in Morocco," the boy answered. Nura smiled at Aviva again making small circles with her tongue.

"Tell Nura I think she should be in school," Aviva said. We collected the beads and left the shop, Nura gesturing after us with her tongue.

Bashir phoned with the news that King Hassan had expressed interest in the pan-Semitic conference. However, the foreign minister, whom the king would have to confer with, was at the U.N. headquarters in New York, debating the Spanish Sahara crisis which Morocco was entangled in. Bashir said that when Irving sent the elaborated conference plans, he would give them to the king for discussion with the foreign minister when he returned from New York. "But it looks good," he said enthusiastically.

Ronit and Jonathan returned to Essaouira and to a much subdued Habib, although Ronit sensed that a suppressed violence still festered. She attempted to curb it by spending some time with Habib. One afternoon while they were strolling on the beach, Habib suddenly turned to her with that dark, intense look she dreaded. "You are a diamond I am holding in my hand, but now the diamond is exploding, it is breaking away from me...soon my hand will be empty." When Ronit tried to reassure him that nothing had changed between them, that they were still friends, he grew threatening. "Jonathan is stealing my diamond. I will not suffer that. I will cripple Jonathan. He will leave Morocco a crippled man." Ronit felt her stomach clench with apprehension and fear. But when she reported the incident to Jonathan he was unconcerned. Ronit thought he dismissed Habib's threats, rather arrogantly, as 'ridiculous'.

Ronit ran a gamut of emotions - guilt tempered by anger, pity by fear. She couldn't bear hurting Habib, but felt she should devote herself to Jonathan, since he had such a short time in Morocco and risk Habib's outbursts and threats. It was an uneasy time for her. But Scott was right. Habib did nothing. He was even cordial to Jonathan waiting patiently for him to go.

As the time drew nearer for Jonathan to leave, Ronit had mixed feelings about his departure. She wanted him to stay but looked forward to the freedom she would have when he left. She missed being with Habib. "Habib is romantic," she told me, "Jonathan is like a buddy. Although I love him more deeply our relationship is predictable, with Habib it's more exciting - anything can happen." Then she added wistfully, "Jonathan is my reality, Habib is my fantasy."

However, after Jonathan left, her relationship with Habib became more complicated, more ambivalent. His signals became unclear. Sometimes he was as before, happy to be with her, affectionate, proclaiming his love; then he'd grow distant, cold. Sometimes Ronit couldn't tell if he wanted to be with her or without her. Often she felt a warm lovingness from him. Then, without warning, he'd ignore her, break appointments, keep her waiting or not show up at all. She felt hurt, rejected, played with rather than loved. Habib always had some flimsy excuse for his behaviour. But nothing was ever discussed openly between them - it wasn't the Moroccan way.

At times it seemed as though Habib was trying to punish Ronit for her time with Jonathan. One evening he got hold of a motor bike and insisted she go riding with him. I begged her not to go. I had a terrible fear of motor bikes since my brother, in his youth, had collided with one while driving his car, resulting in the other driver's leg being amputated. But her desire to be with Habib overshadowed my pleading. They were driving uneventfully through the town, when suddenly Habib, attempting to frighten her, stood up, opened the throttle and raced toward a wall, laughing and singing. Ronit screamed in terror, certain he intended killing them both. The bike leapt into the air with the sudden acceleration, rose on its back wheel like a panicked animal, and flipped over. Ronit was thrown on her back, Habib on top of her and the bike on top of Habib. Miraculously neither was seriously hurt but Ronit was badly shaken. So was I.

I understood exactly what Ronit was going through. My relationship with Mohammed was following a similar pattern. About a week after the teapot night, Mohammed again invited me to his shop after closing. I was half expecting a follow-up evening, treating myself to a bath for the occasion. But this time there were three beautiful young men present, stretched out on cushions, listening to music, languidly stoned. Mohammed waved me to join them. I did. He lit several candles and incense sticks, and then stretched out in an alcove, by himself, coolly absorbed in the music. I lay beside one of the boys, so close I could feel his breath, but careful not to touch him. The atmosphere was purring with sexuality, so sensuous I could rub up against it, yet there wasn't a hint of overt sex. I felt like part of a harem waiting for the sheik's favours. But I didn't mind, I rather liked the feeling. I didn't understand the scene but submitted to it willingly, curious as to its outcome, enjoying its subtle eroticism. When the candles burned out no one moved, we lay in darkness listening to the music through the smell of incense, waiting for Mohammed.

Suddenly Mohammed switched on the lights and announced that we were going for coffee. The sudden bolt of electric light plunged me into an uneasy reality. I felt awkward, estranged. I wasn't even sure if the invitation included me. The boys knew where to go, what to do. For them the ritual was a familiar one. But I, no longer swathed in the mantle of candlelight, felt exposed, not knowing what to expect or even why I was there, my status as mother suddenly weighing heavily. Mohammed ignored me, which didn't help. Befriended by one of the boys, I tagged along, impotent with teenaged angst, in need of salvaging a fast eroding dignity.

After coffee in a small side street café I had never been to, we headed back toward the shop. Mohammed remained silent, aloof. Not a glance graced my direction. Not a wink of reassurance. Was I intruding on his scene? Persisting where I didn't belong? Wasn't wanted? Troubled and humiliated, I said I would be going back to the pension. Nobody objected. Without a word they walked me to the door and wished me a good night. I felt confused, foolish. I couldn't even pretend I was some sort of objective observer. I wasn't. I was a spurned female, resurrecting a hurt I thought I had long ago become immune to. I was playing a game without knowing the rules - an invitation for grief.

In spite of this painful beginning, I couldn't let go. It was as though I'd been allowed a privileged glimpse into some secret circle. I felt drawn into its dark orbit. Despite resolutions to the contrary, several days later when Mohammed invited me to his shop after closing, I was compelled to go. I went again several nights after that, and again after that. Gradually I became an honorary harem member, slipping in, whenever I was asked, to lie among the cushions and the boys and listen to music, and wait for some revelation, secretly pleased by even this minimum contact with Mohammed. Mohammed never singled anyone out for special attention. I assumed the boys, who were always changing, were his lovers, but there was never any indication of this. Nothing was revealed to me. I gained no insights into what the evenings signified, but allowed myself to enjoy their sensuous ambience, their mysterious rhythms, without expectation. However, I made sure to leave while I was ahead.

One night the boys disappeared, whether by design or coincidence, leaving Mohammed and me alone in the shop. In a sudden burst of recklessness I said, "Mohammed, would you be my friend?" The question did not offend or startle him, "I will try," he said simply. "But it is not easy for me. I have no friends. Friends and business do not mix." Then, as though attempting an explanation, he added, "There are two things which make for Moroccans serious problems - money and sex. I cannot have friends because I am in business...but I will try." What was he telling me? Certainly business and money were no obstacles to our friendship, was it sex? I knew I couldn't ask him directly. I chanced a more oblique approach. "Tell me Mohammed, how do Moroccan men feel about women...Moroccan women...how do you feel?"

After a long pause he said, "Women are magic...I am afraid of magic." Then he added on impulse, "Moroccan women do not like sex, sex with a woman is only for children." Lowering his head, as though he had disclosed too much, he was abruptly silent, his fingers clutching the Hand of Fatima

269

under his shirt. Unusually for me, I didn't prod further, pleased he had said this much. And in the candlelight, among the cushions and carpets, with the heady smell of incense, I felt strangely close to him, detecting a sadness which moved me. I wanted to hold him, tell him how I felt, but I didn't dare and closed my eyes tight against the temptation.

When I looked up he was making his bed, making it big enough for two. My heart raced. He put fresh candles in the holders, lit more incense and played music he knew I liked. Then he crawled into bed. I sat a little away from the bed, remembering the feel of his skin, silk under the rough jelaba. I wanted to feel it against me, touch his hair, his eyes, his lips. But I was unable to reach out to him. The risk was too great. What if he was repelled, think I was black magic? I waited for his move. But nothing happened. Did he no longer want me? Had he wanted me just that once? Did being my friend mean he could not be my lover? We were locked in silence. Finally I asked him to let me out. Without a word he unlocked the door. Then he said, "*à demain*". Nothing else. I returned to the pension hurt and bewildered. It seemed the closer I got to Mohammed, the more estranged we became.

My 'Moroccan Code' had cautioned me against being where I was. Now I was paying the price.

That night I began my 'Notes to Mohammed'. The distance between us was so profound I couldn't bridge it in speech. Perhaps I could in writing. I decided to keep a sort of journal written to him. In it I would write the things I couldn't say, thoughts, feelings, reminiscences. I wanted to open myself to him. Perhaps that way he would get to know me, trust me, allow me to know him. With an intensity I couldn't comprehend I longed to be his one friend.

22. Exit Morocco

August was drawing to a close. David's school began in September, so did Aviva's teaching. Irving had to organise his university courses. Cedric was committed to voice-overs for radio and television commercials. Annilee began thinking about September auditions. Rosy and Andrew had to be back in England for work and were already planning on meeting Jos and Bashir in Casablanca, then driving to London. They would deliver Irving's more detailed plans for the pan-Semitic conference to Bashir, and messages from Aviva and me. Suddenly a whiff of exodus was in the air. Words like 'Malaga', 'Toronto', 'London', crept into the conversation, first tentatively, then with increasing urgency. All at once everyone was talking departure. Somehow I hadn't considered departure. It came upon me abruptly, without warning, like a clap of thunder in a clear sky. I began to hate hearing words like, 'travel agent', 'tickets', 'airline schedule', in the same way I used to hate seeing dark autumn clothing replacing summer pastels in shop windows and the appearance of 'back-to-school' displays with school satchels, pencil boxes and exercise books. They filled me with a sense of dread, of bereavement, with the chill of cold grey.

Of course Ronit and I were staying in Morocco. The full departure impact was not yet at hand. We planned on hitch-hiking through North Africa into Algeria and Tunisia, then deep into the Sahara. But not yet. I didn't want that to happen just yet. I wanted time to savour the possibilities of that trip. But mostly I wanted to hold on to our group. I was with my dearest friends in one of my favourite places. Each day was a blessing. We revelled in each other's company. The day-to-day events were like live theatre, enhanced by the wonder of living them together. I was exquisitely alive, exquisitely happy. I didn't want that to change. But I was helpless to prevent it. I watched and listened with a sense of increasing panic as plans were made and then finalised, wretched in the knowledge that our times together were almost at an end.

Rosy, Andrew, Tammy and Jason were the first to leave. David was bereft that night. Not only had he grown attached to them but, like me, felt a terrible rent as the cosiness of our little family was dismembered. Annilee and Richard the Stripper would be driving back to London in Annilee's car, the Azdine adventure on hold. Cedric, Irving, David and Aviva were returning to Canada, flying from Marrakesh to Malaga and from Malaga to Toronto. I could hardly bear it. Desperate to prolong whatever I could, I hit upon an idea. Ronit and I would go to Malaga as well. We would spend a few days there with Cedric, Irving, David and Aviva, seeing them off before returning to Morocco. Postponing the farewell and setting it in another country somehow made things easier. I needed time to adjust.

Actually there were good reasons for my going to Spain. I had to make arrangements for the musicians in England to get to Morocco in time for the opening of Jos's club. This involved complicated financial and ticket negotiations, which in turn involved long distance phone calls, and the transfer of money, tasks close to impossible in Morocco. Because the banking system was incomprehensible - Moroccan money was not a negotiable currency - and because long distance phone operators were a rare occurrence and lines out of Morocco always busy, it was far easier making business arrangements from Spain. Also my prospective sister-in-law, Gitte, whom I adored, would be in Malaga during the last week of August. She had written to me in Morocco telling me where she was staying. It would be a treat to see her. Besides, I wanted to hear news of my brother who was going through a difficult time with his marriage.

The plan was for Cedric, Irving, David and Aviva to spend several days in Marrakesh. Cedric and Irving had airline tickets from Marrakesh to Malaga and Aviva and David had to arrange theirs. David longed to see Mo Mo, Aviva wanted to see Mustafa, Cedric wanted to see the Gnaoua brothers and Irving simply wanted to be in Marrakesh. When they would

272

leave for Marrakesh, Ronit and I would go to Casablanca to arrange money matters with Jos. From Casablanca we would take a bus to Tangier, spend a few days there, then get the ferry to Algeciras and the train to Malaga. Ronit hadn't been to Tangier and I looked forward to sharing it with her. The plan excited me and soothed the imminence of final separation. "We'll have a super time in Malaga," Aviva promised as our bus pulled away and Ronit and I waved *au revoir.*

There was a message from Rosy waiting for us in Casablanca. She had managed to find Bashir, gate-crashing a high-profile party to do so, and had delivered Irving's plans. Bashir was very excited about the pan-Semitic conference and would be meeting some government official in Fez to discuss it. So far so good. Our time in Casablanca was brief and hectic. I wanted to get out quickly, possibly the same day. There was no reason to linger. Jos was up to her ears in club arrangements, Bushta was in France and Bashir in Fez, hopefully on the mission related to the conference.

Jos was prepared for our arrival. Almost as soon as we met she gave me the Moroccan dirham to change into English pounds, to cover air fares and expenses. It was essential to convert the dirham into foreign currency since dirham were not accepted outside Morocco, and their exportation from the country was a serious offence. As a foreigner, I was entitled to convert dirham, whereas a Moroccan was not. However, after spending most of the day rushing from one bank to another with no success, one brave teller confided that I could make the exchange only at the Bank of Moroc's head office - apparently a state secret since no one else had dared convey this dangerous bit of information. We got to the head office ten minutes before closing and were shunted from one department to another. It was late, no one wanted to part with hard currency, the person in charge was busy, I was to come back tomorrow. It was only when I was on the point of hysterics that the papers to negotiate the exchange appeared. I was instructed to fill them in but informed that the actual transference of funds could only be made at the point of departure, in our case, the port of Tangier. To avoid any possible difficulty in Tangier, I insisted on seeing the head teller at the foreign exchange bureau to make sure all my papers were in order and the forms filled in correctly. He assured me they were. It had taken all day to negotiate the money-changing but we managed to leave early next morning.

In Tangier we headed for Pension Miami, a small pension in the old part of town that I liked. We spent two pleasant days in Tangier enjoying being together and enjoying Tangier. We visited the Casbah - the old walled fortress, did some shopping - I wanted to send some gifts with Gitte, sipped mint tea in the elegant Café de France in the new part of town, walked along the beach, gazed at Gibraltar, and wandered in the medina, all totally unmolested. This was nothing short of phenomenal. Tangiers is a city with continuous, short-stay, tourist traffic. Boatloads of tourists are dumped there at frequent intervals for several hours of sight-seeing and shopping, with the inevitable hassle of touts and street urchins pursuing them at fever pitch. But by now Ronit was so at ease with Morocco and Moroccans, exuding such a sense of assurance that we were considered inhabitants, not tourists, and left in peace.

On our last night I took Ronit to my favourite café in the back streets of the medina. Here, ageless men in jellabas sat cross-legged on a raised stage with spiral railings, like a large balcony, and improvised traditional Arabic music on a variety of strange instruments, some no longer made. Anyone who could play music was welcome to participate. Several Westerners with guitars joined them, pleased to play with the old masters, and several younger Moroccans played pipes and drums. The old men nodded encouragement now and again and allowed space for anyone whose music they liked. They leaned into their instruments, communing with them, sensitive to a nod which would signal now one musician, now another, to take the lead.

The café was large with blank green walls and dirty floors, thick with smoke through which a poster of the king wavered, faded and fly speckled, one side of his face buckling as each breeze from an ancient fan induced an attack of palsy. The room was crowded. Moroccan men, and the few westerners who knew about the café, sat on wooden chairs around tables scarred by cigarette butts and crammed with glasses and spilling ashtrays. Sepsis were passed from table to table. Although we were the only females we were accepted easily, without fuss. It was not a place where tourists came. It had no charm. Nothing was sold except mint tea and Coca Cola from a battered, red Coca Cola box. But when the music began, as if by magic, the café was transformed. It spun with colours, shapes and sound. I had spent many evenings engrossed in the music, watching the faces of the old men, like soft leather, wrinkling into smiles when someone's playing pleased them. Now Ronit and I sipped mint tea, listened to the music and smiled as the sepsis were passed. A Westerner at the next table offered us one. He wore a cowboy hat, boots, and a fringed Indian jacket. He looked like I had always known him. He told us his name was Dan, that he was living in Tangier, but was originally from London. Instant friendship. After the music was over he invited us to visit a friend who worked in a circus. Some of the younger musicians would be coming, there would be more playing. We accepted.

Dan got a taxi and we drove to the circus man's house. We found ourselves in a typical Moroccan room, low sofas strewn with pillows, Moroccan wall hangings, carpets woven in the colours of the spices heaped in the market place, golden saffron, orange paprika, earth-coloured kamoun. Circus photos of trapeze artists, clowns and assorted freaks hung on the walls, together with the inevitable photo of King Hassan.

Tea was brewing on a small stove on the floor, glasses and bundles of fresh mint waiting on a tray. There were mainly Moroccans present, a few of Dan's English friends and a Portuguese girl who immediately intrigued me. She looked gentle, self-contained, at ease, yet I found her disturbing. Ronit and I sat beside her. She told us she was travelling alone in Morocco and was staying in Tangier for a while. Her clothes were a medley of colours and textures, collected in the various parts of the country she had been to. She wore a long robe exquisitely embroidered. I asked her who had done the embroidery. "I did it by myself, when I was in prison," she replied, matter-of-factly, then added, "I had much time." She was fragile with delicate features and an abundance of bright copper hair framing her face. She looked like a pre-raphelite model. I didn't want to think of her in prison, and couldn't bring myself to ask for details.

I tried to engage her in conversation but she spoke very little. I saw that Ronit kept glancing at her hand. There was something awkward in the way she held it. She noticed us looking at it. "My hand," she said quietly, spreading it on her knees and contemplating it for a moment. "One night I was making tea, the camping gas turned over and the boiling water was spilled. I tried to fix the fire and by mistake put my hand in it. You see, I had eaten so much opium that I didn't feel my hand in the fire. I burned two fingers but I didn't know." She held up her hand to show us. "There are good doctors in Tangier. They sewed it together very well. Now I have a small hand." She must have been aware of our anguished expressions, because she added, "it doesn't matter too much. You see I didn't use those fingers very much." The doctors had indeed done an excellent job. It was difficult to see that her index finger and the one next to it were missing. She turned away, her profile like a cameo, and hugging her knees, folded into herself. Tea was poured. We sipped tea and picked at little cakes with sesame seeds. The boys played music. We were silent, thoughts spinning in the night.

Before we left, Dan gave us a small lump of something wrapped in paper. "A gift for you," he said. I tried to refuse saying we were leaving Morocco next day and didn't want to take anything with us. He was insistent. "It's so small you can put it anywhere. It's some of the finest opium. Hard to come by." Opium! The word fell like a stone. But it would be insulting to refuse such a generous offer. I decided I would get rid of it later.

When we got back to our room I wanted to throw it out. To my surprise Ronit objected. The Portuguese girl's story, rather than putting her off opium, had increased her interest in it. "Please don't throw it away. I'll take it on the boat. I want to try it once. Just one time. When will I get another chance?" Finally I gave in. If she was to try opium I wanted to be with her. But I refused to let her carry it.

"I'll keep it in my mouth," I agreed reluctantly, "and if there is any problem, I'll swallow it." It was about the size of an aspirin. "The sacrifices mothers make," I sighed, not entirely happy with the arrangement. Although I was a weathered traveller, I had never concealed opium in my mouth before.

Next morning, as we were leaving for the port, I remembered the almond fudge, laced with hashish, Mohammed had given me as a parting gift. A few pieces were left. There was no one in the pension to give it to and we couldn't face the obscenity of throwing it away. We decided that I would eat it - Ronit had the opium. I knew it was mild and pleasant, and by the time its effects were felt, we would be lying in the sunshine on the ship's deck. I munched on the fudge as we walked the short distance to the port.

At the port I went directly to the bank to change my dirham, while Ronit looked after our belongings, and asked to see the head teller. To my horror he informed me, with unconcealed relish, that I had the wrong papers and the dirham could not be converted. My worst fears had materialised. "What am I to do?" I asked in despair. The teller shrugged his shoulders, his face stamped with permanent indifference. "But the bank in Casablanca told me everything was in order," I protested.

"Did I tell you everything was in order?" the teller asked unperturbed.

"Of course not."

"Then what do you want from me? Go to the bank in Casablanca." He proceeded to add up a long list of figures, a task which evidently required total commitment. I was distraught. I had to get the money to London. Contracts had been signed. Musicians were waiting to go to Casablanca. The club had already advertised their arrival. I left the

277

teller frustrated and helpless. My experience with Moroccan officialdom convinced me that further efforts to convert the dirham would be useless.

Suddenly I noticed a man approaching me. He was wearing a Customs Authority badge and some sort of uniform. He looked at least semi-official. Somehow he was aware of my problem, probably working with the bank teller. Yes, he would change my Moroccan dirham into Spanish pesetas, a negotiable currency; yes, he would give me a good exchange, same as the bank, and I would pay him a little extra for his trouble. I didn't trust him. He seemed too polite, too friendly, too eager to help, but I had no alternative. While he was making the arrangements, I calculated how much money I was to receive. But when it came to making the exchange I realised he was giving me less than half of what I should be getting. Aware of my dilemma he was shamelessly taking advantage of me. I was outraged. I detest being cheated.

"No, I will not exchange the money with you. You are a thief."

I grabbed the dirham I had just given him from his hand. He was furious.

"Pay me for my time," he demanded.

"I will pay you for nothing." I turned abruptly, ignoring his threatening gestures, and hiding the money, ran to the customs hall. I vaguely recalled something about Spanish sailors operating a mini black market on the boat to Algeciras. I would try to change my dirham with them.

Ronit was waiting in the customs hall. She looked anxious. The money fiasco had taken much longer than intended. The boat was about to leave. I could see it docked outside the customs shed and last minute preparations being made for its departure. We had to hurry or it would sail without us. I barely had time to tell Ronit what had happened.

My nerves were raw. I couldn't help being aware that the penalty for taking Moroccan currency out of Morocco was prison. The authorities publicised the information with unrelenting repetition throughout the port. And I was approaching the customs officer with a fat wad of Moroccan money tucked into the waistband of my trousers, its unfriendly stiffness jabbing my bare skin. Ronit was getting our passports stamped and was to meet me at the customs desk.

"What are you taking out of the country?" the customs officer asked with practised suspicion.

"Nothing," I answered, unnerved by the bareness of the room, the institutional grey of the walls, the hard leather holster covering his pistol.

"Do you have money?" He got directly to the point.

"No." He moved his badged cap tighter on his head, pinning me with his eyes.

"We know you have money. Better you give it to us." His voice was a visible threat.

"I have no money," I said quietly, a patch of calm emerging in the terror I was feeling.

"Give me the money or we will be forced to find it." The eyes tightened their grip.

Suddenly I knew that the black market man had reported me to the police. Why hadn't I considered that possibility? My stomach twisted painfully. "I don't have any money," I persisted, the calm patch dissolving. It was too late now. Even if I gave them the money I would be considered a smuggler. Ronit had returned with our passports stamped, 'Exit Morocco'. "I must catch the boat. I have a train connection on the other side." I could feel my words making no impact.

The customs officer summoned four policemen, all with holstered pistols. "Search the bags," he ordered. Then glancing at me with sinister calm he said, "we will find the money. I have a woman officer coming to search your body." His French was excellent. The policemen gathered around me and began searching my bag, opening my maps, my letters, going through every pocket, reminding me, lest I forgot, that they would find the money. My anxiety was compounded by an awful taste in my mouth. It was the opium. The paper it was wrapped in had disintegrated and the dissolving opium was excruciatingly bitter. I tried to swallow it in anticipation of the body search. But my mouth was like blotting paper with the combined bitterness of fear and opium. The tiny lump felt the size of a boil. I couldn't swallow.

Meanwhile Ronit engaged the police officers and customs official in conversation. With her gift for languages she had, by now, acquired a significant amount of Arabic. She spoke to them in Arabic, a tactic which never failed to bring results. "We have no money. Please let us go. We will miss our boat." At the sound of Arabic the formality crumbled. Her incredibly long hair falling in waves to her thighs, helped.

"You speak Arabic?" the customs officer said, unbuttoning his jacket, "where did you learn?" I thought he was going to embrace her, declare her an instant Muslim. He began to joke with her while the search continued. The atmosphere was perceptively less tense, although I was still struggling with the duel malignancies of impossibly bitter opium and the wad of illegal dirham. Finally I was told I could close my suitcase. Nothing had been found.

But the worse was yet to come. I could see the policewoman approaching with another customs officer. Prison was minutes away. Perhaps I would improve my embroidery. While Ronit was distracting the policemen with her Arabic and long hair, I tried a desperate manoeuvre. I reached under the Moroccan shawl I was wearing, withdrew the wad of money from the waist-band of my trousers, covered it with my hand and, in front of four policemen, one policewoman and two customs officials, slipped it into the suitcase I was closing. I felt strangely calm.

The officers proceeded to search Ronit's knapsack while I was told to follow the policewoman into a cubicle. My Arabic was good enough to understand the instructions she was given. "She has money. Find it." The woman searched me efficiently and would certainly have found the money. I had none. Fortunately the search for illegal dirham did not include my mouth. The opium remained undetected. I left the cubicle vindicated. The officers were bewildered, one even scratched his head. Perhaps he would arrest the informer instead. After an attempt to propose marriage to Ronit, offering one hundred camels, a price I had no way of evaluating, they conceded defeat and let us go.

There was no time to rejoice. We could see the ship's crew about to lift the ramp and raced from the customs shed to a steep flight of stairs leading to the boat. Ronit didn't even have time to put her knapsack on her back and carried it bulging in her arms along with unpacked bits and pieces. As we began our frantic rush down the stairs, Ronit's knapsack slipped from her arms. We stood helplessly watching as it bumped down the stairs, rolled a few feet along the dock and dropped into the sea. It floated for a few seconds and then began to sink. All her belongings were in the knapsack, clothes, passport, money. We remained on the stairs paralysed.

At the bottom of the stairs a man was dismantling his little cart of souvenirs. He sprang into action, shouting something to the men on the ship. Instantly someone threw a hook. By now the knapsack had sunk, only one strap remained above water. As though born for this moment, the souvenir man threw the hook, and in the one try he had, hooked the knapsack by the strap and pulled it up to the dock, sopping wet. People on the boat cheered and applauded. We ran down the stairs jubilant. Ronit shook the man's hand again and again. I kissed him. We rushed onto the ramp which was kept lowered for us, knapsack dripping. Everyone was waving and shouting. A man on the ship yelled, "you must kiss me too, I threw the hook."

"Yes!" I shouted up to him. I kissed the hook thrower as soon as we climbed aboard. Proudly he informed me that he was a Moroccan policeman, sent to accompany the ship out of Moroccan waters.

"Oh no, not another policeman," I whispered to Ronit, regretting the kiss.

He helped us find a place on the ship where we could lay the clothes to dry. I was so ecstatic about the recovery of the knapsack, I hardly noticed that the opium had dissolved in my mouth. It was no more, paper and all. The policeman adopted us. He brought us drinks and chocolate and talked incessantly. He had an uncle in Toronto and, although we were from Montreal and living in London, he described the uncle in minute detail, so that we wouldn't fail to recognise him in case we should bump into him. We had to get rid of him. I was anxious to change the Moroccan dirham into Spanish pesetas. Once I left the ship the money would be worthless. I made a mental note never again to kiss a policeman. Once kissed, they never quit the case.

By now I was high on a combination of fudge, opium and sheer good fortune. But I couldn't enjoy my state of elation, an enormous task loomed before me. I had to find a Spanish sailor willing to change Moroccan money illegally, and I had to hurry. There was only an hour left before we docked in Algeciras. My problem was compounded by the fact that sailors looked like everyone else, and none of them like the policeman's uncle.

After sending the policeman for drinks we didn't want, I left Ronit on deck drying clothes and recuperating from multiple trauma, without the aid of opium or even fudge, and gingerly made my way along the ship looking for a corrupt sailor. I noticed two men hunched in a corner. They looked adequately suspicious. Pretending to tie my shoe, I listened to their conversation. They spoke in subdued tones in Spanish which I couldn't understand, but I kept hearing the magic word, "*pesetas*". They must be my men. One of them was a sailor, at least he had dirty finger nails. I approached him. He spoke no English, French or Arabic, only Spanish. I spoke virtually no Spanish. "*Pesetas, dirham,*" I said, shifting my eyes deviously. He understood. "*Si,*" he said, "*quanto?*" How much did I want to change. I wrote the amount of dirham I had, followed by the word pesetas with a question mark. He wouldn't say how many pesetas he would give me, but indicated I was to follow him.

I tailed him at a safe distance beginning to feel unfocused, trying to concentrate on the business at hand, forgetting the procedure, if indeed there was one, distracted by sounds which suddenly accosted me, by people moving strangely, as though poised between steps, by waves floating onto the deck in slow motion. My senses were becoming seriously flawed.

There was a thing like a haze swirling inside my head. One moment I could see through it, crystal clear, flashes of coloured light glinting like a prism in sunlight, sparkles of sound, vibrant. The next moment shapes and sounds were swathed in coils of mist, diffuse, nebulous. To compound my difficulties, I felt I was being watched and tried to act nonchalant, pretending I was strolling on deck looking for the Rock of Gibraltar. The swaying of the ship didn't help my composure. I kept stumbling. People would think I was drunk. I had to get hold of myself. I musn't arouse suspicion or I'd end up in jail after all.

Suddenly, to my horror, the Moroccan policeman appeared. Of course, he had been following me. He had been sent by the customs men in Tangier. They knew I had the money. I wouldn't get away with it. In his hand he carried a greasy paper bag which he ceremoniously handed to me with a pleased grin. I held it away from me, opening it carefully, suspiciously. It contained a cooked chicken. I thanked him. A chicken was the last thing I needed. "Toilet", I whispered urgently, and rushed off with my chicken, desperate to locate my sailor, fearing I had lost him. To my relief I spotted him about to descend a flight of metal stairs. I followed him.

The stairs were slippery and went on forever, the clang of our footsteps echoing loud somewhere beneath us. Suddenly I was hit with panic. What if he planned on killing me and taking the money. He knew I had it. It would be easy to dispose of my body in the ocean. Nobody would ever find me. I'd just vanish. I was descending into hell, unable to stop.

Miles later we came to the boiler room, perfect place for a murder. The ship's engines were pounding so loud my screams would never be heard. The air was stifling, and smelled of dirty oil. The room was filled with a huge blistered tank beside which stood a dwarfed table with a chair on either side - an improvised banker's office. I was drowning in sweat. The sailor signalled me to sit. He didn't kill me. Instead he began to count money off a large roll of pesetas which appeared from nowhere. "*Quanto pesetas*?" I asked, trying to impose order on my unruly senses and act business-like, efficient, as though I was at an interview with the bank manager finalising a loan. He couldn't hear me.

I tried to remember the official exchange rate. Dollars and pounds and dirham and pesetas danced together in my head executing a crazy jig. I would have no idea if I was being cheated. Perhaps he was offering me even less than the Moroccan black market man that distant time ago in Tangier. Perhaps the whole trip had been in vain and I had risked prison for nothing. I made a mental note to accept being cheated now and again.

I tried to appear in control. It would be harder to cheat a person who was self-possessed and efficient. "*Quanto pesetas*?" I screamed. He shouted a number in Spanish which I couldn't understand, then continued counting out money. I indicated he was to write down the amount he was offering me. I kept insisting, thumping on the table, interfering with his count. Reluctantly he scribbled a figure. I had no idea what to do with the information. He continued counting the money with great concentration. The engines were roaring, my head was reeling, the smell of oil was pickling my brain. I struggled to keep things from slipping away, the facts, the furniture, myself, most of all the pesetas. A fat pile of money was growing in front of me. I watched fascinated as the bills mounted each other and reproduced. He was the banker. He was chanting a mantra. "Go to jail, go directly to jail, do not pass go, do not collect two hundred dollars."

Finally he stopped, handed me the pile and prepared to leave. "*Encore pesetas*" I shouted above the pounding engines. I knew one thing for certain, whatever he was giving me was not enough. "*Encore pesetas*!" I screamed. Hastily he added a few more bills to the pile, anxious to get rid of me. "*Encore pesetas*," I screamed again, encouraged by my success. He added a few more bills hoping to end the encounter. I could see his pleasant face darkening with annoyance, but I couldn't stop. "*Encore, encore pesetas*," I screamed louder, growing wild with excitement. But he had had enough. Angrily he began to reclaim the money. I realised, through all the din in my head, that I had gone too far. I wasn't in the Grand Opera House, shouting 'encore' between curtain calls. I was in a grease-stained boiler room, making a sleazy black market deal. *"Bueno, bueno,"* I shouted, reaching for the money, and pulling out my comparatively thin wad of damp dirham from the waistband of my trousers. We made the exchange. I clung to the thick pile of pesetas, not knowing what to do with all the bills. They would look like a cancerous growth tucked in my trousers. Finally I plunged them into the bag with the chicken.

My blood thumping and roaring with the engines, I began the long ascent to safety. The sailor remained below, glad to see the last of me. He probably made a mental note to avoid crazy ladies with stained paper bags. I emerged from the churning bowels of the ship into the calm of the upper deck, trying to appear casual, as though I had spent my life ascending from boiler rooms. I paused for a moment. Yes, everything was in its place, business was as usual. The case was closed. I no longer had illegal currency. I could see the outline of Algeciras. No one could get me now. I was engulfed by a wonderful serenity. The traumatic exit from Morocco was over. I tucked my greasy bag under my arm and prepared to saunter off, anxious to tell Ronit the good news.

Waiting for me at the top of the stairs was the Moroccan policeman. He put his hand on my shoulder and smiled. I lowered my head to escape his smile and saw his heavy black boot threatening my lavender linen sandal with the embroidered flowers. I had a passionate urge to rescue the delicate violet and pink flowers from the black assault and shifted the paper bag to free my right hand. But my fingers were paralysed, they refused to operate. I watched in horror as the paper bag slid slowly through my numbed hand and thudded on his black boot. Like a shot he reached down and seized the bag. His fingers burned on my shoulder blade as though I was being branded. The evidence was now in his possession.

My brain, like a tape reeling at fast speed, quacked like Donald Duck in an echo chamber. Of course! He wanted that bag. The policeman was working with the sailor, if the sailor was a sailor. There was no limit to my naivety. I hadn't suspected the black market man. I hadn't suspected the policeman. I hadn't suspected the sailorman. If I was to engage in criminal activity I'd have to smarten up, suspect a little. Now they really had me. The policeman had the evidence. The sailor was a witness. We were probably still in Moroccan waters. Moroccan waters, Spanish waters, such details were unimportant to a repressive police force. The point was they had tricked me good and solid. Snatches of my defence exploded in my muddled mind. I would deny everything. What sailor? I never saw a sailor. What was I doing in the boiler room? What boiler room? I never saw a boiler room. What about the chicken co-habiting with the pesetas? What pesetas? I never saw pesetas. Do I usually keep my money with chickens? What chicken? The man gave me a bag. I never even looked inside. No good. My fingerprints were on the dirham and the pesetas and the bag. Damn. Why hadn't I worn gloves?

The policeman looked down at me. "Change dirham? Yes?" The question was more sinister posed in English and accompanied by a tranquil smile.

"Dirham," I croaked hysterically, the word turning solid in my throat. My god. He knew everything. "No. No. I don't change dirham. I have no dirham. I have no money to change. I brought no dirham from Morocco. Nothing. Only a few coins. Look!" I couldn't stop talking, my denials becoming more obsessive as I fumbled in pockets for coins I didn't have, growing increasing flustered. "My friend has the coins. Just a few. You know, the one with the knapsack. Not really money. Souvenirs." My rambling was frantic, the jumble of English and French incoherent. I knew I had to gain control of myself or I didn't stand a chance.

Unperturbed by my escalating hysteria, the policeman, reverting to French, said, "no problem, the man who works in the bank on the ship

286

is my cousin. He will change your dirham at the bank rate. He is a good man." I was raving at full speed when what he said crashed through my delirium-denial. I did a Marx Brothers double take. In slow motion I turned to face him. "You can get dirham changed?" My words were about a mile apart.

He nodded. "No problem." I saw his face for the first time. He looked like my favourite uncle. How come I hadn't noticed? I stood very still feeling the sunshine spread warm between my shoulder blades. All at once, overcome by sudden passion, I threw my arms around him and hugged for real. "You know I don't do anything illegal," I said, reaching for the bag, my shoe meeting his. He smiled as he returned the hug, the stuffed paper bag pressed securely between us.

23. The Enticing Beyond

The day after Ronit and I arrived in Malaga, ecstatic at having escaped a Moroccan jail, Irving and Cedric were due to leave for Toronto. Aviva and David had a three day reprieve. Cedric had already made the decision to return to Spain in early October. He had arranged to collaborate on material for a concert with a musician friend who was spending a year in Spain. But mostly he wanted more of Morocco. The country intrigued him and he needed another go to probe deeper.

Irving too had been smitten by Morocco and viewed returning to Canada with distaste. He bemoaned 'the horror of Toronto....the pale graceless ways of white Anglo-Saxia...the gimme attitude of the children' and compared 'the perpetual pout on their faces' to the smiles of Moroccan children who had so much less to smile about. He had chided me at one of our Essaouira dinners, 'why didn't you tell me about Morocco before....I'll never go back to Greece.' The possibility of the pan-Semitic conference heightened his enthusiasm and I promised to inform him as soon as there was any news from Bashir.

Ronit and I didn't go to the airport with the others. Our farewells were made in an outdoor boulevard café lined with palm trees, where we were to meet my future sister-in-law, Gitte. The goodbyes were without trauma, tempered by sunshine and sangria, but mostly by the unexpected bonus of time alone with Aviva.

Gitte moved into our pension to be with us, but ended up entertaining David and Ronit to facilitate that bonus. She was phenomenal. Without a hint of complaint she took them to the beach, played round after round of 'fish', a tedious card game David adored, and helped Ronit learn Spanish - having gone to school in Venezuela her Spanish was fluent. Instead of sleeping on the terrace with Aviva and me, she shared David and Ronit's room - an act based not only on altruism but on self-preservation, since Aviva and I chatted incessantly. But our non-stop talking fascinated her. "How come you have so much to say to each other," she marvelled. "I bet if you were left on a desert island you'd hardly notice, you'd just go on talking." However, she seemed to enjoy making our being together possible and contented herself with our company over the long evening dinners - a concession we made to family life.

Aviva and I were in the throes of a last-ditch desperation knowing we had less than three days together before an indefinite separation. We wanted to pack every minute full to bursting with our being together, and were grateful to Gitte for freeing us from the interferences of motherhood. David was to remember Gitte as his Malaga guardian angel. Although he thrived on her attention, he stored the event in his armoury of recriminations to be hurled like darts in future tirades against me. "And in Malaga you and my mother didn't care if I lived or died, you were too busy blabbing. Thank god for Gitte, she was the only person who noticed I was alive. She told us stories, explained things, took us to the beach, played cards with me, and when we went to sleep at night she always said, 'dream with the angels', I'll never forget that, 'dream with the angels', that's a beautiful thing to say to a kid. She acted like a mother, she did all the things you and Aviva were supposed to do, at least once in a while." I had to concede that when he was right, he was right.

When our last day came, David, Aviva, Ronit and I made our way to the airport as if to a funeral. Gitte had left earlier, ever cheerful, ever smiling, to rejoin friends. We entered the departure lounge like mourners shrouded in misery, at a loss as how to negotiate the final separation. Fortunately, the check-in hall had its own demands, its own agenda which, with a sense of relief, we obliged. Ronit and David went in search of a luggage cart, Aviva organised the tickets and passports and I located the check-in queue. As we were arranging the bags on the trolley, Ronit said to David, "I promise to write and tell you everything that happens." Her words had the intensity of a declaration of eternal love.

289

David burst out with, "promise you'll visit me soon...and promise me you'll visit Mo Mo...and promise me you'll feed the kitten on the beach...and don't forget the black one with the chopped off tail," he pleaded, turning from Ronit to me and back to Ronit, allocating the appropriate duties. "OK, OK." I interrupted, "if you promise me to stick to one Coca-Cola a day." He nodded vigorous assent. We shook hands all around, sealing the bargain, and Ronit took him to buy his third Coke. "Come on David," she said, "I'll treat you to a Coke. You know something, you're not as much of a brat as you used to be." David didn't argue the point.

Aviva and I were unusually quiet, emptied, as though in the three days of talking we had drained our souls. She went through the motions at the check-in counter on automatic, her mind elsewhere. But just before going through immigration she turned to me, suddenly animated, sprung to life, as though life-bearing thoughts were flooding a parched psyche causing it to flower.

"I don't know what will happen between Irving and me but what I do know is that I'll be able to deal with whatever it is. I feel so much calmer, so much stronger so much surer of myself. I feel as though I've been given a kind of permission to believe in my own instincts. And for that I have to thank Morocco, and for Morocco I have to thank you. Thanks so much, Niemale." We embraced and I felt tears hot on my neck.

"I'll miss you terribly," I said, "and I'll miss my David. It wouldn't have been the same without you."

"Honest?"

"Honest. It's been so good."

"It's been so good," she repeated. Then in a wisp of a voice, "kiss my prince for me....he's a beaut guy...tell him I won't forget him."

"I will. I promise. And he won't forget you either."

After a final round of hugs and surreptitious tear-blotting, David and Aviva disappeared through the gate. Gone. Ronit and I waited, unwilling, unable, to leave. We located their plane on the tarmac and kept our eyes glued on it as though if we stared long enough we would somehow be able to see into it. As it began to move away we waved frantically, hoping for a last moment of contact. But we knew they couldn't see us.

On the bus back from the airport Ronit and I hardly spoke, overwhelmed by a sense of loss. Although we would probably see Cedric in October, we knew it would be a long time before we saw David and Aviva again, even if the conference plans worked out. From now on it was just Ronit and me. I felt suddenly orphaned, bereft, and incredibly weary.

Before going to the airport Ronit and I had decided to spend the night in Malaga, then take the morning train to Algeciras and the evening boat to Tangier. But the thought of returning to the pension, still warm with the shapes and sounds of the others, was unbearable, like returning alone to the honeymoon bed knowing the groom had gone. I felt gutted. Ronit must have felt the same way because suddenly she said, "mum, maybe we can get a boat to Tangier today. Let's not stay in Malaga, it's too lonely in Spain. Let's get back to Morocco. Morocco is like home."

It was as though she had sprung some psychic trap. All at once my weariness slipped away like I was shedding a weighty suffocating skin. I became animated, alive. "Wonderful idea, Ronchick. I'm sure there's a boat we can catch today. We'll pick up our things and take the first train or bus to Algeciras." The sense of relief was so great it was like having averted a fatal blow. I gave Ronit a hug, leaned into my seat, which suddenly felt soft and welcoming, and closed my eyes, restored.

As I was drifting into reverie I heard Ronit say, "you know mum, we should be really thankful that we're going back to Morocco and not to Toronto or London." How right she was. I should be rejoicing instead of grieving. "You're absolutely right, Ronchick, we're so lucky, so privileged... thanks for reminding me." I brushed a rebellious strand of hair from her forehead and was overwhelmed by a surge of affection, an exquisite empathy. She was, after all, my favourite travelling companion.

Gradually Morocco seeped into my consciousness, full-bodied, pungent. I could taste it, smell it, breathe it. I folded into it, allowing its sensuality to engulf me, suffuse my senses. We would be in Tangiers that night, then Essaouira and then the Sahara, Algeria, Tunisia, the enticing beyond. I dared to imagine the possibilities in the adventures awaiting us and a flicker of excitement ignited my reveries, a glimmer of the promises of travel shone in my soul. True, one part of our journey had ended, but another was just beginning.

Also by Niema Ash

Touching Tibet
Foreword by His Holiness The Dalai Lama
ISBN: 0953057550
R.R.P: £7.99

Despite the determined efforts of the Dalai Lama to publicise the Tibetan cause, for many of us the country, its people, culture and traditions remain mysterious.

Niema was one of the first Westerners to enter Tibet when its borders were briefly opened. In this highly absorbing and personal account, she relates with wit, compassion and sensitivity her encounters with a people whose humour, spirituality and sheer enthusiasm for life have carried them through years of oppression and suffering.

This book gives a fresh insight into the real heart of Tibet

"Excellent - Niema Ash really understands the situation facing Tibet and conveys it with remarkable perception."
Tenzin Choegyal (brother of The Dalai Lama)

"Mesmerising"   The Sunday Times

"Thought-provoking and enjoyable...it will evoke a deep desire to go to Tibet"   Geographical Magazine

Other Titles from TravellersEye

Desert Governess

Author: Phyllis Ellis

Editor: Gordon Medcalf

ISBN: 1903070015

R.R.P: £7.99

In 1997 badly in need of a new start in life, Phyllis answered an advertisement: *English Governess wanted for Prince and Princesses of Saudi Arabian Royal Family.* She soon found herself whisked off to the desert to look after the children of HRH Prince Muqrin bin Abdul Aziz al Saud, the King's brother. In this frank personal memoir Phyllis describes her sometimes risky reactions to her secluded, alien lifestyle in a heavily guarded marble palace, allowed out only when chaperoned, veiled and clad from head to foot in black.

"Fascinating...Desert Governess throws light on a way of life that has hitherto remained almost literally under a veil."

The Sunday Express

Discovery Road

Authors: Tim Garratt & Andy Brown

Editor: Dan Hiscocks

ISBN: 0953057534

R.R.P: £7.99

Their mission and dream was to cycle around the southern hemisphere of the planet, with just two conditions. Firstly the journey must be completed within 12 months, and secondly, the cycling duo would have no support team or backup vehicle, just their determination, friendship and pedal power.

"It's power comes from the excellence of writing."

The Independent

"Readers will surely find themselves reassessing their lives and be inspired to reach out and follow their own dreams."

Sir Ranulph Fiennes, Explorer

Fever Trees of Borneo

Author: Mark Eveleigh
Editor: Gordon Medcalf

ISBN: 095357569
R.R.P: £7.99

This is the story of how two Englishmen crossed the
remotest heights of central Borneo, using trails no
western eye had seen before, in search of the
legendary 'Wild Men of Borneo'. On the way they
encounter shipwreck, malaria, amoebic dysentery,
near starvation, leeches, exhaustion, enforced alcohol
abuse and barbecued mouse-deer foetus.

*"Mark has the kind of itchy feet which will take more than a bucket of
Johnson's baby talc to cure... he has not only stared death in the face, he
has poked him in the ribs and insulted his mother."*

Observer

*"Mark's unique blend of enthusiasm and humour is genuinely absorbing
and immensely readable"*   Global Adventure

Frigid Women

Authors: Sue & Victoria Riches
Editor: Gordon Medcalf

ISBN: 0953057526
R.R.P: £7.99

In 1997 a group of twenty women set out to become
the world's first all female expedition to the North
Pole. Mother and daughter, Sue and Victoria Riches
were amongst them. Follow the expedition's
adventures in this true life epic of their struggle to
reach one of Earth's most inhospitable places,
suffering both physical and mental hardships in order
to reach their goal, to make their dream come true.

*"This story is a fantastic celebration of adventure, friendship, courage
and love. Enjoy it all you would be adventurers and dream on."*

Dawn French

*"They embrace an experience that many people would prefer to only
read about."*   Daily Express

Riding with Ghosts

Author: Gwen Maka

Editor: Gordon Medcalf

ISBN: 1903070007

R.R.P: £7.99

This is the frank, often outrageous account of a forty-something Englishwoman's epic 4,000 mile cycle ride from Seattle to Mexico, via the snow covered Rocky Mountains. She travels the length and breadth of the American West, mostly alone and camping in the wild. She runs appalling risks and copes in a gutsy, hilarious way with exhaustion, climatic extremes, dangerous animals, eccentrics, lechers and a permanently saddle-sore bum.

We share too her deep involvement with the West's pioneering past, and with the strong, often tragic traces history has left lingering on the land.

"A beautifully written book which achieves the delicate balance between poetic description, gritty humour and well-paced storytelling."
Manchester Evening News

Slow Winter

Author: Alex Hickman

ISBN: 0953057585

R.R.P: £7.99

Haunted by his late father's thirst for adventure Alex persuaded his local paper that it needed a Balkan correspondent. Talking his way into besieged Sarajevo, he watched as the city's fragile cease fire fell apart. A series of chance encounters took him to Albania and a bizarre appointment to the government. Thrown into an alliance with the country's colourful, dissident leader, he found himself occupying a ringside seat as corruption and scandal spilled the country into chaos.

"It is full of a young man's enthusiasm, thirst for adventure and search for identity... an engrossing and illuminating read."   Yorkshire Post

"Slow Winter, offers a human view of great political change. As a evocation of the modern Balkans, it is the better of any academic work."
The Times

Tea for Two…with no cups

Author: Polly Benge
Editor: Dan Hiscocks

ISBN: 0953057593
R.R.P: £7.99

Four months before her 30th birthday Polly finds
herself in a quandary. Fed up with dancing a swan
or woodland nymph every night, failing to impress
Barry Manilow with her singing abilities and falling
in love with a New Zealander with a rapidly expiring
visa, she needs to come up with some answers quickly.
She decides the only way to do this is by embarking
on a 'love test'. With a yet uncalloused bottom she
joins Tim and Lee on a bicycle ride from Kathmandu
to Assam in the hope of finding some answers.

"infectious"   The Daily Telegraph

*"This colourful paperback is tailor made to give armchair adventurers
hope. If Polly, who secretly packs her eye repair gel, can manage a few
months on the road, so can anyone!"* On Your Bike Magazine

The Jungle Beat – fighting terrorists in Malaya

Author: Roy Follows
Editor: Dan Hiscocks

ISBN: 0953057577
R.R.P: £7.99

In search of adventure, Roy joined the Malay police
at the height of a bitter ten year campaign against
communist terrorists. He was 22 and had no
experience of jungle warfare. Within a year he had
become the youngest ever commander of a jungle
fort and platoon operating deep within enemy
controlled territory. Faced by this deadly enemy, Roy
was also forced to confront an unknown but equally
threatening environment. Stampeding elephants,
swarming ants and prowling tigers competed with
the terrorists for the lives of his men.

*" It tells the story with no holds barred: war as war is. A compelling
reminder of deep jungle operations."* General Sir Peter de la Billière

"Lively, accurate... this book is one of true adventure"
                                Medal News

Heaven & Hell

Travellers' Tales from Heaven & Hell

Author: Various
Editor: Dan Hiscocks
ISBN: 0953057518
R.R.P: £6.99

More Travellers' Tales from Heaven & Hell

Author: Various
Editor: Dan Hiscocks
ISBN: 1903070023
R.R.P: £6.99

An eclectic collection of real life travel stories which range from the bizarre and extreme to the amusing and anecdotal. The Heaven & Hell series is compiled using the best entries to our annual competition to find the most 'heavenly' or 'hellish' travelling tales.

- An elderly lady forced to stay in a brothel
- A tiger biting a dinner guest
- A biker mothered by the Mafia
- A dusty afternoon with an incontinent Vice President

"an inspirational experience. I couldn't wait to leave the country and encounter the next inevitable disaster."
The Independent

"It is tempting to assume the further you go, the more exotic the trip. From reading entries it is clear to see that adventurous travel can happen anywhere." Lonely Planet

"readers will delight in the entries as they grin and grimace their way around the world." STA Travel

A Trail of Visions

Route 1: India, Sri Lanka, Thailand, Sumatra

Author/photos: Vicki Couchman
Editor: Dan Hiscocks
ISBN: 1871349338
R.R.P: £14.99

Route 2: Peru, Bolivia, Ecuador, Columbia

Author/photos: Vicki Couchman
Editor: Dan Hiscocks
ISBN: 093505750X
R.R.P: £16.99

A Trail of Visions is an intimate portrait of one person's travels, on a shoestring budget, through exotic and exciting lands. Covering India and South-east Asia in Route One and South America in Route Two, beautifully illustrative photographs elucidate the joy of travel, and the lives and passions of the people met along the way. Whether they are indigenous to the country or other travellers from around the globe.

Using her expertise as a professional photographer Vicky captures images that many see, but never take. Her photographs seize the action, emotion and poignancy of the moment and are fantastic insights into the foreign cultures that she visits.

Guide books tell you where to go, what to do and how to do it. The Trail of Visions series shows and tells you how it feels.

"A Trail of Visions tells with clarity what it is like to follow a trail, both the places you see and the people you meet."   Independent on Sunday

"The illustrated guide."   The Times

"stunning"   Marie Claire

What is TravellersEye?

TravellersEye was set up in August 1996 by Dan Hiscocks. His vision was to publish books which showed that great things can be achieved by ordinary people.

Dan lived, worked and travelled in over forty different countries in his early twenties. During this time he met many people who had achieved things against the odds, and with little recognition.

He saw that the value of the achievements was not only for the achiever, but the receiver (in this case himself) as they motivated and inspired him to have belief and desire to stretch himself in order to achieve. As he says:
"Don't ever let anyone tell you the world is small … it is absolutely huge and out there for the taking. The world has never had more opportunities and been more exciting. We no longer need fantasy for dreams, we can achieve this aspiration with reality – we just need to push ourselves as individuals to our own limits."

TravellersEye has a list of books which show that 'ordinary people can achieve extraordinary things'.

TravellersEye Club Membership

Each month we receive hundreds of enquiries from people who've read our books or entered our competitions. All of these people have one thing in common: an aching to achieve something extraordinary, outside the bounds of our everyday lives. Not everyone can undertake the more extreme challenges, but we all value learning about other people's experiences.

Membership is free because we want to unite people of similar interests. Via our website, members will be able to liase with each other about everything from the kit they've taken, to the places they've been to and the things they've done. Our authors will also be available to answer any of your questions if you're planning a trip or if you simply have a question about their books.

As well as regularly up-dating members with news about our forthcoming titles, we will also offer you the following benefits:

Free entry to author talks / signings
Direct author correspondence
Discounts off new and past titles
Free entry to TravellersEye events
Discounts on a variety of travel products and services

To register your membership, simply write or email us telling us your name and address (postal and email). See address at the front of this book.